The Belt and Road Initiative

The Belt and Road Initiative (hereafter BRI) of China has attracted world-wide attention and participation, causing a lot of debate over its implications for international society. Although it is still in a budding stage, the BRI seems to afford a framework for an increasing number of countries to explore jointly new international economic governance mechanisms and offer significant opportunities for them to cope jointly with global challenges. Taking a globalization perspective and tracking the ancient silk roads, this book tries to examine the general context in which the BRI is raised and implemented, arguing that this Chinese initiative, instead of replacing existing international cooperation mechanisms, is a call for the reform and development of neoliberal globalization and will open up a new era of inclusive globalization.

Inclusive globalization is neither an overturning nor a simple continuation of neoliberal globalization but rather a proposal capable of addressing the problems of existing globalization. The difference between them lies in the fact that globalization cannot only serve the "spatial fix" of capital but also has to meet the needs of living people. The book also addresses a number of major issues on building the Belt and Road and contains Chinese media's interviews with the author on various BRI issues. Given the author has been intensively involved in the study of and planning for the BRI, the book offers a valuable academic insight into this Chinese initiative.

Weidong Liu is a professor in Economic Geography at the Institute of Geographical Sciences and Natural Resources Research, Chinese Academy of Sciences. His research interests include regional development and regional policy, foreign direct investment (FDI), multinational corporations (MNCs), Global Production Network (GPN), the automobile industry, and the Belt and Road Initiative of China. His previous publications include *The Geographical Transformation of China* (Routledge, 2015).

China Perspectives

The *China Perspectives* series focuses on translating and publishing works by leading Chinese scholars, writing about both global topics and China-related themes. It covers Humanities & Social Sciences, Education, Media and Psychology, as well as many interdisciplinary themes.

This is the first time any of these books have been published in English for international readers. The series aims to put forward a Chinese perspective, give insights into cutting-edge academic thinking in China, and inspire researchers globally.

Titles on economics include:

The Belt and Road Initiative
A Pathway towards Inclusive Globalization
Weidong Liu

Regulating Effect of Tax on Chinese National Income Distribution
GUO Qingwang, LV Bingyang, YUE Ximing

Internationalization of the RMB
Establishment and Development of RMB Offshore Markets
International Monetary Institute of the RUC

Chinese Macroeconomic Operation
Liu Shucheng

The Chinese Path to Economic Dual Transformation
Li Yining

Hyperinflation
A World History
Liping He

For more information, please visit www.routledge.com/series/CPH

The Belt and Road Initiative

A Pathway towards Inclusive Globalization

Weidong Liu

Routledge
Taylor & Francis Group
LONDON AND NEW YORK

商務印書館
The Commercial Press

This book is published with financial support from the Chinese Fund for the Humanities and Social Sciences

First published in English 2019
by Routledge
2 Park Square, Milton Park, Abingdon, Oxon OX14 4RN

and by Routledge
52 Vanderbilt Avenue, New York, NY 10017

First issued in paperback 2020

Routledge is an imprint of the Taylor & Francis Group, an informa business

Translated by Wu Qiaofang 伍巧芳, polished by Michael Dunford

British Library Cataloguing-in-Publication Data
A catalogue record for this book is available from the British Library

Library of Congress Cataloging-in-Publication Data
A catalog record has been requested for this book

ISBN 13: 978-0-367-66088-8 (pbk)
ISBN 13: 978-1-138-33160-0 (hbk)

Typeset in Times New Roman
by Newgen Publishing UK

Contents

Figures

Tables

Acknowledgments

The author, Weidong Liu, acknowledges the support of the Chinese Academy of Sciences (XDA20010100) and the China National Natural Science Foundation (41530751) for the research related to the book, and wishes to extend special thanks to Michael Dunford for his help with the editing of the English of the translated manuscript. However, the author remains responsible for any errors in the book.

Preface

On May 14–15, 2017, China successfully held the Belt and Road Forum for International Cooperation (hereafter Forum). Fifteen hundred participants from more than 130 countries and 70 international organizations attended the Forum, including 29 heads of foreign states or governments, nearly 100 high-ranking foreign officials above the ministerial level, and the heads of 60 international organizations, which made the Forum the largest and highest-level diplomatic event held by China as the host country since the New China was established in 1949, promoting the development of the Belt and Road Initiative (hereafter BRI) to new heights. At the Roundtable Summit of the Forum, 30 heads of state and the Secretary General of the United Nations (UN) as well as the president of World Bank and the managing director of the International Monetary Fund reached a broad consensus and signed the *Joint Communiqué of the Leaders Roundtable of the Belt and Road Forum for International Cooperation* (hereafter *Joint Communiqué*). The *Joint Communiqué* pointed out that the BRI offers significant opportunities for all countries to deepen cooperation and jointly cope with global challenges, and helps promote a globalization path that is open, inclusive and beneficial to all.

In the Forum, many national heads of state pointed out in their speeches that the BRI, with its strong inclusiveness, will allow more regions to share the benefits of globalization. For example, then-Pakistan prime minister Nawaz Sharif noted that the BRI had praised cultural diversity and inclusiveness, providing development opportunities for people at the margins of globalization. Former French prime minister Dominique de Villepin stated that the BRI is a bridge that connects the past, the present and the future, aiming to "leave no one behind" on the path of development. President Michelle Bachelet Jeria of the Republic of Chile, President Recep Tayyip Erdoğan of the Republic of Turkey, President Milos Zeman of the Czech Republic and President Mulatu Teshome of Ethiopia, among others, also expressed the same high expectations. Secretary General António Guterres of the United Nations pointed out in an interview with China Central Television (CCTV) on the eve of the Forum that the BRI is significant, and that it will unite the world to drive globalization in a more equitable direction. Meanwhile the *Joint Communiqué* proposes to promote free and inclusive trade. It can be fairly said that supporting inclusive globalization is an important consensus reached by the heads of state at the Forum.

Economic globalization has been the main driving force for global economic development and transformation of the world structure over the past three decades, not only having promoted the overall growth of the world economy but also having brought prominent problems of unbalanced development and social polarization. Economic globalization is a historical phenomenon resulting from the combined effects of market forces, technological progress and institutional factors, the root of which are neoliberal policies. More and more politicians and scholars now have realized the limitations of economic globalization directed by neoliberalism and its harmful effects on the sustainable development of the world, and therefore have been advocating the need for exploring new paths of globalization. In this macro context, the BRI, based on the "spirit of the Silk Road", provides new thinking for promoting reform and deepening the development of the governance mechanisms of economic globalization, and has the potential of leading to an inclusive model of globalization. So-called "inclusive globalization", compared with neoliberal globalization, is a new concept and a new model of global economic governance. The notion will be elaborated in many parts of this book and thus will not be discussed here in the Preface.

"Inclusive globalization" is a theoretical concept proposed by the author in an article entitled "The Scientific Connotations and Scientific Issues relating to the Belt and Road Strategy", published in May 2015 (included in this book). "The Belt and Road Initiative is a significant framework for promoting the in-depth development of economic globalization . . . a new manifestation of globalization with a prominent feature of integrating cultural connotations of the Silk Road, rather than a simple continuation of past economic globalization". To put it simply, the BRI is an embodiment of inclusive globalization. The author proposes in his article entitled "Discussion of Misunderstandings about the Belt and Road Initiative", written in January 2016 upon the invitation of *Journal of Chinese Academy of Governance*, that "the BRI advocates anew globalization that will open up a new era of inclusive globalization". In November 2016, the author, cooperating with Michael Dunford, published an essay entitled "Inclusive Globalization: Unpacking China's Belt and Road Initiative" in *Area Development and Policy*, further elaborating that the BRI is the embodiment of inclusive globalization. In a BRI special issue of the *Bulletin of Chinese Academy of Sciences* in April 2017, the writer published a paper entitled "The Belt and Road Initiative: Leading Inclusive Globalization". In addition, in the book entitled *A Study of the Belt and Road Initiative*, published in January 2017, the author also elaborated the concept and connotations of inclusive globalization. At dozens of domestic and international academic conferences and in a large number of media interviews, the writer has constantly elaborated on the concept of inclusive globalization, which, gladly, has been increasingly recognized by more and more scholars. In particular, after communicating on dozens of occasions with foreign colleagues, the author found that the concept of inclusive globalization makes it easier for them to understand the essence of the BRI.

Inclusive globalization surely is still a brand-new theoretical concept, which requires further study by the academic community jointly so as to improve its theoretical content. It is exactly for this reason that, with the help of the Commercial Press, the author has put together this compilation of chapters of his books, papers and media interviews published or presented over the past three years on the subject of the BRI and *Inclusive globalization*, providing a basis for future discussions.

Compared with the international impact and sound progress of the BRI, academic research is still falling behind. It might be said that practice lies far ahead of academic research and discourses. On the one hand, the academic community has not yet developed a complete academic discourse to support the BRI, while various interpretations and voices have been emerging at home and abroad, including misinterpretations and misunderstandings, and even attempts to discredit it. On the other hand, Chinese studies of countries along the Belt and Road are still inadequate. To date, studies of their geographical environment, social and economic structures, legal systems, business and operation environments, religion, cultures and so on, are not sufficient to support enterprises seeking to "go global". To solve these problems, long-term and joint efforts of the academic community with other communities are required.

July 12, 2017

1 The Silk Road and the Silk Road Spirit[1]

Originally proposed by Chinese president Xi Jinping in September and October 2013, respectively, the Belt and Road Initiative (hereafter BRI) refers to building the Silk Road Economic Belt (the Belt) and the 21st-Century Maritime Silk Road (the Road). At present there is increasing consensus among a growing number of countries in the world that the BRI affords a framework to explore jointly new international economic governance mechanisms. Both the Belt and the Road use the notion of "Silk Road" (or the Silk Routes), a term expressing long-lasting historical relationships between different parts of the Eurasian Continent, to put the BRI at the forefront of top decision-making and public discussions.

To understand correctly the BRI, one has to first comprehend "Silk Road" and what it really implies. Two key points must be noted before any discussion of this term. First, although the Silk Road has always been specifically deemed to refer to historical phenomena, such as ancient trade routes, historical monuments or cultural relics, the use of this term in relation to the BRI does not lie in those specific phenomena but in its historical and cultural connotations, or what is called the Silk Road Spirit. The Silk Road Spirit refers specifically to the key values mentioned in the *Vision and Actions on Jointly Building Silk Road Economic Belt and 21st-Century Maritime Silk Road* (hereafter *Vision and Actions*) that is, the pursuit of "peace and cooperation, openness and inclusiveness, mutual learning and mutual benefit". Second, the Silk Road, though it seems to refer to a Chinese "legend", is indeed a historical and cultural heritage shared by many Eurasian and even African countries. The BRI, by taking advantage of this historical and cultural heritage (i.e., the Silk Road Spirit), roots today's economic and trade cooperation among countries along the Belt and Road and the accompanying spirit and models of cooperation in the history of the Silk Road and what one can learn from it.

Cross-border and long-distance trade has existed for thousands of years. Recorded ancient long-distance trade can be traced back to around 3000 BC, mainly in Mesopotamia and the Indus Valley Civilization (IVC), where the goods traded were largely ancient luxuries such as spices, textiles and precious metals, among others. It was the geographical advantages of being the hub of regional trade networks that brought prosperity to many international cities in ancient times. As these cities had great concentrations of spices, textiles, jewelry, dresses and other luxury goods, they could meet the needs of surrounding areas to buy the above-mentioned products. For instance, Cyprus, known for its abundance of Cyperus papyrus and wool, had already become the trade center of the coastal area of the eastern Mediterranean and Egypt circa 2000 BC; Phoenicia, famous for navigation, grew into the center of the Mediterranean in the trade of cedar and linen dyes. The Silk Road across Eurasia is the representation and symbol of cross-border trade and cultural exchange in ancient times, which could be called the ancient version of globalization to some extent.

The Silk Road refers to the general term for long-distance commercial trade and cultural exchange routes gradually developed from ancient times, stretching through Eurasia and even reaching northern and eastern Africa. The Silk Road is a product generated from the interaction of material and spiritual culture between ancient China and other countries and nations, the result of collisions of Eastern and Western civilizations, and also an embodiment of the Chinese nation's pioneering spirit in history. The Silk Road, from the perspective of history, connecting Eastern and Western cultures, enriched people's material life of those ethnic groups and countries along the Road and facilitated the civilization process of the world. It was, looking back to the history of more than 2,000 years, not some fixed trade route but a bridge for communication between the West and the East. The specific routes of the Silk Road constantly changed as geographical conditions changed and the political and religious situation evolved. The opening and the prosperity of the Silk Road have promoted the socioeconomic development of a large part of the world's most densely populated area in terms of politics, economy and culture. And the history of the Silk Road is the history of goods exchange, trade intercourse, and cultural interactions among the countries, ethnic groups, and various regions along the Road, which benefit greatly from such exchanges.

The Silk Road has profound economic and cultural foundations, and is the result of the highly developed human civilization. The great economic and cultural development of these countries and ethnic groups along the Road laid the foundation for the Road. Without the emergence and development of the Eastern and Western civilizations along the Road, there would be no Silk Road. The great development of economy and culture in countries along the Road created great material foundations for the emergence and opening of the Silk Road, while the differences in natural endowments and economy generated a strong desire and demand for material and cultural exchanges among people in those regions.

Political factors have also had a significant impact on the development of the Silk Road. Some dynasties in China often adopted more proactive policies and measures toward the opening of the Silk Road. The prosperity and development of all the major countries along the Silk Road also played an important role in the formation and smooth operation thereof. For instance,

Zhang Qian's two diplomatic missions to the Western Regions (*xiyu*) at the time of the Han dynasty; Ban Chao and his son Ban Yong's administration over the Western Regions, Central Asia, and West Asia in the Eastern Han dynasty period; many envoys such as Han Yangpi being sent to Central Asia and Persia in the Northern Wei dynasty era; and the administration over the Western Regions, Central Asia, and West Asia by the Sui and Tang dynasties all contributed substantially to the exploration and sound operation of the Silk Road.

Technology development is another important element of the vicissitudes of the Silk Road. With the development of shipbuilding and navigation technology, the safety and cost of shipping greatly improved, and thus maritime transport was widely employed in international trade. Against the background in which the economic, industrial and cultural center of ancient China shifted for a while to coastal regions with the founding of the Southern Song dynasty (1127–1279) in Hangzhou in southeastern China, the Maritime Silk Road, accompanied by the development of maritime transport technology, increasingly flourished. The treasure voyages, the seven Ming-era maritime voyages of the treasure fleet commanded by Admiral Zheng He between 1405 and 1433, symbolized the flourishing of the Maritime Silk Road. The trade along the Maritime Silk Road was much more developed than that achieved on the backs of camels in the time of the land Silk Road.

I. The origin of the term "Silk Road"

Since *The Travels of Marco Polo* was published in Europe in the late thirteenth century, myths and legends about China and the Orient have attracted a lot of Europeans and led to a great number of works about China written by missionaries in their pursuit of the Kingdom of Prester John, even causing the trend of Sinomania. From the Serica, Sinae, and Mahacina before Christ to Tabgach and the Kingdom of Prester John, the passion of the West to explore the path toward China and the Orient never stopped growing. The Silk Road expedition in the nineteenth century was exactly an extension of such a tradition. Before the nineteenth century, people's understanding of cultural exchanges between the East and the West were relatively superficial, and their awareness of the nature and significance of the Silk Road, acting as a major artery of economic and cultural exchanges between Asia and Europe and an important trade route between China and the West, was even more vague. The nineteenth-century expedition outlined the basic route of the Silk Road.

The term *Seidenstraße(n)* ("Silk Road(s)" or "Silk Route(s)") was first invented by Ferdinand von Richthofen (1833–1905), a German geographer. In 1860, Richthofen joined in the expedition to the Far East with a German economic mission and later conducted geographical and geological studies in China for almost four years starting in 1868. Back in Germany, Richthofen successively served as president of the Berlin International Geographical Society, president of the University of Berlin, professor of Geology at the University of Bonn and professor of Geography at the University of Leipzig, and he devoted the rest of his life to writing his master work, *China; Ergebnisseeigener Reisen und daraufgegründeter Studien* (China: The results of my travels and the studies based thereon; hereafter *China*), sharing his experiences and findings from his previous trips to the Eastern world. It took 35 years to complete and publish this five-volume masterpiece, the first two volumes of which were written by Richthofen in person and the rest compiled by his students based on his findings and materials accumulated before his death. In the first volume of the book, published in 1877, Richthofen first proposed the concept of *Seidenstraße* (Silk Road). This word was not something he imagined, but it related to his habit of focusing on study of the transport routes. In each survey, apart from documenting goods and products, he paid special attention to the routes for transporting them. Therefore, wherever he arrived in an area, Richthofen first had to describe the land and maritime traffic conditions of local places, and then record the towns and commercial routes formed on the basis of such conditions, which, thus, consisted of the main framework of Richthofen's findings.

Richthofen gradually refined the historical context of the Silk Road by recording the transport routes in China, studying the routes of commerce and trade in Chinese history and referring to the records about Serica (the country producing silk) in the West. He found that as early as the Qin and Han dynasties, Chinese silk had been transported through today's Xingjiang to Central Asia and then to Europe. At that time silk was called Ser, and China Serica, meaning the nation of silk. After the establishment of the Han empire, especially after Zhang Qian's missions to the Western Regions, the frequency of occurrence of the term "Silk" increased greatly in Western literature. A trade route to Serica eastward from the Euphrates ferry was recorded by an ancient Greek geographer, Marinus of Tyre, and was included in the *Geography* compiled by Claudius Ptolemy, also an ancient Greek geographer living in first–second century AD. Matteo Ricci, S.J., who visited China in the Min dynasty, once said that "I also have no doubt that this is the country known as Serica". By the nineteenth century, Sir Henry Yule, the British geographer known for his study *The Travels of Marco Polo*, published *Cathay and the Way Thither: Being a Collection of Medieval Notices of China*. As such, the term *Seidenstraße* was just about to come alive.

On the basis of those previous studies and research, Richthofen first referred to the term *Seidenstraße* in his work *China*. However, he used this term in a quite prudent way, mainly to demonstrate his proposed railway line from Chine to Germany (starting from Xi'an, passing through the Hexi Corridor or the Gansu Corridor and Southern Xinjiang to Kyrgyzstan, Turkmenistan, and Iran, and ending in Europe). Though Richthofen had been clearly aware of the existence and importance of other trade routes and maritime trade, the *Seidenstraße* in his conception still only referred to the Eurasian trade routes in the Han dynasty, or even more specifically, to the Eurasian transport routes from 128 BC to 150 AD. The German historian

Albert Herrmann afterward developed Richthofen's ideas in the book *Die Alten Seidenstrassen zwischen China und Syrien* (The Ancient Silk Road between China and Syria), published in 1910. And then after Sven Hedin, a student of Richthofen, published the book *Die Seidenstraße* (The Silk Road) in 1936, the term *Seidenstraße* became more and more recognized by the public and spread rapidly.

The expedition to Central Asia reached its peak at the time from the mid-nineteenth century to the early twentieth century when almost all orientalists, geographers, and archaeologists from European and American countries, represented by Sven Hedin, Aurel Stein, Albert Grünwedel, Nikolay M. Przhevalsky, and Pyotr Kozlov, visited China now and then. This period was an important stage in the study of the Silk Road. For the first time, scholars from various countries conducted in-depth studies with more scientific methods of the modern age. At that time, those Western explorers not only carried out geological, geomorphologic, and hydrological surveys in the central part of Asia that was a geographically unknown area, but also conducted investigations and studies of the ethnic groups, races, cultures, ancient sites, historical relics, the change of transport routes, the ups and downs of cities and towns, economy, and society along the Silk Road. In modern times, it was the first large-scale, systematic and scientific study of the history of Central Asia, Mongolian studies, the history of the Western Regions, Dunhuang Studies, the history of communications between China and the West, the history of northwestern ethnic groups and the history and geography of borderlands, which not only enriched the knowledge of the Silk Road from various aspects but also substantially influenced the methods and directions of the study on the Silk Road.

Building on translations of *Die Seidenstraße* written by Sven Hedin, the term *Seidenstraße* created by Richthofen, was translated from German to various languages, such as Silk Road or Silk Route in English, Routes de la Soie in French and "绢道" in Japanese. In the early twentieth century, French sinologist Édouard Chavannes in his work *Documents sur les Tou-kiue (Turks) occidentaux* (Documents on the Western Turks) first included the maritime trace into the realm of Silk Road, and then was followed by a number of Japanese and Chinese scholars. By the second half of the twentieth century, "Silk Road" had become the general term for long-distance business, trade and cultural exchange routes stretching through Eurasia and even reaching northern and eastern Africa in ancient times, and a synonym for amicable channels of exchange between the East and the West in economy, culture, and politics. Silk Road, as an academic term in studies on the exchanges between ancient China and countries in Central Asia and South Asia through the Hexi Corridor and Xinjiang, soon became widely used by international sinologists along with a continuous expansion of its contents from northwest land trade routes to southeast maritime trade routes, and the occurrence of derivations such as "Maritime Silk Road", "Porcelain Road", "Spice Route", and "Tea Road".

II. The background of the Silk Road

1. Zhang Qian's diplomatic missions to the Western regions triggered strong motivations of the Han Dynasty to trade with Western countries

Around the late Qin dynasty and the early Han dynasty, the Huns[2] expanded their forces from what is now the west of Korea to the east of Xinjiang, directly controlling the northern and southern Gobi Desert and cutting off the trade path between China and the West. The Huns frequently attacked the Central Plains over the Great Wall and to the south. With the growth of national power during the reigns of Emperor Wen and Emperor Jing of the Han dynasty, Emperor Wu of the Han dynasty, in order to defeat the Huns, dispatched Zhang Qian to the Western Regions to make contact with Darouzhi, who was expelled by the Huns from their original homeland, for the purpose that Darouzhi could persuade countries in the Western Regions to build an alliance with the Han dynasty. After Zhang Qian, who returned from his first mission to the Western Regions, reported the specific situations about the Western Regions to Emperor Wu, the Han dynasty changed its purpose of controlling these areas from defending the country against the Huns to the strong desire to rule the vast land with Han dynasty's power and benevolent rule but not military forces.[3] In order to promote the exchanges between the Western Regions and Chang'an (the capital of the Han dynasty), Emperor Wu recruited a great number of small merchants from the underclass of society to conduct business in the Western Regions with the goods assigned by the government, attracting more people to engage in land trade activities. Though failing to achieve its political ends of allying with Darouzhi, Zhang Qian's mission to the Western Regions was of great historic significance to Hexi, the Western Regions, and even Central Asia as it broadened the horizons and visions of the Han imperial court and facilitated the opening and operation of its path to the Western world. Meanwhile, at that time silk goods, characterized by practicability, artistry, portability, and high value, became the best choice of goods in long-distance trade and the most representative goods exported from China. The name of this trade route, therefore, was called the Silk Road by later generations.

2. The economic and cultural development of countries and regions along the Silk Road laid the foundation for the emergence of the Silk Road

The Silk Road fundamentally was a trade route built on the basis of the economic and cultural development of countries and kingdoms along the Road, which were the origins and most developed areas of ancient civilization of mankind. The western end of the Silk Road was the east coast of the Mediterranean where the earliest development of human culture emerged, including ancient Egypt, ancient Greece, and Mesopotamia, which had the most ancient human civilization in the world with the most developed economy and culture in the world at that time. At the eastern end was China with a developed ancient civilization, which, in particular, produced silk that could be easily transported as early as dozens of centuries before Christ. The central section of the Silk Road plays a pivotal role in the Silk Road. These West Asian and Central Asian countries such as ancient Persia, Bactria (or Bactriana) and Khwarezm (or Chorasmia), and ancient India became important hubs of the Silk Road stretching tens of thousands of miles. The great development of comprehensive national strength from politics to economy and culture of countries along the Road created prerequisites for the emergence and opening of the Silk Road.

3. The ethnic minorities in ancient China provided the impetus for the smooth operation of the Silk Road

Prior to Zhang Qian's missions to the Western Regions, the Darouzhi and Wusun, who were originally living in what is now the Hexi Corridor in Gansu, migrated from the north foothills of the Tian Shan Mountain to the Ili River basin and the west Tian Shan Mountain in about 201 BC and in the midterm reign of Emperor Wen of the Han dynasty, taking eastern products and economic information with them. Moreover, the Huns also played an important role in and made special contributions to the opening of the Silk Road. As the Huns constantly invaded and harassed the frontiers of the Han dynasty, the Han government had to pay such tributes as lots of silk, food and drink, and other products to the Huns. As the Huns did not need silk as nomadic tribes, they traded such silk from the Central Plains with people in Central Asia and Iran for greater benefits. The role of the Huns in the Silk Road later repeated itself with the Turks. In the Northern and Southern dynasties, the northern Chinese tribe Turks was rising with great power when the Khagan of the Turkic Khaganate took the opportunity to extort silk and other properties from its rival powers in the Central Plains, the Northern Qi dynasty, and the Northern Zhou dynasty. However, the silk robbed by the Turks, though considered as luxuries used by the Khagan and a few high-ranking officials, were largely exchanged with Central Asia, Persia, and other regions. Therefore, these kinds of silk trade activities as mentioned above played a supplementary role in the development of the Silk Road.

III. The evolution of the Silk Road

Under the narrow definition proposed by Richthofen, the Silk Road started from the ancient capital Chang'an (today known as Xi'an), a political, economic, and cultural center of ancient China, connecting Asia, Africa, and Europe. It stretched across the Longshan Mountains and the Hexi Corridor to Xingjiang through the Yumen Pass (or Jade Gate) and the Yangguan Pass (or Yangguan), and then through the Central Asia, West Asia, and North Africa along oases and foothills of the Pamir Mountains (or the Pamirs) before finally arriving in Africa and Europe (See Figure 1.1). Generally

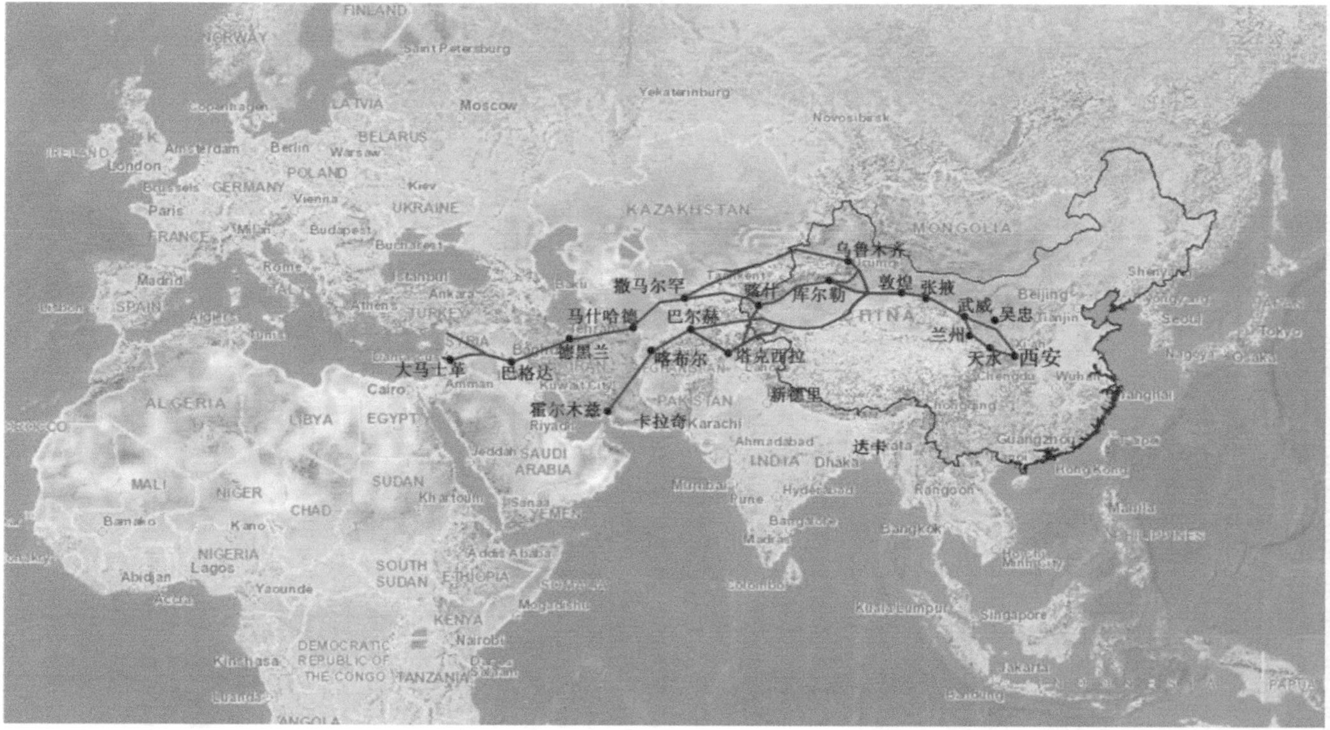

Figure 1.1 Ancient Silk Road in the Han dynasty

speaking, the land Silk Road, though without a strict historical definition, could be divided into the North Road, Middle Road, and South Road, all of which consisted of numerous trunk routes and branches. Overall, the general development of the Silk Road is divided into the following stages.

1. The opening of the Silk Road in the Western Han Dynasty

The Western Han dynasty started a brand-new era in the exchanges between China and foreign countries, lifting the barriers between the East and the West. At that time, the Silk Road started from Chang'an, traveling westward through Wuwei and the Hexi Corridor to Dunhuang and entering Xingjiang through the Yumen Pass (or Jade Gate) and the Yangguan Pass (or Yangguan). It ran along the northern and southern margins of the Taklamakan Desert and converged on the Pamir Plateau, and then it entered Central and West Asia before finally reaching the east coast of the Mediterranean (See Figure 1.1). The Silk Road spanned various countries and ethnic groups, resulting in diverse cultures, which, as a blend of spirits and materials, linked those people of different countries and different ethnic groups along the Road together.

Chinese and foreign businessmen on the Silk Road transported a large amount of silk to western countries. When the Han government had normal relations with bordering countries, it would open up *Guanshi*, trading markets in fortresses and passes on the borders, particularly for people from different ethnic groups to conduct business transactions. With the setting up official posts in the Western Regions by the Han dynasty as a symbol, countries or kingdoms therein claimed allegiance to the Han dynasty one after another and dispatched envoys to visit Chang'an. Relying on the dynasty's strong national power and based in Chang'an, Emperor Wu took aggressive policies on both land and maritime silk routes, and thus the Silk Road started its first era of prosperity. At that time, with the continuous movement of goods and officials all year around, the cultural exchanges and trade among China, India, Southeast Asia, Sri Lanka, the Middle East, Africa, and Europe underwent rapid development, with numerous novel goods, technologies and ideas starting to flow into countries in Europe, Asia, and Africa.

2. The reopening of the Silk Road in the Eastern Han dynasty

In the late Western Han dynasty, the relationship between the Central Plains and the Western Regions was suspended due to Wang Mang's dictatorship (8–23 AD). Emperor Ai of the Han dynasty renounced control over the Western Regions. Various wars and conflicts continued in the Western Regions. Afterward the prolonged wars between Jushi[4] and the Huns made the trade routes through the Taklimakan Desert inaccessible. The Han government often closed the Yumen Pass to spare itself from the disturbances of the Western Regions. In addition, the trade route along the southern foot of the Tianshan Mountains was blocked from time to time due to a variety of reasons. In one word, trade exchanges during this period were on and off as a result of continuous wars and disputes.

Although the Eastern Han dynasty relocated its capital from Chang'an to Luoyang, Chang'an, still governed by Jingzhaoyin (the governor of the capital) as in the Western Han dynasty, remained an important distribution center for goods to be traded from the East to the West or vice versa along the Silk Road. In the Eastern Han dynasty, Ban Chao and his son Ban Yong recovered the Western Regions from the Huns. They reestablished the Protectorate of the Western Regions, seized control over the Hexi Corridor and the troops stationed at the southern foot of the Tianshan Mountains. Ban Chao used diplomatic and military means to make more than 50 kingdoms subordinate to the Eastern Han dynasty. After he succeeded in pacifying Central Asia, the transportation and trade on the Silk Road were further developed. Until the midterm reign of Emperor Ming of the Easter Han dynasty following decades of recuperation, the Eastern Han dynasty, having a solid material foundation to resist the threat of the Huns, finally restored the Silk Road in its entirety.

During the 300 years from the late Eastern Han dynasty to the demise of the Northern Zhou dynasty, Chang'an, though no longer possessing its former prosperity, never stopped business transactions with the West. The Han dynasties in East Asia, Rome in Europe, Anxi (Arsacid empire[5]) in West Asia, and the Kushan empire[6] in Central Asia were all flourishing during this period, actively seeking expansion and exchanges with other countries and kingdoms.

3. The rise and fall of the Silk Road in Wei, Jin, and the Southern and Northern Dynasties

During the Wei, Jin, Southern, and Northern dynasties, mainland China, with no centralized government, was stuck in a tumultuous era of 16 kingdoms and the Southern and Northern dynasties. However, since the Western Regions (today's Xinjiang), Hexi and Qinghai remained relatively stable, and the ethnic minorities in power valued foreign trade and exchange, the interactions between West China and Central Asia and South Asia were never cut off. Furthermore, the migration of noble families and intellectuals to Hexi in order to escape chaotic wars promoted the culture of the Hexi Corridor, embodying interaction between China and the West, to an unprecedented level of development. After the founding of the Five Liang dynasties, the cultural advancement and emergence of a large number of intellectuals and scholars laid the foundation for the import and acceptance of foreign cultures by local people in the Central Plains.

During this period, a new branch of the original North Road along the southern foot of the Tianshan Mountains was opened up on the basis of the previous silk routes. And Persia, as one of the countries having the most frequent interaction with China, became the main hub for the collection, distribution, and transit of Chinese silk. The king of Persia had sent envoys multiple times to Pingcheng (in the northern region of modern Datong, Shanxi) during the Northern Wei dynasty, and to Luoyang and Chang'an during the Western Wei dynasty. And in return, Emperor Xiaowen of the Northern Wei dynasty (his name is Tuoba Hong), had once also sent Han Yangpi to visit the capital of the Sasanian empire (located on the eastern bank of the Tigris about 35 km southeast of modern Baghdad, Iraq). Though without the backup of a unified country, the Silk Road was operated well in general during this period as travelers never stopped taking their steps on the Silk Road, whether in the Eastern Jin dynasty, in the Sixteen Kingdoms of five non-Han people (ruling most of China 304–439) or later in the Southern and Northern dynasties.

4. The flourishing of the Silk Road in the Sui and Tang Dynasties

The Silk Road reached unprecedented prosperity in the Sui and Tang dynasties, being more prosperous than in the Han dynasty. With the unification of northern China and southern China by the Sui dynasty, Chinese feudal society entered its prime. The Sui dynasty adopted a basic national policy of promoting interactions with the Western Regions and the development of trade along the Silk Road. Emperor Yang of the Sui dynasty even led his troops personally to the northwestern regions of the country, expelled the Tuyuhun[7] people who impeded interactions along the Road, and also supported trade fairs, contributing to another wave of exchanges between China and the West. The Silk Road then connected China with the eastern Rome, Persia, and India. The Sui dynasty laid the foundations for the flourishing development of the Silk Road in the Tang dynasty.

History witnessed social stability and trade prosperity in the Tang dynasty. The rulers of the Tang dynasty, seizing opportunities brought by the victory against the Turks, took control over the whole territory of the Western Regions, reopened these commercial routes and in 648–658 established the Four Garrisons of Anxi (in Qiuci (Kucha), Yutian (Hotan), Shule (Kashgar), and Yanqi (Karashahr)) as its administrative bodies of the Western Regions. Moreover, the Tang government renovated the Yumen Pass, reopened all the passes along the routes, and opened up branches of the Silk Road along the northern slope of the Tianshan Mountains. Furthermore, the West Road was extended to Central Asia, the eastern route of the Silk Road was opened again and new branches of trade routes were opened one after another. From Tang Emperor Taizong to Tang Empress Wu Zetian, the Tang Imperial Court, with its domination over the kingdoms of the Western Regions in the Tarim basin, became the suzerainty of kingdoms to the north of the Tianshan Mountains and west of the Pamirs (Figure 1.2).

During this period, the Uyghurs, who once replaced the Turks and assumed control of the Mongolian Plateau for a short time, gave up their nomadic lifestyle and started to settle down in a more stable environment. The Western regions reached an unprecedented era of stability due to a sound relationship between the Tang dynasty and Uyghur Khaganate. Under such circumstances,

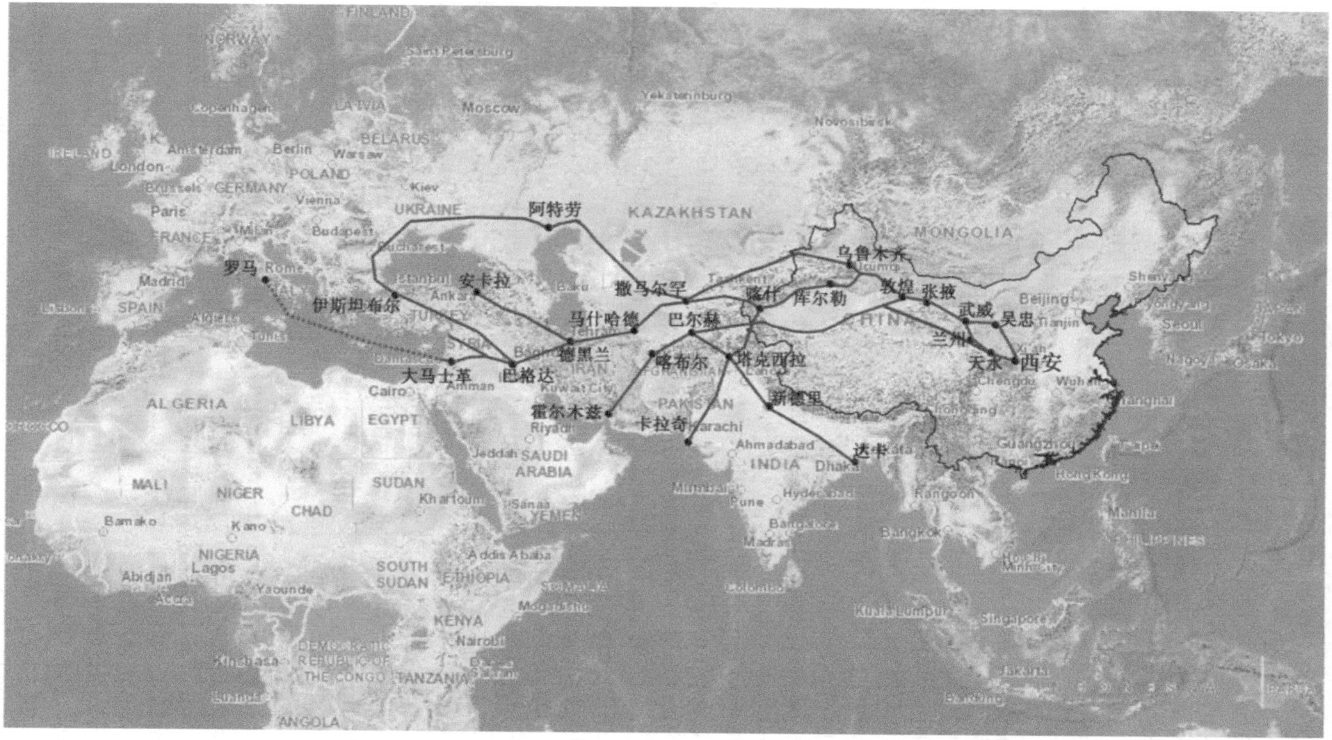

Figure 1.2 Ancient Silk Road in the Tang and Song dynasties

the Silk Road in the Tang dynasty, therefore, reached its heyday when every road led to Rome, with no hindrance to the interactions between China and the West and better development of trade than in the Han dynasty. Thus had arrived the second golden age of the Silk Road. However, unlike the Silk Road in the Han dynasty, the Tang dynasty controlled some areas of the Western Regions and Central Asia along the Silk Road and established a stable and effective order for its rule therein.

5. *The emergence of the Maritime Silk Road after the Tang Dynasty*

After the Tang dynasty, the shift of the economic center southwards increased foreign trade in southern China, where it had been relatively stable. Along with the booming of southern and maritime trade, Guangzhou and Quanzhou grew into two major economic cities in southern China. At the same time, maritime transport, with advantages brought by the reliability and safety of ships, enrichment of the sailing experience and the lessening of hardship and costs, gradually replaced freight on the land Silk Road (Figure 1.3). On the other hand, in the late Ming dynasty, the commodity economy was rising accompanied by the rapid development of agriculture and handicrafts while the Western world was immersed in a commercial revolution and a subsequent phase of colonial expansion. However, the Silk Road lost its position of official monopoly in "tributary trade", since the Ming imperial court, in order to consolidate its feudal rule and resist the trend of economic and social development, spared no effort to impede nongovernmental foreign trade. In the early Qing dynasty, namely from the reigns of Shunzhi emperor to Kangxi emperor, the isolation policy adopted by the Qing government in order to consolidate its ruling and prevent a series of such activities as "restoring the Ming dynasty" and "allying with foreign states", led to a fall in the foreign trade on the Silk Road.

The maritime Silk Road started from the southeastern coast of China, passed through Indochina and countries on the South China Sea, the Indian Ocean, and the Red Sea, and ended in Eastern Africa and Europe. As a major maritime route of trade and cultural exchanges between China and foreign countries, this Silk Route promoted the common development of the countries along it. The maritime route originating from Guangzhou on the southeastern coast of China and heading for countries in Southeast Asia, on the northern Indian Ocean, on the Red Sea coast, in northeast Africa and in the Persian Gulf, even could be traced back to the Tang dynasty. In the Song and Yuan dynasties, the great development of shipbuilding and navigation technology in China, as well as the wide use of the compass in navigation, comprehensively improved merchant ships' capability for long voyages. Also at that time, China maintained maritime trade relationships directly with more than 60 countries in the world, while the maritime Silk Road gradually replaced the land Silk Road, becoming the main channel for China's foreign exchange.

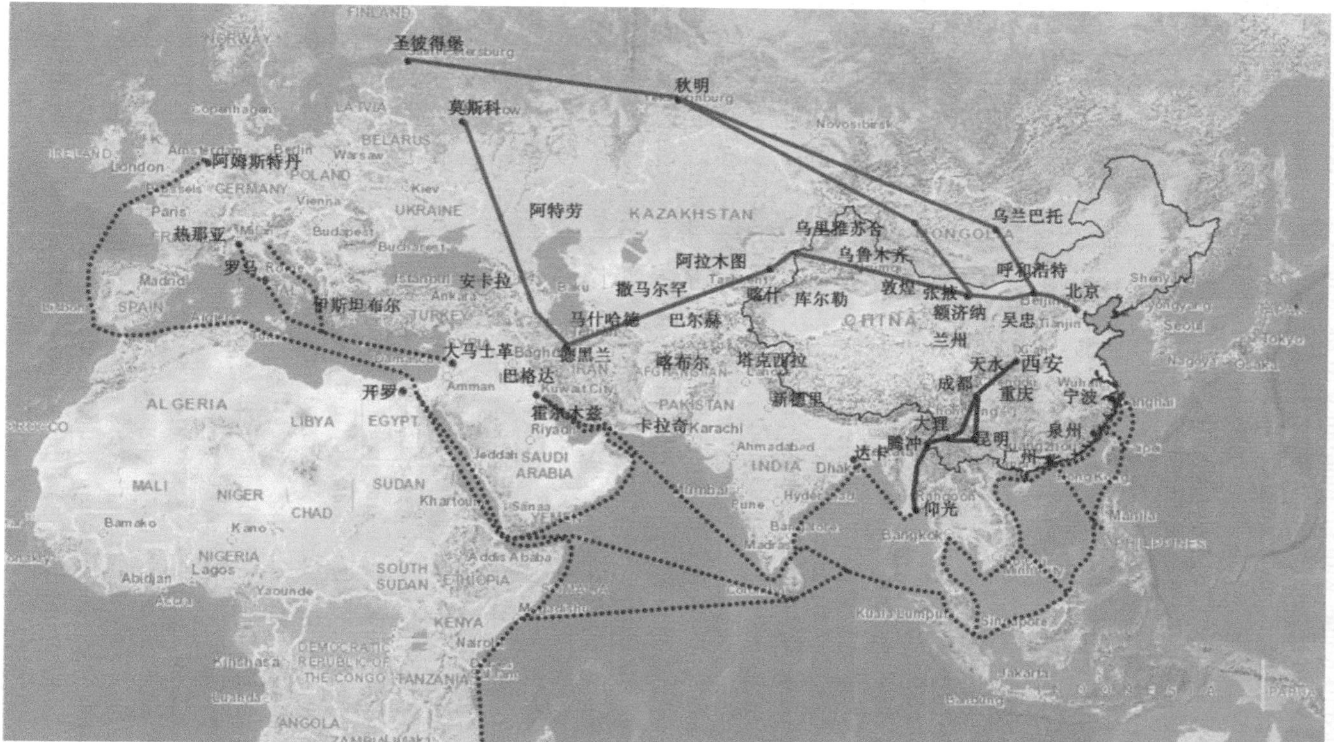

Figure 1.3 Ancient Silk Road in the Yuan and Ming dynasties

In the Ming dynasty, the maritime Silk Road reached all around the world. With respect to westward expansion, Zheng He commanded seven expeditionary voyages to the "West", which were large-scale sailings, organized by the Ming imperial court, and that reached 39 countries and regions in Asia and Africa. As for eastward extension, the Guangzhou-Latin America route (1575), initiated from Guangzhou, entered the sea via Macau and passed through Manila Port in the Philippines, the San Bernardino Strait and the Pacific Ocean before reaching the western coast of Mexico. Maritime trade, beginning from the Han dynasty, reached its peak in the Ming dynasty after long-term development in the Tang, Song, and Yuan dynasties. At the time dominated by the Haijin (sea ban) policy[8] of the Ming and Qing dynasties, Guangzhou became the only trade port on the maritime Silk Road that was open to foreign countries, shaping an unprecedentedly great global cycle of trade that lasted until the eve of the Opium Wars. After the Opium Wars, China lost its sea power, and its coastal ports became markets for the dumping of goods by the West after they were forced to open up. Meanwhile, the Western powers came to monopolize the export trade of China's silk, porcelain, and tea, among other commodities. This was the time that the maritime Silk Road started declining.

IV. Enlightenment from the Silk Road: The Silk Road Spirit

The Silk Road is the bridge and tie of political, economic, and cultural exchange between mainland China and the Western Regions as well as between China and other countries in Asia, Africa, and Europe. From the perspective of material exchange, abundant products from the Central Plains were, with the flourishing of trade along the Silk Road, transported to the Western Regions, Central Asia, India, Persia, the Arab world, and the European parts of the Mediterranean. Through the effort made by the Sogdians[9], Turks, Uyghurs, Arabs, and Persians, a wide range of products, such as exquisite silk and porcelain, tea, paper, bamboo wares, ginger, and rheum palmatumr were exported into the West in huge quantities. While Chinese goods were largely introduced into the West through the trade along the Silk Road, a lot of Western products and goods, such as grassland livestock and their fur, woolens, corals from Western Asia, jades, jewelry, glassware, various spices, alfalfas, Jerusalem artichokes, grapes, pomegranates, peppers, and herpetospermum pedunculosum (an annual climber whose seeds are used in Tibetan medicine), were also imported into China, which have enriched China's material civilization.

In terms of cultural exchange, Buddhism, Nestorianism, Islam, and related arts were introduced to China through the Silk Road. The influence of the Western Regions' civilization brought by the Silk Road was embodied and reflected in every aspect of society and culture in China, from customs and fashions, such as diet, costumes, residences, festivals, and entertainment, to music and dance, literature and art. The Silk Road was the mother of major cultures in the world that cultivated a number of ancient civilizations such as the Mesopotamian civilization, the Egyptian civilization, the Khwarazmian Persian Sunni civilization, the Indus civilization, and the Chinese civilization. Furthermore, the introduction of science and knowledge from the Eastern Roman Empire, the Arab empire, India, and the Persian empire, such as astronomy, medicine, construction technology, sugar technology, and the technology of sewn boat building, promoted the development of science and technology in China. And in addition, since Buddhism was brought into China in the first century AD, the economic and cultural exchanges between China and the West had become increasingly closer with the influx of various foreign religions into China, such as Islamism, Manichaeism, Nestorianism, Zoroastrianism, Judaism, and Christianity, which fundamentally influenced the social structure and ideological philosophy in China.

The Silk Road has promoted the process of communications between nations and strengthened the friendship of people along the Road. The Silk Road began at about the same time as a wave of national migrations occurred. And it was the hinterland of Eurasia, including China, especially Central Asia, which had been a crossroads of national migration and integration since ancient times. The Silk Road then has become a channel and link for national integration and interaction, in which the activities of ancient Saca, the Huns (Xiongnu), Darouzhi, Sogdians, Arabs, Turks, Persians, Tubo, Tuyuhuns, Xianbei, Tangut, Uyghur, Tiele, Rourans, the Di ethnic minority, and the Qiang ethnic minority in this area have profoundly influenced the history of Eurasia, those kingdoms and historical sites they established, having become a significant part of the history of civilization. Owing to the civilizations of the various ethnic groups that originated and developed there, the hinterland of Eurasia presented a pluralistic social structure and facilitated the formation of various modern ethnic groups during the historical process of national integration. In particular, the integration of ethnic groups into western China based on the Han culture and on the background of the Silk Road formed a unified Chinese national psychology and sense of nationhood. The cultural identity has essential and far-reaching significance for the pioneering and stabilizing of the northwestern and southwestern borders of China.

As Chinese president Xi Jinping pointed out, "spanning thousands of miles and years, the ancient silk routes embody the spirit of peace and cooperation, openness and inclusiveness, mutual learning, and mutual benefit". It can be said that the "Silk Road Spirit" is the essence of the ancient Silk Road, which provides the cultural foundation and core concept for the BRI. In a speech at the opening ceremony of the Belt and Road Forum for International Cooperation (hereafter "B&R Forum") held on May 14–15, 2017, President Xi comprehensively elaborated the Silk Road Spirit in depth. And in the opening speech of the Roundtable Summit, he further emphasized that the world may well draw wisdom and strength from the ancient Silk Road, which features the spirit of peace and cooperation, openness and inclusiveness, mutual learning, and mutual benefit, so as to promote cooperation and jointly pursue a brighter future.

Peace and cooperation. The history, given the fact that the ancient Silk Road was connected in peacetime but disrupted during wartime, has proved that peace is the premise of exchange, cooperation, development, and prosperity. Generation after generation, Silk Road travelers, from Zhang Qian in the Han dynasty, to Du Huan, Marco Polo, and Muhammad ibn Battuta in the years of the Tang, Song, and Yuan dynasties, then to Zheng He in the Ming dynasty, have built a bridge for peace and East-West cooperation. President Xi pointed out that "these pioneers won their place in history not as conquerors with warships, guns or swords. Rather, they are remembered as friendly emissaries leading camel caravans and sailing treasure-loaded ships". Humankind now has reached an age of great progress, great transformation and profound change. Although peace and development are the mainstream of the age, conflict and turmoil still happen frequently. The spirit of peace and cooperation left by the ancient Silk Road is the best choice for us to balance the "deficit" in peace.

Openness and inclusiveness. The ancient silk routes connected the birthplaces of the Egyptian, Babylonian, Indian, and Chinese civilizations as well as the lands of Buddhism, Christianity, and Islam. These routes enabled people of various civilizations, religions, and races to interact with and embrace each other with open minds. In the course of exchange, they fostered a spirit of mutual respect and were engaged in a common endeavor to pursue prosperity. This part of history shows that civilization thrives with openness, and that nations prosper through exchange. Only by seeking common ground while putting aside differences and embracing each other with an open mind may people, on this basis, find a conjunction of interests, jointly develop cooperation plans and take corresponding actions, and build a new pattern of cooperation featuring policy coordination, connectivity of plans, inclusive development and shared benefit.

Mutual learning. The ancient silk routes were not just for unilateral export but also for bilateral exchange and mutual learning; they were not for trade only but also boosted the flow of knowledge as well. Through these routes, Chinese silk, porcelain, lacquer work, and ironware were shipped to the West; China's four great inventions and silkworm breeding spreading to other parts of the world, while pepper, flax, spices, grape and pomegranate, Buddhism and Islam, and Arab astronomy, calendars, and medicine found their way to China. There is no hierarchy among human civilizations, and equal exchanges make the world colorful. As President Xi noted, "more importantly, the exchange of goods and know-how spurred new ideas . . . Herein lies the appeal of mutual learning". Therefore, pursuit of the BRI means achieving a complementarity of strength, exchange and interaction, cooperation, and innovation.

Mutual benefit. The ancient silk routes witnessed bustling scenes of visits and trade over land and ships calling at ports. President Xi stressed that along these major arteries of interaction, capital, technology, and people flowed freely, and goods, resources, and benefits were widely shared. It has been proved by history that exchange creates new opportunities, and that cooperation brings promising prospects. Jointly building the Belt and Road aims at seeking the "biggest common denominator" for development, collectively making a bigger cake of development, sharing the fruits of development, and avoiding the cliché of geopolitical confrontation, so as to add a splendid chapter to win-win cooperation.

Notes

1 Special thanks go to Fan, Yuting and Song, Tao for providing material.
2 Translator's note: the Huns refer to an ancient nationality in China, which was "a confederation of warrior bands" ready to integrate with other groups to increase their military power, in the Eurasian Steppe in the fourth to sixth centuries AD. The Huns were a nomadic people who lived in Eastern Europe, the Caucasus and Central Asia. It is widely thought that the Huns who appeared on the borders of Europe in the fourth century AD were descendants of the Xiongnu ("howling slaves") who had invaded China from the territory of present-day Mongolia between the third century BC and the second century AD. After defeat at the hands of the Chinese Han dynasty, the northern branch of the Xiongnu retreated north-westward and their descendants may have migrated westward through Eurasia.
3 Translator's note: the literal meaning of "广地万里，重九泽，威德遍于四海" is "China's territory can be expanded thousands of miles, people from afar will be presented at the Han's imperial court with the help of translators, and the emperor's power and benevolent rule will be spread all over the world".
4 Translator's note: The Jushi (車師, Jūshī) were a people who established a kingdom during the first millennium BCE in the Turpan basin (modern Xinjiang, China).
5 Translator's note: The Arsacid empire (247 BC–224 AD), also known as the Parthian empire, was a major Iranian political and cultural power in ancient Iran and Iraq. The ancient Chinese called it Anxi.
6 Translator's note: The Kushan empire was established in the early first century and spread to encompass much of Afghanistan, present-day Pakistan and then the northern parts of India.
7 Translator's note: Tuyuhun (313–663) is an ancient country established by Eurasian nomads and located in the Qilian Mountains and the upper reaches of the Yellow River from the Western Jin dynasty to the Tang dynasty.
8 Translator's note: Hanjin was a general term for a series of restrictive policies relating to maritime affairs undertaken by the Ming government during the fourteenth century.
9 Translator's note: Sogdians was an ancient Iranian civilization that at different times occupied territory in present-day Tajikistan and Uzbekistan

2 Economic globalization and its limitations*

Though the term "economic globalization" was not frequently used until the 1990s, economic globalization has existed for several centuries. International trade in ancient times, limited by the development of productivity and transportation, was basically dominated by regional trade and luxury goods. The trade between East and West, involving long distances and great risks, was much more like a business of adventure. The variety and volume of goods in circulation were limited due to high transportation costs, and expensive goods were only affordable by the upper classes able to pay for luxury lifestyles. In the thirteenth to the fourteenth century, feudal lords in Europe, in pursuit of pleasure, bought luxury goods in bulk from the East, creating a huge trade deficit for Europe with the East. The need for precious metal currencies, such as gold, indirectly led to Europeans' exploration of new sea routes. The start of massive exploration overseas led by the Western European countries in the late fifteenth century and early sixteenth centuries was the prelude to the great geographical discoveries.

European exploration overseas was initiated by two Atlantic coast countries, Spain and Portugal. In the fifteenth century, the Portuguese opened up a new sea route from Europe to India, controlling the southbound channel along the western African coast. The Spanish crossed the Atlantic Ocean, discovered the New World, and accomplished a global voyage, opening up a new transportation route between the East and the West. Afterward, other countries like the Netherlands, England, France, and Denmark started to participate proactively in world exploration. The land area of the world known by the Europeans in the late seventeenth century was five times larger than that in the fourteenth century.[1] It means that there was unprecedented expansion in the size of the global market and trade, and that "transoceanic trade" with Asia and the Americas was developed along the new routes by Europeans with different purposes. For Asia, the reduction of transportation costs brought by the new route made former "luxuries" affordable ordinary goods. As for the New World of the Americas, relations with Europe were more a matter of colonization, with the plunder of raw materials, the dumping of products and slave trading becoming growing segments of European trade.

In the meantime, European trade routes and economic centers also evolved. With the economic center shifting from the Mediterranean to the Atlantic Ocean due to the opening up of new routes, Italian city-states, which had relied on their location advantages at earlier stage, fell into decline. In the mid-sixteenth century, Antwerp, Belgium, became the "commercial center of the world". However, shortly afterward, when transcontinental trade system was replaced by maritime trade, the Netherlands became the trade center of the world. With two crucial commodities in international maritime trade, sea salt, and grain, under the control of Dutch transporters, Amsterdam became the busiest port in the world. By the end of the seventeenth century when the global demand for trade in grain fell, Holland's dominant position in commercial sector was gradually replaced by the British.

During 300 years after the Great Geographical Discoveries, Western European merchants gradually connected the regional markets of Europe with Asia, the Americas, Africa, and Oceania, creating a global market centered on Western Europe. The decisive role that trade had played in the sixteenth to eighteenth century was of great significance in European and even human history. The importance of trade went far beyond other economic activities and the shift of trade routes made Europe the economic center of the world. It was afterward that the modern history of capital started.

I. Global economic expansion and ebbing before World War II

1. The age of laissez-faire capitalism(1780–1873): Free trade, commodity exchange, and colonial expansion

If the Great Geographical Discoveries was the start of global economic expansion, then the industrial revolution may be deemed as the beginning of high economic dependence and integration. The exploration of foreign lands and the world's oceans had broken the relative isolation of world regions and connected the whole world. However, features of economic globalization, such as change in the global production and trade map, and the increasing scale and complexity of foreign investment, did not occur until after the industrial revolution.

From the late eighteenth century to the mid nineteenth century, the first industrial revolution started in Great Britain and rapidly spread to Western Europe and North America, and even other regions around the world. Great Britain consolidated its dominance by taking advantage of being the first industrial country. The major change brought by industrialization was a rapid growth of productivity. The types of goods available for trade increased dramatically when manual work and workshops were gradually replaced by mechanized factory production. Measured by value, 99 percent of the goods in the world did not enter the global trade market in 1820.[2]

The increase in productivity enabled industrial countries to export goods. In order to further expand the market for more profit, they turned colonies into raw materials suppliers, markets for product dumping and destinations for capital export. As such, economic activities were geographically expanded to the global in a real sense. Whether from the perspective of convergence in the prices of products from different regions or of the increase of trade volumes, the magnitude of international economic interactions increased unprecedentedly, with large flows of capital and giant financial trust and joint stock companies emerging.

At that time, the primary international division of labor and the formation of a world market were associated with a core-periphery structure of geographical specialization. On the one hand, led by industrialized countries, fast-emerging manufacturing industries produced a great number of surplus products. Great Britain, as the factory of the world at that time, exported more than half of its industrial products, yet the raw materials it needed were largely imported from other regions. On the other hand, the nonindustrialized countries (usually colonies), supplying raw materials and foodstuffs and serving as markets for these manufactured products, developed one-sided economies producing agricultural products and minerals, which made them highly dependent. For instance, Egypt was an important producing area for cotton, wool, and other raw materials for Great Britain.

It is notable that, though global trade at that time was always referred to as free trade, this freedom was actually based on colonialism. European colonists, backed by military force and in the name of free trade, were trying to make colonial and semicolonial countries their sources of raw materials and export markets by imposing reductions in or even eliminating tariffs. For example, in Algeria, a colonial country at that time, all products imported from France were exempted from tariffs starting in 1835. Algeria also eliminated tariffs on most of the products exported to France after 1851, and extended exemptions to all products in 1867. Another semicolonial country, Tunisia, after suffering a military defeat, was forced to end its policy of self-isolation and became a free trade market for European colonists with import tariffs of only 3 percent on products from its colonizers.[3]

Industrial civilization enabled European countries to increase their knowledge and economic power, while civilizations in other regions fell into serious crisis since they were unable to resist Western invasion. Asia, Africa, and Oceania, after being forced to open up to European countries, were incorporated into an international political and economic system. Japan was compelled to open up to trade with the West in 1854. China, after the two Opium Wars in 1840 and 1856, had to open its ports and became a semicolonial country, losing much of its independent sovereignty. India, already reduced to a colony, was directly controlled by the British East India Company. In Africa, most coastal areas were already occupied by Spain, Portugal, France, and Britain by the middle of the nineteenth century. Although at that time inland African countries still remained independent, they were soon colonized in the next half century. During that era, global economic expansion was founded on colonialism.

Table 2.1 Share (%) of major industrial countries in world industry and world trade from 1820 to 1870

Year	Great Britain		France		Germany		United States	
	Industry	Trade	Industry	Trade	Industry	Trade	Industry	Trade
1820	50	27	15~20	9	—	—	10	6
1840	45	25	—	9	12	8	11	7
1850	39	22	—	11	15	8	15	7
1870	32	25	10	10	13	10	23	8

Source: Kuczynski, Translated by Chen Dongxu: "Research on the World Economic History of the Capitalism", SDX Joint Publishing Company, 1955; W. W. Rostow, *The World Economy: History & Prospect*. The Macmillan Press Ltd., 1978, pp. 70–71.

Great Britain, being the largest country in terms of capital output and colonial reach, was the dominant force in the world economy until the second industrial revolution. In 1870, its coal production accounted for 51.5 percent of world output, its pig iron production for 50 percent, cotton consumption for 49.2 percent and trade volume for 25 percent. There is no doubt that Great Britain was at that time the core of the "core countries" (Table 2.1). With the arrival of the second industrial revolution, however, it gradually lost its leading position as an empire on which the sun never set.

2. *The second industrial revolution (1873–1913): The emergence of monopoly capitalism and the new imperialism*

From the late nineteenth century to the early twentieth century, a new wave of inventions and innovations led to a second industrial revolution. Driven by electricity, which gradually replaced steam as a source of power, growth accelerated in the United States and a number of European countries. Many countries seized the opportunity of this second industrial revolution to develop. Britain was surpassed by the United States and Germany. And the United States, taking the place of Great Britain, became the world's number one industrial power. By 1913, Britain's share of the world's total industrial output fell to 14 percent, while that of the United States rose to 36 percent.[4]

The revolutions in transportation and communications boosted global economic expansion. With respect to technology, cars, planes, and telephones were invented, along with great development in international railways, canals, telegraphs and postal services. Great Britain, with a saturation of domestic railway lines, began to invest in railway building in other countries and colonies that were in the process of industrialization. The United States, catching up from its relatively backward status as an industrial country, started to introduce large amounts of foreign capital for railway construction and public works, which effectively improved its transportation and communication industries. In 1866, the transatlantic submarine cable was successfully laid; in

1869, the Suez Canal controlled by the Great Britain and France was formally opened; in 1876, Alexander Graham Bell invented the telephone; in 1914, the Panama Canal, under the control of the United States, was officially opened. People were able to transport goods and exchange information more rapidly and over greater distances more efficiently and at lower cost, while economic activities in the world were linked much more closely than ever before in terms of both time and space. Of course, it also made it easier for Western powers to gain benefits worldwide.

With the massive increase in productivity, laissez-faire gave way to monopoly capitalism in the major industrialized countries. During the first industrial revolution, Great Britain established a free trade system to meet the needs of international trade and capital flows. This system subsequently expanded to other countries in Europe[5]. As tariffs and consumption taxes were reduced or even eliminated, previously privileged companies, such as the East India Company, lost their monopoly position in trade, while the number of small private enterprises gradually grew, facilitating the integration of the world economy. However, a market economy of free competition grants greater advantages to those large enterprises with larger amounts of capital and larger scales of production. With increasingly brutal competition in the industry, the economic crisis of 1873 saw the bankruptcy of a lot of small to medium-sized enterprises, while a large number of monopolies and even international monopolies emerged. Around the same time, Japan, which had embarked on industrialization after adopting a series of reforms, also joined the camp of looters. By the early twentieth century, the world market had been basically divided up by capitalist powers.

Industrialization also provided new opportunities for foreign investment. The international capital market, like the market for goods and services, was undergoing rapid expansion. In 1900, total foreign investment in the world was 4.75 billion pounds (about 23 billion US dollars), and in 1914 it reached 9.5 billion pounds (about 43 billion US dollars). As it industrialized, the United States also started to make a large number of foreign direct investments (FDIs), including investment in mining and manufacturing in Canada, Mexico, and South America, so as to provide raw materials for the development of domestic industries and to assume a dominant market position. The volume of US foreign investment rose from less than 75 million US dollars before 1870 to 685 million US dollars in 1899, and reached 3.514 billion US dollars in 1914. It can be said that it was a prime time of global economic expansion. As shown in Figures 2.1 and 2.2, the proportion of world trade and FDI in the world gross domestic product (GDP) rose starting in 1870, and reached a peak on the eve of World War I.

3. Two World Wars (1914–1945): The ebbing of global economic expansion

Two World Wars from 1914–1918 and 1939–1945 and the Great Depression in 1929–1933 significantly influenced the international economic order.

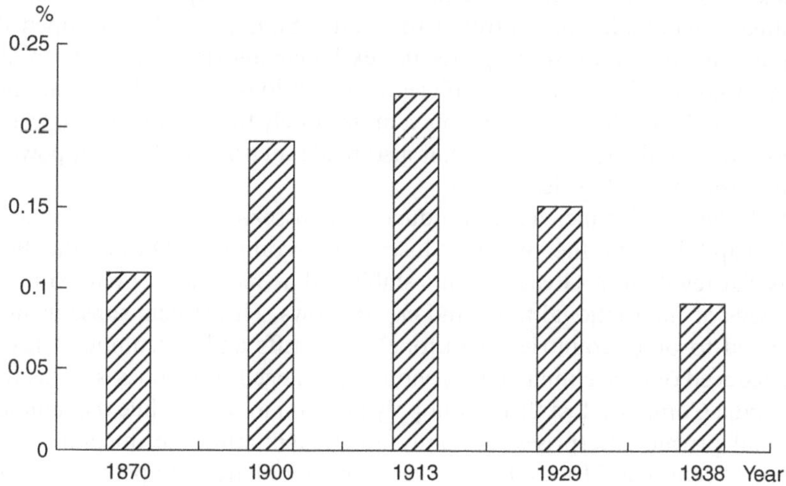

Figure 2.1 Proportion of world trade in world GDP from 1870 to 1938
Source: A. Estevadeordal, A. M. Taylor, “The Rise and Fall of World Trade, 1870–1939”. *Quarterly Journal of Economics* 118, no. 2 (2003): 359–407.

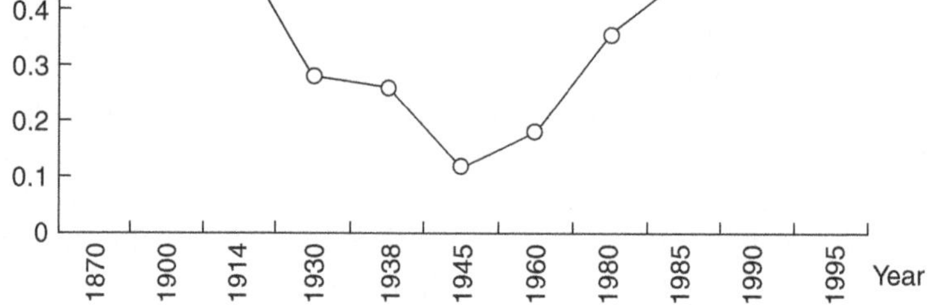

Figure 2.2 Proportion of foreign direct investment in world GDP from 1870 to 1995
Source: M. Obstfeld, A. M. Taylor, “Globalization and Capital Markets”. *NBER Chapters* 15, no. 2–3 (2002): 233–248.

Before World War I, with a basically open world economy, international trade continued to grow. With the start of World War I, growth was interrupted since governments, whether their countries were at war or not, strengthened their control over products, prices, output and labor. World War I saw international trade volume decline by 40 percent. At the same time, the countries carrying out substantial outward foreign investment such as Great Britain and France suffered serious losses (15 percent and 20 percent, respectively). The international financial order and the gold standard collapsed.

Though the world economy suffered a severe setback, the economic strength of the United States had grown dramatically during the war. Due to its remote location from the battlefields and neutral position in the early stages of World War II, the United States avoided losses and made a fortune by providing supplies and arms. In addition, it also attracted a large number of talented people during the war, who subsequently made essential contributions to its development.

Generally speaking, the early global economic expansion was small in scale as the patterns of manufacturing production, international division of labor, trade, and international capital flows were relatively simple. From the birth of the capitalist market economy to the eve of World War II, the map of the world economy presented a core-periphery structure. Whether dominated by Great Britain as in the first industrial revolution or led by the United States as in the second industrial revolution, manufacturing production was concentrated in core countries. Until the outbreak of World War II, the four largest countries in manufacturing accounted for 71 percent of world output and the top 11 countries had 90 percent. The manufacturing of Japan, the only industrialized country in Asia at that time, accounted for only 3.5 percent of world output. A clear international division of labor persisted. The core industrial countries exported 65 percent of manufactured goods to peripheral countries and regions, and absorbed 80 percent of primary products from them. In addition, international direct investment came from companies in core countries, and 65 percent of overseas investment went to developing countries.

At that time global economic expansion basically involved the invasion, looting and exploitation of underdeveloped countries by developed countries by virtue of colonial hegemony, which embodied a nature of severe exploitation. A variety of issues brought by this kind of "core-periphery structure" still exist even today. The two World Wars destroyed the global economy and the original structure and order of the world. Though most of the world's industrial production capacity was undermined by war (except in North America), many industrial technologies were reformed and improved during the war, such as aircraft manufacturing, laying the foundation for the subsequent development of the world economy and the shaping of the world structure.

II. Economic internationalization after World War II

The capitalist market economy system gradually developed by Western countries after World War II led economic internationalization into a new stage, yet the process of this was limited by differences in ideologies within the political landscape of the Cold War. It might be said that the progress of economic internationalization during the 30 years after World War II manifested epochal features to a large extent.

1. The establishment of a global institutional framework and the progress of economic internationalization

After World War II, the United States became the world's largest economy, while Continental Europe was left in a state of devastation that increased from west to east. In 1945, US GDP accounted for about one-half of world GDP and stood at 27 percent, with over 60 percent of the world's gold reserves, even when the economies of Continental Europe had largely recovered in 1950. In this context, the United States played a leading role in the establishment of international organizations and international financial rules. In order to match the West, the socialist camp, led by the Soviet Union, also strengthened organized international cooperation. The organizations and rules that emerged at that time (Table 2.2) contributed to a rapid subsequent restructuring of the world economy.

The Bretton Woods system, comprising the World Bank and the International Monetary Fund, set up as a result of agreements made at the Bretton Woods Conference, and the subsequent General Agreement on Tariffs and Trade (GATT) saw the emergence of a US dollar-centered international currency system, ensuring the unshakable dominance of the United States.

Table 2.2 Important international economic organizations and institutional framework agreements after the war

	Time	*Founding Countries*	*Nature*
World Bank	1944.7	US, UK, etc.	International financial organization
IMF	1944.7	29 countries, including US and UK	International financial organization
GATT	1947.10	23 countries, including US, UK and China	Multilateral international agreement
Comecon	1949.1	6 countries, including the Soviet Union and Bulgaria	International political and economic cooperation organization
OECD	1961.9	20 countries, including US, Canada and some European countries	International political and economic cooperation organization

After the dissolution of the Bretton Woods System in the 1970s, the United States, relying on the special position of the US dollar, still acted as the leader of the Western world. Of course, for other countries, postwar reconstruction needed a loose and active economic environment, and the liberalization of foreign exchange, capital, and trade under the Bretton Woods system did create the second golden era of global economic expansion. This phase may also be called the stage of economic internationalization.

Earlier global economic expansion was more like a spontaneous process, a natural product of human development that met the needs of national economic development and benefited from the advancement of transportation technology. In contrast, the international organizations and agreements after World War II were deliberately planned and established to advance economic global expansion in depth, greatly expanding international trade and capital flows, and laying the foundation for the prosperity of multinational corporations. At the same time, however, these interacting international institutions institutionalized the unequal relations between Western developed countries and most underdeveloped countries. The theoretical basis behind the new institutional system established by Western countries was a free market, and differed radically from the planned economy model of socialist countries such as the Soviet Union. Long-term political confrontation between these two sides resulted in economic separation between each other. Internationalization was undoubtedly one-sided, and given the absolute dominance of the United States international integration and economic expansion were forced to follow routes arranged by the United States. So-called "freedom" was actually a tool that served the interests of strong capitalist countries.

2. The spatial manifestations of internationalization: opposing international political and economic forces

Economic internationalization during this period was obviously politically colored. The world was divided into three camps: the capitalist camp, the socialist camp, and the developing countries. Comprising mainly the old capitalist countries in North America and Western Europe, the capitalist camp was concentrated in the Western world. The United States, taking advantage of the accumulation of capital during World War II, became the leader of the capitalist camp, and initiated the Cold War against socialist countries, relying on its political and military alliance with Western European countries. With the help of the United States, the economies of these Western European countries quickly recovered. In 1948, the United States launched the Marshall Plan to help countries in Western Europe revive their economies that had been damaged during the war. In the meantime, tariffs and trade barriers between these countries declined, leading to a dramatic increase in international trade and accelerating the process of European integration. It only took a few years after World War II for most Western European countries to reach prewar levels of economic output. In the next 20 years, with the rapid development of a new scientific and technological revolution, capitalist countries experienced postwar booms. From 1950 to 1973, average GDP growth rate of Western capitalist economies doubled that of the industrialization period before World War I. Another remarkable record was the export growth rate reached 8.6 percent in the same period, which also doubled that in the prewar period and eight times that in 1913–1950.

Another significant change was the rise of the red camp (socialist countries), mainly in Eastern Europe and Asia. These countries, whose economic foundations were relatively weak due to the severe damage they had suffered during World War II and the fact that they were relatively less developed before it, formed alliances led by the Soviet Union. After the war, most of these countries followed the Soviet model of socialist public ownership, a highly centralized planned economy management system and emphasis on the development of heavy industries. The Soviet model achieved remarkable results in the 30 years after the war. The socialist camp in the 1950s and 1960s maintained relatively high economic growth rates, which were almost as fast as those of rapidly growing Western countries. However, it was in the 1970s that most socialist countries reached their limit, especially the Soviet Union. Though the Cold War with Western countries had largely hindered the economic internationalization of Eurasia, the integration process among socialist countries never stopped. The Soviet Union, Bulgaria, Hungary, the Czech Republic, and other countries established the Council for Mutual Economic Assistance (Comecon) in 1949, and formed a military alliance under the Warsaw Pact in 1955. The establishment of Comecon had promoted economic cooperation among the socialist member states, especially in trade and investment. In particular, high shares of trade of Comecon member states with the Soviet Union strengthened the dependence of Eastern European countries on the Soviet Union. A distinctive feature of the trade structure at that time was that most import and export trade was conducted between nonopposing countries. For example, in 1950, the socialist countries and the developing countries accounted for 85 percent of the Soviet Union's total trade, and Comecon countries for 69 percent of its trade with socialist countries. As political relationships were directly reflected in trade relationships, the internationalization process during this period was tinged by strong political colors.

With unprecedentedly fast economic growth, this period was called a "Golden Age". Yet, it was "golden" only for a few countries in the world. Instead of sharing in this golden age, most developing countries were involved in struggles for national liberation designed to get rid of the colonial rule from which they had long suffered and to establish independent nation-states. During the Cold War, the countries of the "non-aligned movement" were independent third-party forces rather than parts of the two major camps that dominated the world's political structure. These countries were caught in the middle of a tug-of-war between the United States and the Soviet Union, both of which strategically competed for the support of the developing countries by providing military assistance and economic aid. The countries that received help to a large extent followed the development model of the countries that assisted them. Most of them, influenced by Western ideas, adopted import-substitution and export-oriented development strategies under the guidance of the World Bank and the International Monetary Fund. At times the result was a rapid growth of exports and foreign capital. Nevertheless, these countries, lacking sufficient primitive capital accumulation, not only failed to enjoy the expected benefits brought by joining the international market, but also lost control over their own national economies due to a lack of competitiveness, and found themselves marginalized in relation to the progress of economic internationalization.

III. The arrival of the era of economic globalization

In the postwar boom, major Western countries, considering government regulation and interventionist measures necessary, adopted Keynesian policies. At the same time, economic prosperity and high profitability relaxed pressures on capital accumulation, reducing the motivation to export their capital overseas. In addition, during the Cold War, international trade and investments took place mainly in different ideological circles, not globally. Thus this period is featured by economic internationalization. In the 1970s when the postwar boom came to an end, serious issues of stagflation[6] emerged in major Western developed countries. In order to find a way out of the crisis, Western countries represented by the Reagan and Thatcher governments shifted from a Keynesian policy to Friedrich Hayek's neoliberalism, largely reducing government intervention, privatizing state-owned enterprises, and liberalizing investments and trade. The new policies allowed capital to flow more freely for profitability and witnessed large-scale FDIs from developed countries to developing countries. This movement was called by Peter Dicken a "global shift". In particular, after the end of the Cold War in the early 1990s, FDIs of developed countries grew explosively, and the world thus entered the era of economic globalization.

Since the 1980s, the term "economic globalization" has gradually become a buzzword in fields from the media to academia and politics. For the masses, globalization might be just a popular term for the availability of a wide range of products and information from all over the world. For politicians, globalization, commonly used in diplomatic contexts, is a clarion call that drives change in the world and is a powerful tool for world politics. For the media, globalization is a major contextual situation that always links to attractive news and events. However, for scholars, globalization is a serious topic of research and study. Although the various forms of "globalization" mentioned above can be traced back to the birth and expansion of capitalism four centuries ago, and even to the cross-border trade in the "Silk Road" era, the decisive turn to a global economy took place in the 1970s, and was associated with several landmark events including the disintegration of the Bretton Woods system and a surge in cross-border direct investment. Fundamentally, however, globalization is combination of a "spatial fix" for problems of capital accumulation and neoliberalist policy. Of course, the end of the "Cold War" and the rapid advancement of transportation and communications technology were also crucial driving forces of the globalization process.

1. The origin of globalization

Over the past 30 years, the concept of globalization has been widely used, and even deemed historically inevitable by many people. In fact, globalization, though driven by certain objective forces, is more a development mechanism shaped by politicians, entrepreneurs, and scholars, a widely acknowledged system in which most countries in the world participate. As Dicken wrote in the opening chapter of his book *Global Shift*, "When we talk about globalization, we must keep in mind that it is a trend, not a certain final state. Regardless of geographical space or organizational structure, these trends are uneven. There are neither established paths nor definitive end points".[7] Of course, globalization has its own dynamic power and embodies a certain degree of inevitability, as David Harvey's notion of "spatial fix" implies. According to Karl Marx's *Das Kapital*, technological progress and spatial transfer can delay the occurrence of cyclical economic crises during the process of capital accumulation. The former is the so-called "technological fix" and the latter a "spatial fix". Drawing on Marx's analysis of geographical features of capital accumulation in *Das Kapital*, Harvey developed a theoretical account of the geographical mechanisms of capital accumulation, at the center of which is the concept of a "spatial fix" of capital[8]. Harvey considers that since it is difficult to sustain capital accumulation without spatial expansion, a constant search for spatial fixes is necessary. Therefore, restless movement is a prominent feature of capital accumulation.

Since spatial expansion is a fundamental characteristic of capital, why did the concept of "economic globalization" not appear until the 1970s? A core reason is possibly the existence of relatively intact national boundaries regulated by governments that confine the flow of capital within the governments' cages. Marked by the two oil crises in the 1970s, the postwar boom period ended, and the Western developed countries entered an era of severe stagflation and economic crisis. In the 1970s and early 1980s, in order to resolve the crisis, governments in developed countries, especially the governments of the United States under Ronald Reagan and the United Kingdom under Margaret Thatcher, abandoned Keynesian policies and embraced neoliberalism, which provided academic grounds for opening government regulatory boundaries. It is the liberalization strategies adopted by both developed and developing countries in trade and investment that allow the global free flow of goods, capital, information, and labor. The multilateral trading system and its underlying organizational structures (the World Trade

Organization and numerous multilateral trade agreements) aim to move in the direction of an increased liberalization of trade and investment. Thus, to put it briefly, the combination of a "spatial fix" of capital accumulation and neoliberal policies opened the way to a large-scale global spatial expansion of capital and the process of economic globalization that the last 30 years have witnessed.

Early globalization dreamers believed that capital would be free from regional and national restrictions and would flow with absolute freedom and flexibility. For example, Korton once described the ideal state of the "global dream": the world's currency, technology, and markets would be controlled and managed by giant global companies; people would share a unified consumer culture on the basis of average material satisfaction; companies might take any action at their own discretion for greater profit regardless of national and local consequences; the relationship between the individual and an enterprise would be completely determined by the market.[9] It is a portrayal of capital supremacy that, though a little extreme, does reflect the nature of capital's spatial expansion. Despite the continuous efforts that later scholars have made to question such an understanding of globalization and to try to correct it, today definitions and understandings of globalization have, instead of exploring its inner essence, become more and more superficial. Under such circumstances, while some people dream of globalization, its inherent contradictions have been overlooked. Capital may freely flow to the best production location in the world (whether for a market or resources, or even cheap labor). However, it is difficult for the labor force (at least blue-collar workers) to enjoy such freedom. In other words, the neoliberal globalization mainly satisfies the need for a "spatial fix" for capital accumulation rather than the needs of ordinary people. Therefore, although scholars have long recognized the influence that globalization and the rapid flow of capital will have on the balance of global political power, they have overlooked the social consequences brought by globalization, namely, the widening gap between the rich and the poor.

Technology is another important factor that should never be ignored in the understanding of economic globalization. On the one hand, the dramatic progress of transportation and communication technologies over the past half-century has resulted in strong "time and space compression", reducing the cost to capital of space displacement, and providing necessary conditions and "catalysts" for the large-scale spatial expansion of capital. On the other hand, enterprises have constantly adjusted the organization of production, from the vertical integration and mass production of the Fordist model to post-Fordist components outsourcing and flexible production. This shift has caused a gradual extension of supply chains and increasingly specialized division of labor in the production of parts and components, bringing substantial growth in the supply chain trade. For example, despite the growing popularity of industrial clusters, more than 70 percent of internal trade in East Asia today is in intermediate products.

Large-scale foreign investment by developed countries, changes in the organization of production, advances in information technology, and the prevalence of neoliberalism have jointly made the world an increasingly closely integrated socioeconomic space. Throughout history, the spatial expansion of capital has been the fundamental driving force behind global economic expansion, while technological progress is the "catalyst", and national controls and interventions are the "gates". It is a combination of the "spatial fix" of capital accumulation and neoliberalism that have propelled the large-scale global spatial expansion of capital, a process of which has been accelerated by the advancement of transportation and communication technology.

Of course, the spatial scope, direction, and "friction" affecting a "spatial fix" depend on national intervention. Therefore, capital, technology, and the state play different roles in global economic expansion, the former two being the driving forces, while the latter acts as a "mediator" and is the only entity that can adjust the pace and direction of globalization. In the past 30 years or so, the influence of neoliberal ideas has led governments to play a major role in creating favorable political and economic environments for the global flow of capital. At the same time, only powerful countries have managed to assume the role of leaders of global economic expansion or globalization.

2. *The appearance of globalization*

Economic globalization is a phenomenon that involves a wide range of issues, including not only the global flow of capital, information, and commodities but also the global strategy of enterprises, the global economic impact of some noneconomic events (such as immigration, terrorist incidents) and the influence of global organization and culture on the flow of economic factors. In general, globalization is a continuous phenomenon in which the world, jointly driven by economic and technological forces, is made into a close socioeconomic space where the economic decisions of one subject may have a profound impact on economic or social groups in other regions. In the economic field, globalization has been associated with an ever-expanding scale and with constantly changing modes of cross-border flows of goods, services, factors of production, and information. Through the international division of labor and cross-border investment, the efficiency of resource allocation within the world market has continued to increase, while the dependence of economies on each other has been deepening. Thus, the Organization for Economic Cooperation and Development (OECD) defines economic globalization as a dynamic process of increasing interdependence of markets and production in different countries on the basis of trade in goods and services, capital flows, and technology transfer and diffusion, which is a process of an extensive flow of production factors on a global scale to achieve the optimum allocation of resources.

During this process, the global economic system undergoes tremendous changes. For example, the separation of financial capital and industrial accumulation has led to a rapid flow of capital on a worldwide scale and caused an increasing concentration of financial institutions in space. Knowledge is an essential factor of production, and its production, distribution, and flow in production systems have become more and more important. The internationalization of research and development (R & D) along with the rapid development of technology has emerged. The monopolistic positions of multinational corporations (MNCs) have deepened. Many nations have adopted policies to welcome globalization. MNCs, among others, are the core force of economic globalization, which can be reflected by their substantial growth of FDI and international (goods and services) trade. In brief, it might be more specific to understand economic globalization through the following symptomatic phenomena.

First, global trade has been growing faster than GDP. As Figure 2.3 shows, since 1970, the rate of growth of world exports was in most years higher than the nominal rate of GDP growth (at current prices). From 1970 to 2014, the world's total economic output increased 26.5 times, while exports increased 62.2 times (Figure 2.4, at current prices). The volume of world exports of goods and services, which only accounted for 18.4 percent of global GDP in 1990, rose to 28.5 percent of it in 2015. Two factors mainly contribute to this phenomenon. On the one hand, economic globalization has enabled capital to seek, to a large extent, the lowest-cost production locations on a global scale, causing a notable spatial concentration of global production activities.

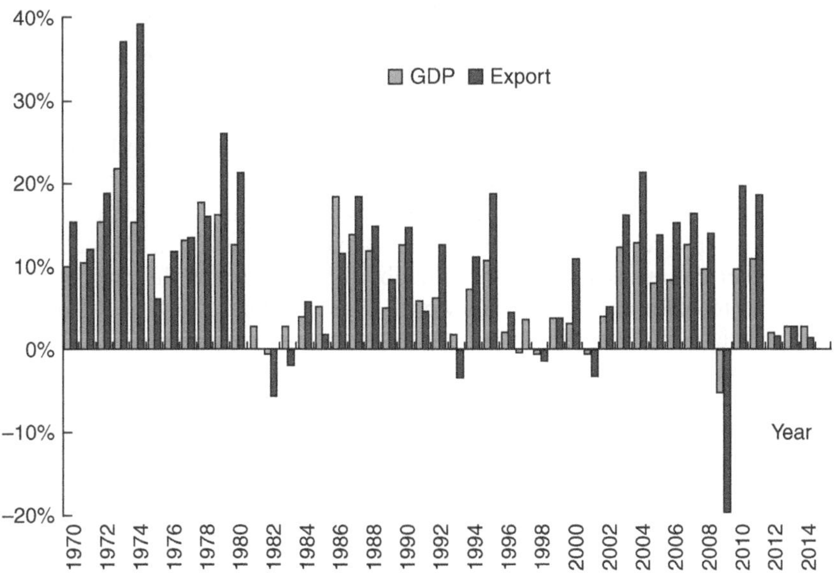

Figure 2.3 World GDP growth rate and export growth rate
Source: World Bank World Development Indicators.

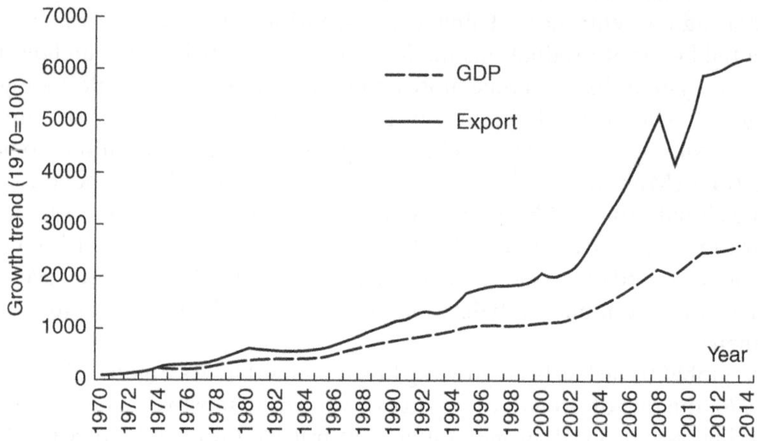

Figure 2.4 World GDP and export growth
Source: World Bank World Development Indicators.

For example, in manufacturing industry, most of the more than 80 percent of information technology products such as mobile phones, laptops, and desktop computers, and more than two-thirds of the world's white goods, produced in China, are exported and sold to countries all over the world. On the other hand, the end of Fordist mass production, the prevalence of lean (flexible) production and refined divisions of labor, along with the increasing proportion of "outsourcing" of production activities, has brought a rapid development of supply chain trade over the past 30 to 40 years. For instance, intermediate product trade represented about 70 percent of the total trade within East Asia. Taking Apple's mobile phone as an example, although product assembly is completed by Foxconn in mainland China, 70 percent to 80 percent of its components, including touch screens, memory, processors, and cellular wireless systems, come from Japan, South Korea, China Taiwan, and other countries and regions, and about 80 percent of the final products are sold to other countries in the world. This is a typical case of the division of labor in manufacturing today, although it is an extreme case.

Although highly volatile, with increases of up to 50 percent to 60 percent in some years and reductions of 30 percent to 40 percent in others, the growth rate of global FDI does present a long-term upward trend that is obviously higher than that of exports (Figure 2.5). From 1970 to 2013, the annual flow of global FDI increased 93.8 times, while exports increased 62.2 times (both at current prices). This growth trend at the early stage was due to the capital export from developed countries in Europe and America, which was partly related to addressing "stagflation" in these countries in the 1970s. This led to the phenomenon that Dicken calls a "global shift", which is the inevitable

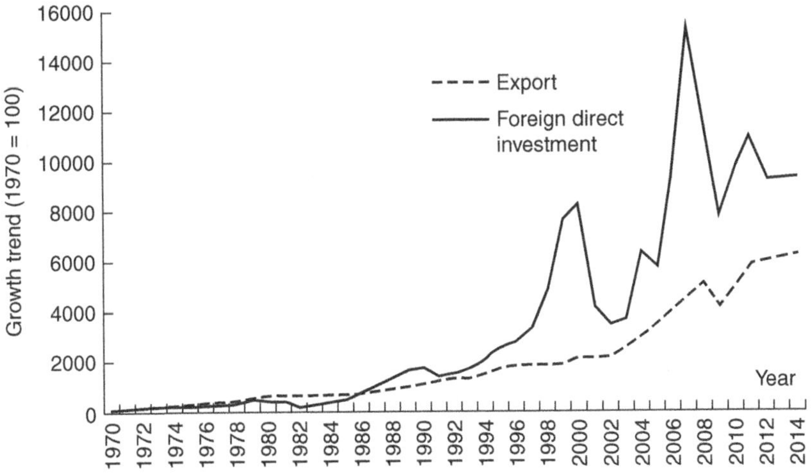

Figure 2.5 Growth of exports and foreign direct investment in the world

Sources: World Bank World Development Indicators and Foreign Direct Investment Database of UNTCAD.

result of the "spatial fix" of capital accumulation in these countries. Since the global financial crisis in 2008, the growth rate of direct foreign investment in developed countries has slowed down, while that in developing countries has increased dramatically. According to statistics published by the United Nations Conference on Trade and Development (UNCTAD), FDI in developed economies, which accounted for more than 85 percent of the world total before 2008, fell to 61 percent in 2014 and rose to 72 percent in 2015.

Third, the number and monopoly positions of MNCs have increased. MNCs, referring to companies that are engaged in production and business activities in two or more countries, set up headquarters and business establishments in one country, and production and operation establishments in other countries. With the rapid growth of direct foreign investment, the number of MNCs in the world has been exploding. In the early 1950s there were fewer than 2,000. The numbers had increased to more than 7,000 by the late 1960s, and reached 15,000 in the early 1980s and 53,000 in 1997. According to estimates in the UNCTAD's *World Investment Report*, today there are approximately 70,000 to 80,000 MNCs, controlling700,000 to 800,000 subsidiaries in more than 180 countries and regions. These companies directly control two-fifths of the total world output, and, through their global production networks, indirectly control over three-quarters of the world economy, two-thirds of world trade (the trade volume of their overseas subsidiaries accounts for 38 percent of the world trade), and more than 90 percent of FDI. The wealth of many MNCs is comparable to that of many states, giving them great influence over the world economy. For example, in 2015, Greece's GDP was about US$240 billion, while Apple had a profit of US$53.4 billion. Today's world thus has shifted from governance by states and supranational institutions (international organizations) to an era of "co-governance by MNCs, states, and supranational institutions". At this time it would be difficult to clearly understand the organizational model of the world economy without a deep knowledge of the operating mechanism of MNCs.

Fourth, integration and fragmentation of the global economy coexist. Economic globalization has promoted the liberalization of investment and trade, and driven it in the direction of a closer integration of global economy. Especially in the framework of the World Trade Organization (WTO), countries around the world are closely connected through trade, forming an increasingly integrated global division of labor. The six principles adhered to by the WTO, namely, the principles of reciprocity, transparency, market access, promotion of fair competition, encouragement of economic development, and non-discrimination (most-favored-nation treatment and national treatment), are the foundations of a complete (including goods, services, and trade-related investment and intellectual property), more dynamic and lasting multilateral trading system. By the end of 2015, the WTO had 164 member states, whose total trade volume accounted for 98 percent of the world total. Although the WTO has provided a positive and significant platform for the integration of the global economy, it is still quite difficult to reach consensus among many member states, which is exactly why limited progress has so far been made in the Doha Round negotiations.[10] In the meantime, small multilateral and bilateral trade negotiations are in full swing around the world. It is estimated that more than 1,000 small multilateral and bilateral trade agreements have been signed or are under negotiation in the world, and that 167 trade agreements have been reached or are under negotiation among just the 53 member states of the United Nations Economic and Social Commission for Asia and the Pacific. The coexistence of integration and fragmentation of the global economy makes the question as to how to protect the achievements of economic globalization and promote the integration and revitalization of the global economy a prominent issue challenging the world's major economies.

Fifth, global production networks have become the main organizational form of the world economy. Accompanied with the trend toward investment and trade liberalization, the global economy, supported by new information technologies, has undergone a new spatial restructuring as the spatial organization of MNCs' production activities has become more complex and active, and the formation of global production networks has accelerated worldwide. Since the 1970s, with the prevalence of lean (flexible) production, the specialization of production activities has gradually deepened. The "segmentation" of the industry chains is noticeable, and production segments that were originally scattered all over the world have been integrated into production networks at various scales. What are called global production networks

(GPNs) are the value creation networks centered on lead firms occupying controlling positions.[11] Though called a "production network", a GPN does not only refer to the manufacturing process but also covers the entire process from R & D and financing, to production, distribution, consumption, and recycling. The study of GPNs, which mainly focuses on analysis of the spatial organization of complex production activities from the perspectives of the creation and capture of value and the distribution and "embeddedness" of power in the network, is a powerful analytical tool for understanding the relationships between MNCs and states (regions), and an effective theoretical framework to understand how global economic integration takes place. The OECD estimates that more than 80 percent of global trade today takes place in various global production networks.

IV. The limitations of economic globalization

Economic globalization has had a positive effect on the overall growth of the world economy. From 1980 to 2015, the average annual growth rate of the world economy reached 2.86 percent, and the total size of the economy increased by 5.2 times; the world's import and export volume of goods reached 33.28 trillion US dollars, an increase of 7.3 times; the net flows of FDI worldwide amounted to 2.1 trillion US dollars, an increase of 40 times. However, in this period the global economy also experienced the 1997 and 2008 financial crises, and it has not yet recovered from the 2008 financial crisis. The average annual growth rate of the world economy was only 2.24 percent from 2009 to 2015, with negative growth in world GDP at nominal prices in 2009 and 2015.

Moreover, in the context of the global transfer of industrial activities disparities between continents decreased. From 1980 to 2013, the average annual economic growth rate of Asia, Africa, and Oceania as well as the average world growth rate were higher than those of Europe and the Americas. In particular, Asia's GDP grew at more than 4 percent, per year on average and increased 9.3 times to 25 trillion US dollars. In terms of the total GDP of the five continents in 1980, Europe accounted for 41.9 percent, followed by the Americas, accounting for 32.1 percent, and Asia, Africa, and Oceania respectively for 20.6 percent, 3.7 percent and 1.7 percent. In 2013, Asia ranked first, accounting for 33.3 percent of world GDP, and the Americas followed with 32.7 percent, while Europe fell to 28.6 percent (Figure 2.6).

Nevertheless, contrary to the claims made for free trade and globalization by a large number of scholars, globalization has, at many spatial scales, led to increased inequality and social polarization. It is always stated in economic studies that free trade and free investment will benefit all parties involved, and mainstream economists use mathematical models to argue that free trade enables countries to achieve balanced development. The reality, however, is quite the opposite (at least at many spatial scales). In fact, as early as the mid nineteenth century, Great Britain, after abolishing its own Corn Laws, encouraged Western European countries to implement completely free trade.

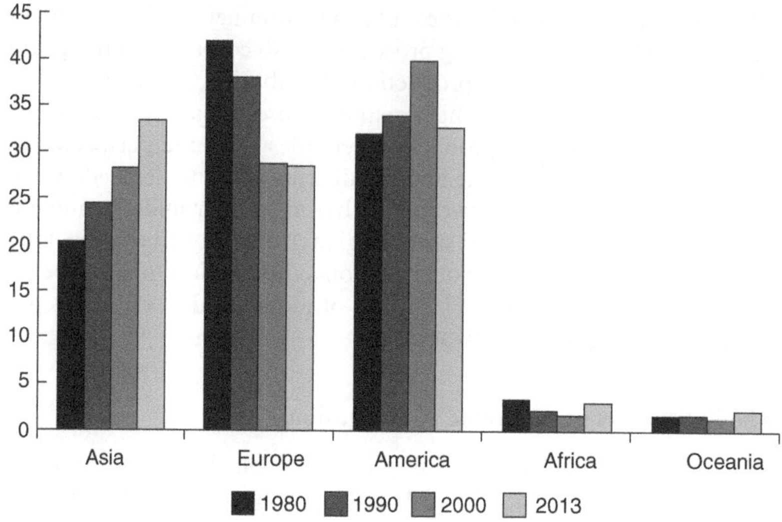

Figure 2.6 Five continents' share of world's total GDP from 1980 to 2013
Source: World Bank.

Only after a few years did they realize the harm to their interests and start to adopt protectionist measures.[12] In addition, mainstream free trade theory is based on epistemological individualism, by which the income of the grass roots is easily "averaged". In fact, variable and often limited connectivity and the diversity of "society and space" mean that the extent that different regions can benefit from globalization varies considerably, especially when many developing countries have not yet been able to fully participate in the globalization process.

World Bank data shows that the ratio of GDP per capita between the richest country and the poorest rose to 336:1 in 2015 from 272:1 in 1982 (the per capita GDP of Luxembourg, the richest country, was \$102,000, while that of Burundi in Africa was only \$303.7). There are large imbalances not only between European countries and the United States and African, Asian, and Latin American countries, but also between developed and developing countries as well as among developed countries themselves. In recent years, the poverty rates in Japan, Germany, the United States and other countries have been rising, reaching about 15 percent today. The latest research shows that from 1970 to 2014, the proportion of workers under 30 years old in the United States whose income exceeded that of their parents has dropped from 90 percent to 41 percent, with the middle class experiencing the greatest decline. In other words, since the 1970s, US income growth has been mainly concentrated on high-income families, while that of middle- and low-income families has made little progress. The main reason behind this outcome may be the continuous loss of stable manufacturing jobs. For example, the number of manufacturing jobs in the United States decreased by 40 percent from 19.43 million to 11.53 million from 1979 to 2010. In 2016, the middle class declined to 40 percent of its total population.

In addition, the gap between the rich and the poor has continued to widen across the globe. Wealth has been concentrated in the hands of a small number of people, while the share of the poor has declined. An Oxfam report states that the total wealth of the world's richest 62 individuals is equivalent to that of half of the world's poorest population. This report identifies the "1 percent economy" phenomenon, that is, the world's richest 1 percent of the population owns more wealth than the remaining 99 percent. Furthermore, in the last five years the wealth of the world's poor has not increased but instead decreased. Increasing interdependence caused by globalization has also led to a rise in vulnerability and risk associated with disease, events that disrupt the flow of goods and services and so on. Management of these risks depends on political and social stability.

Therefore, economic globalization over the past three decades has been associated with a set of international economic governance mechanisms developed on the basis of neoliberalism by developed countries in Europe and America to allow their capital to find a "spatial fix" overseas. Having adopted the path of neoliberalization, developed country governments and elites, convinced that a one-size-fits-all market solution related to the development they had taken was the first-best solution for all developing countries, sought to export it in the shape of the "Washington Consensus" of the 1990s. It was the adoption of the neoliberal Washington Consensus that caused the Soviet Union and Eastern European countries to fall into deep economic recessions of variable length after the fall of communism. Although neoliberal economic globalization involves a set of mechanisms that mainly meets the needs of capital's spatial expansion and has delivered enormous benefits to capital and large companies, it has also been the cause of serious social problems and imposed high costs on lower-income groups in developed countries. Neoliberal globalization is also a bittersweet process in that, while capital is allowed to flow freely, the labor force does not enjoy the same freedom to move. If unregulated, these mechanisms could cause increasing social conflict around the world and make global sustainable development goals and objectives harder to achieve.

After more than 200 years of global economic expansion, the world entered the era of economic globalization under the combined impact of institutional, economic, and technological factors. However, after more than three decades of development, economic globalization has arrived at a "crossroad". Answers to the questions as to how and where it will proceed are essential for global sustainable development. Economic globalization is extensively debated with both strong advocates and sharp critics. Although China, as to a large extent a beneficiary of the economic growth economic globalization delivered, has been called on by many scholars and media in China and abroad to lead globalization, it cannot take the old path due to the limitations of neoliberal globalization. First, the problems brought about by economic globalization must be taken seriously in looking for a solution. Second, it was the organic integration of market forces and the actions of a strong Chinese government, rather than Western development models, that enabled China to benefit from economic globalization. Therefore, China should make full use of its own development experience in participating in the reform of economic globalization mechanisms and contribute a Chinese solution for international economic governance.

Notes

* The author thanks Gao Boyang and YeerkenWuzhati for their assistance.

1 Debu Gao and Jue Wang, *An Economic History of the World* (Beijing: China Renmin University Press, 2001).

2 J. G. Taylor and A. M. Williamson, *Globalization in Historical Perspective* (Chicago: University of Chicago Press, 2005).

3 Charles Issawi, *An Economic History of the Middle East and North Africa* (New York: Columbia University Press, 1982), 464–465.

4 Peter Dicken, *Global Shift: Mapping the Changing Contours of the World Economy*, 6th ed. (New York and London: Guildford Press, 2010).

5 In fact, in the mid nineteenth century, Great Britain, after abolishing its own Corn Laws, encouraged Western European countries to implement free trade. Only after a few years did they realize the harm to their interests and begin to adopt protectionist measures. So-called "free trade" was subsequently mainly trade terms that colonial countries were forced to accept.

6 Stagflation was a very complicated phenomenon and a surface manifestation of the crisis of Western economies in the 1970s. It involved a combination of increased unemployment, a low growth rate and a high inflation rate. Stagnation was arguably due to a significant decline in business investment as a result of a decline in profitability and productivity growth and an increasing wage share negotiated by trade unions. Rapid exchange rate movements after the collapse of the Bretton Woods system also played a role. In these circumstances, business investment moved offshore to less developed countries where rates of return on investment were higher. Stagflation played a role in undermining standard Keynesian economic models as they indicated that stagflation should not happen. In this volume, when reference is made to stagflation, it refers to these deep issues behind more superficial phenomena in addition to stagflation itself.

7 Peter Dicken, *Global Shift: Reshaping the Global Economic Map in the 21st Century*, trans. W. D. Liu (Beijing: The Commercial Press, 2007).

8 See D. Harvey, "The Geography of Capitalist Accumulation: A Reconstruction of the Marxian Theory", *Antipode* 2, no. S (1975): 9–12; D. Harvey, "The Spatial Fix: Hegel, Von Thunen and Marx", *Antipode* 13 (1981): 1–12; D. Harvey, *The Limits to Capital* (Oxford: Blackwell, 1982).

9 Peter Dicken, *Global Shift: Reshaping the Global Economic Map in the 21st Century*, trans. W. D. Liu (Beijing: The Commercial Press, 2007).

10 The Doha Round is the latest round of multilateral trade negotiations among the WTO membership. It aims to lower trade barriers among member states and to

facilitate the economic development of the world, especially the relatively poor countries, through a fairer trade environment. Though these negotiations cover eight subjects of agriculture, nonagricultural market access, trade in services, WTO rules, dispute settlement, intellectual property, trade and development, trade and environment, only the Bali Package has been adopted in the Doha Round during the last 18 years.

11 For more information on the global production network, see N. M. Coe and W. C. H. Yeung, *Global Production Network* (Oxford: Oxford University Press, 2015).

12 E. Sheppard, *Limits to Globalization: Disruptive Geographies of Capitalist Development* (Oxford: Oxford University Press, 2016).

3 General context of the Belt and Road Initiative

Scholars and media may miss the key point when discussing the BRI and attribute it to a certain or single objective. According to the official statement, the BRI is a major and long-term vision of open development that the Chinese Communist Party Central Committee and the State Council have proposed to coordinate the overall domestic and international situation. In other words, it is not a single factor or purpose, but changes in the general context as a result of a series of complicated factors that led to the proposal of BRI. Basically, the BRI is the result of the combined effects of the development of economic globalization, changes in the world economic pattern, and the transformation of China's own development model, along with other factors such as the goal of creating peace and stability in the surrounding environment and seeking diversity of the natural resources supply.

I. The changing global context

The past 30 years have witnessed major changes in the global socioeconomic context that, from a world perspective, are mainly driven by economic globalization. On the one hand, the world has gradually evolved from a binary structure of "core (developed countries)-periphery (less-developed countries)" to a ternary structure of "developed countries-emerging countries-less developed countries". On the other hand, the gap between the rich and the poor continues to expand at various scales while the global poverty issue remains prominent. In particular, since the outbreak of the global financial crisis in 2008, the world economy, with slow and even negative growth in trade and a frequent occurrence of precarious events, has continued to slump. Protectionism and populism have been rising along with increasing questioning of economic globalization. It might be said that BRI has been proposed against the background of economic globalization having reached a "crossroad".

Over the past three decades, economic globalization has had a profound impact on the socioeconomic development and spatial process in different regions. On the one hand, economic globalization has promoted the growth of the global economy, manifesting in the global optimization of production factors and the liberalization of trade and investment. From 1970 to 2010, the average annual growth rate of the world economy reached 3.16 percent, and the total scale increased by 3.47 times. However, the average annual growth rate since the global financial crisis in 2008 was only 2.2 percent, while a negative growth rate of 5 percent to 6 percent in nominal prices even occurred in 2009 and 2015. On the other hand, economic globalization has intensified the uneven development of countries (regions) in the world. The gap between the rich and the poor has widened dramatically at various scales due to the inherent contradiction of the economic globalization mechanism. That is, capital may freely flow to seek production locations with the lowest cost in the world, while it is difficult for the labor force to enjoy such freedom. According to studies by Oxfam (a charity for alleviation of poverty), the 1 percent rich of the global population in 2016 will have more wealth than the remaining 99 percent[1]. The World Bank estimates that, with one USD/day as the poverty line, the world's total poverty population was reduced by 639 million from 1981 to 2005, of whom 624 million were reduced in China, and only 15 million in other regions. Or taking 1.5 USD/day as the poverty line, the 519.5 million total poverty population was reduced in the world over the same period, of whom 627.4 million were reduced in China, while there was actually a net increase of 108 million poverty population in other regions. In addition, some countries that once were proud of their high average income levels, such as Germany and Japan, which remain a 15 percent proportion of total poverty population today, have also experienced a continuous widening of the income gap in recent years. In the United States, the proportion of the middle class has fallen below 50 percent of the population. Therefore, in general, in the process of economic globalization based on neoliberalism, capital is the biggest winner, while societies have paid a huge price.

It is undeniable that China's rapid economic development over the past three decades has benefited from economic globalization. And in return, China has also made tremendous contributions to the growth of the global economy and changed the world economic landscape (Figure 3.1 and Figure 3.2). At the beginning of the reform and opening up, China's GDP only accounted for 5 percent of the world's share (calculated in purchasing power parity, i.e., PPP), while its exports accounted for less than 1.5 percent of the world's total exports. By 2015, the share of China's GDP in the world had risen to 15.0 percent (converted to the average US dollar exchange rate of that year), and its share of exports had also risen to 13.8 percent. Correspondingly, China became the second-largest economy in the world in 2010, the world's largest country of trade in goods in 2013, and the second-largest foreign investor in the world in 2015. At the same time, China is currently the world's largest manufacturing country, accounting for 24 percent of the world's manufacturing output (while the proportion of the United States has dropped to about 20 percent).

Moreover, since the global financial crisis in 2008, China's contribution to world economic growth has remained around 30 percent on average. Although China's economy is still large but not strong, such a large economy

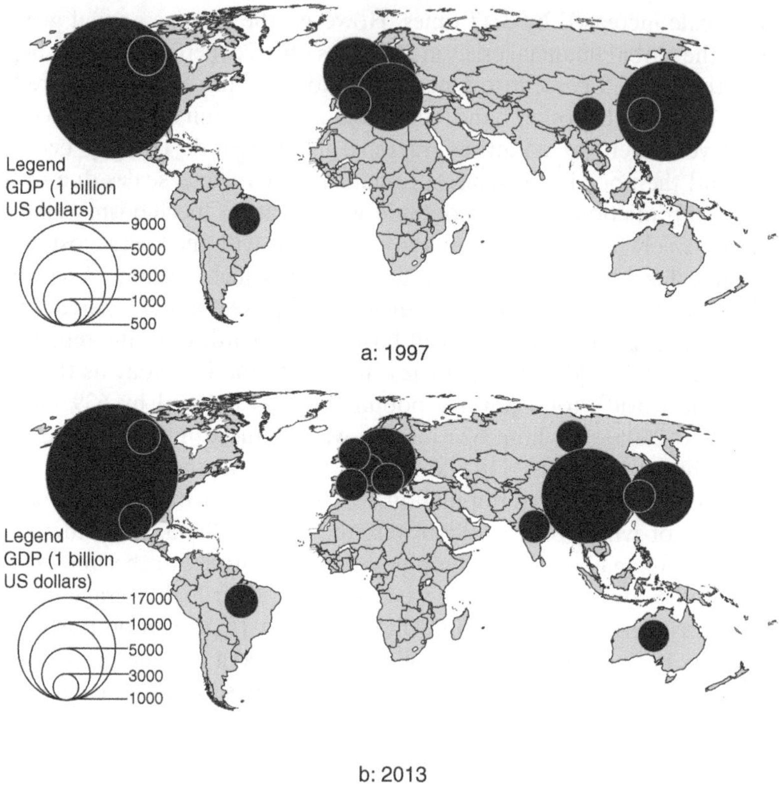

Figure 3.1 Distribution of GDP in major countries
Source: World Bank Database.

(10.8 trillion US dollars in 2015) is enough to make it one of the major forces shaping the global context. Furthermore, within the trend of increasingly close economic linkages among countries in the world, it is inevitable that the development of and changes in such a large economy will substantially influence other relevant countries.

From the perspective of a longer historical period, the rise of the Chinese economy in the past three decades has been the biggest change in the world economic landscape in the past 100 years, and is also one of the few major events that have occurred in the world landscape in the past 300 years. According to estimates by Angus Madison, former chief economist of the OECD, at the beginning of the eighteenth century when the United States' share of the world's economy was negligible, China's GDP accounted for nearly one-third of the world's total. However, more than 200 years later, at the time of the founding of the New China, China's proportion in the world GDP had fallen to 4.6 percent, while the United States' rose to 27 percent (Figure 3.3). Until

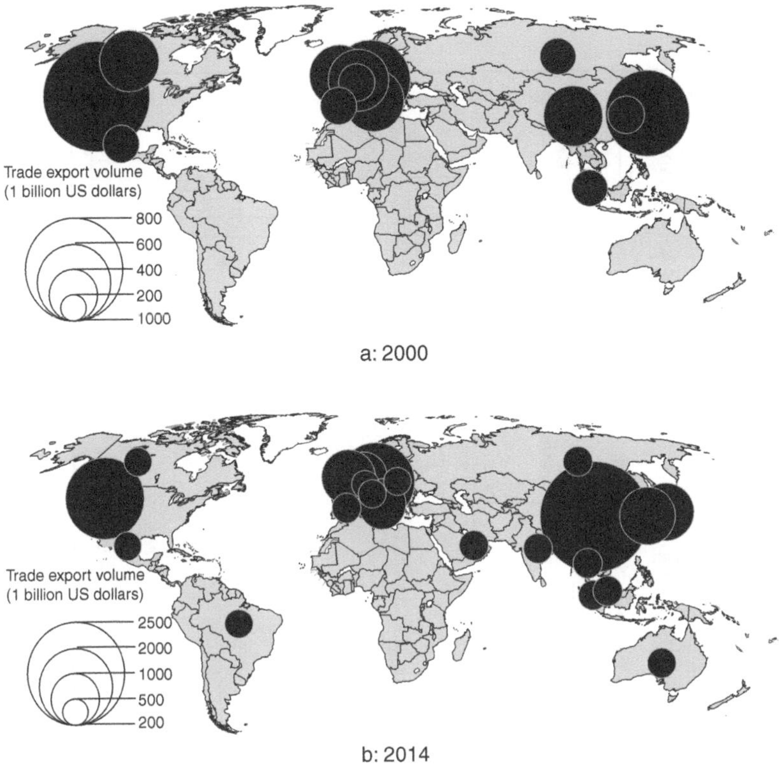

Figure 3.2 Distribution of export size in major countries
Source: World Bank database.

the beginning of the reform and opening up, China's GDP still accounted for only 4.9 percent of the world's total (Figure 3.4; this figure would be only about 2 percent if calculated on the basis of the official exchange rate). After rapid development during more than 30 years of the reform and opening up, China's share of GDP in the world has recovered to 15 percent (based on the official exchange rate, and this figure would be 20 percent or so if estimated on the basis of PPP), while the share of the United States has dropped to 22.5 percent. Along with the rise of China, East Asia (including mainland China, Hong Kong SAR, Macau SAR and the Taiwan region, Japan, and South Korea) today accounts for more share in the world economy than the United States. Overall, the world economy tends to be balanced in triple poles as North America (the United States and Canada) accounts for 27 percent of the world's economy, the European Union (EU) for 26 percent, and East Asia for 25 percent (calculated in official exchange rates). This means a huge shift in the world economic landscape and the arrival of the "Asian Century".

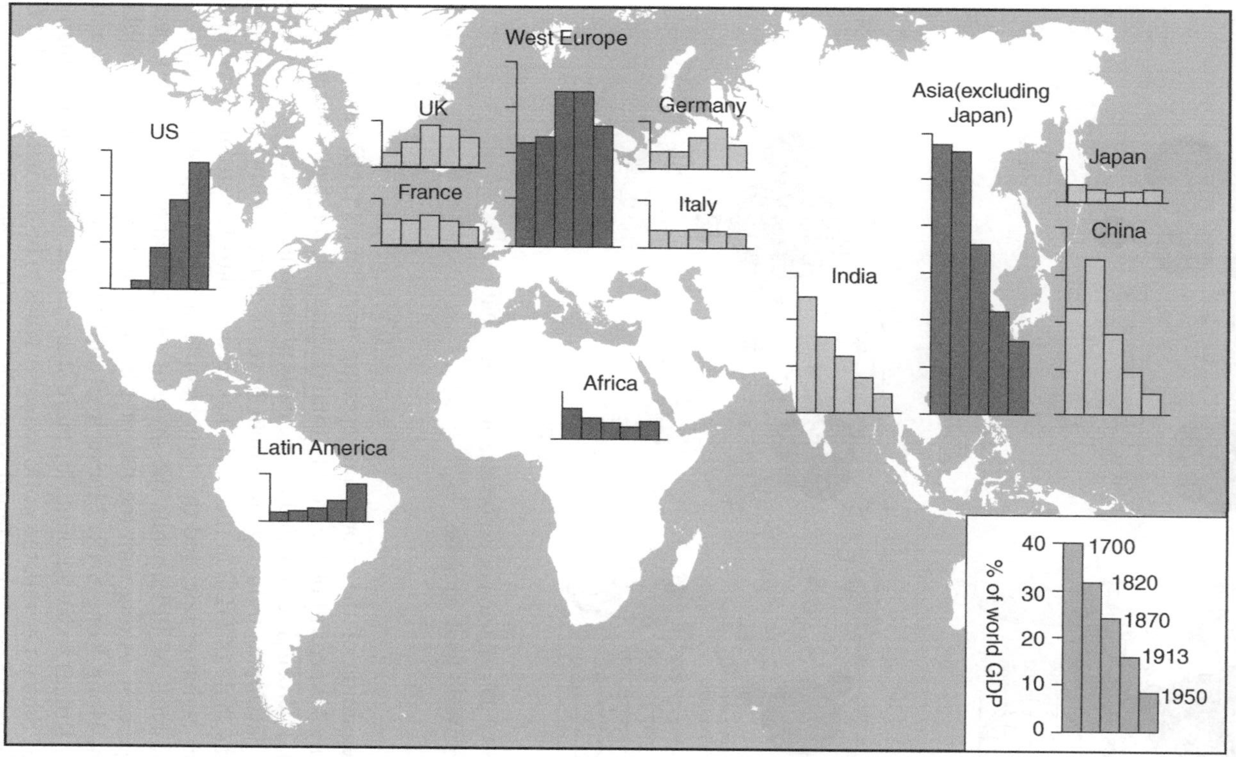

Figure 3.3 Changes in the world economic landscape (1700–1950)
Source: cited from Dicken (2010).

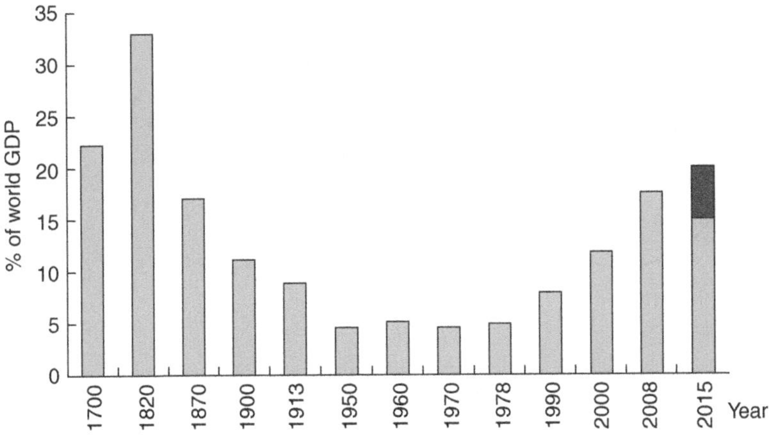

Figure 3.4 Changes in the proportion of China's total economic output (GDP) accounting for the world's total from 1700 to 2015

The data for 2015 are estimates by the author (the slash part is calculated on the basis of official exchange rate, and the dotted part is calculated on the basis of PPP).

Source: Maddison (2009).

In the rather long period after World War II, the division of labor in the world was simplified as a "core-periphery" model under which developed countries acted as the "core", mainly engaging in manufacturing industry while developing countries acted as the "periphery", serving as the provider of raw materials and agricultural products as well as the market for manufactured goods from developed countries. It is from the "core-periphery" model that the buzzwords "South-South cooperation" and "North-South cooperation" in world politics and media originated. Nevertheless, this binary structure, driven by economic globalization, has undergone tremendous changes during the past three decades. On the one hand, developed countries have transferred traditional industries to some developing countries (such as China), "hollowing out" their manufacturing industries and enabling them to shift their focus of economic development to the financial industry and high-tech industries; on the other hand, some developing countries, represented by China, have risen to become emerging economies and major manufacturing powers, while many other developing countries, mainly providing primary products in the division of labor, remain at a low income level with lagged manufacturing industries. Therefore, a ternary structure of "core-middle-periphery" has formed in the world such that the emerging economies as the middle layer have played an increasingly important role in world economic ties (Figure 3.5). How to promote reform of the global economic governance system and achieve sustainable development of the world in this ternary structure is a new topic for the next few years.

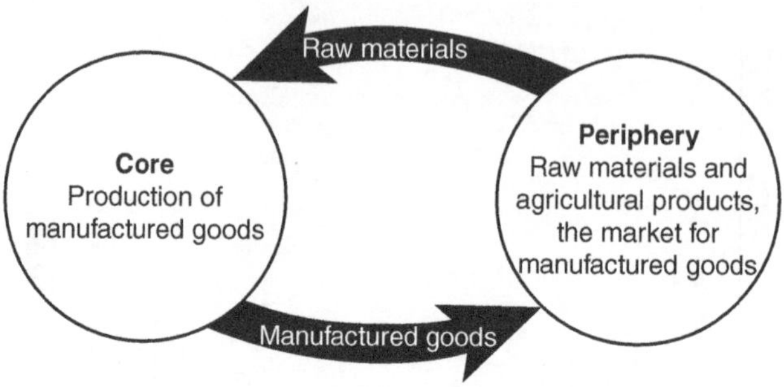

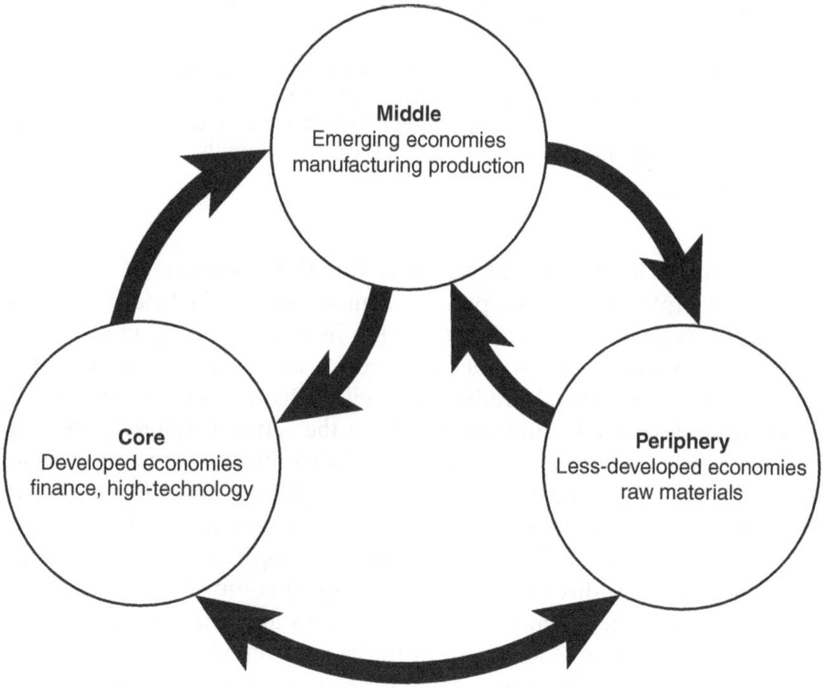

Figure 3.5 Schematic diagram of the world structure

II. The transformation of China's development model

Since the reform and opening up, China has maintained a high-speed economic growth rate for more than 30 years, and the average annual growth rate of GDP reached 9.6 percent from 1978 to 2015, having created a miracle of economic growth that was not previously seen in the history of the world. During this period, China, with the increase of GDP from more than 200 billion US dollars (based on the official exchange rate) to 10.8 trillion US dollars, and an increase of total economic output by more than 30 times at comparable prices, became the second-largest economy in the world. Moreover, with its per capita GDP rising from more than 200 US dollars to nearly 8,000 US dollars, and its poverty population falling from 770 million (based on the poverty line of 2,300 yuan, unchanged in 2010) to 55.75 million, China has grown from one of the poorest countries in the world to an upper-middle-income country. Nevertheless, such remarkable achievements of economic growth have attracted a lot of debate among domestic and foreign academics about the "Chinese miracle", including such perspectives as China's success can mainly be attributed to the introduction of market mechanisms, or to the important role played by its "strong government", or to economic globalization. Overall, economic globalization has provided a beneficial international environment and the possibility of facilitating development. However, it is China's own efforts, especially the combination of "effective markets" and "active government" and progressive reform that have essentially contributed to its success. From the external perspective, the "strong government" of China still plays a crucial role in economic growth; from the internal perspective, the market mechanism has been the foundation of its success as China has changed from a planned economy to a market economy. Despite a lot of controversy, the rise of China's economy and its approach to overall poverty alleviation can still have significant implications for other developing countries, which is exactly the reason that Francis Fukuyama, a well-known American expert on international issues, once commented that "the Belt and Road Initiative" is a competition between different development models. The outcome will determine the fate of Eurasia in the coming decades.[2]

Of course, China has also paid a huge price in resources and the environment for its achievements in economic growth. China's total energy consumption was only 570 million tons (standard coal, the same below) in 1978, rising to 2.3 billion tons in 2004, and 4.3 billion tons in 2015. This was an increase of 6.5 times in 36 years. In 2013, China became the world's largest energy consumer and the largest carbon emitter (annual emissions, nonaccumulated emissions). With the slowdown of economic growth and structural transformation (especially the removal of production capacity) in recent years, China's energy consumption and carbon emissions have been gradually slowing too (Figure 3.6). In addition, economic growth has dramatically accelerated the occupation of land, especially cultivated land, which has been occupied nearly 576,580 acres (i.e., 2333.45 square kilometers) per year since 2001. Furthermore, inefficient use and overutilization of land have also brought prominent problems. Meanwhile, a series of ecological and environmental issues such as atmospheric pollution (especially fog and haze), water pollution, soil pollution, the disappearance of wetlands, and the degradation of grasslands have seriously threatened the sustainable development of China. Thus, it is imperative for China to change its economic development

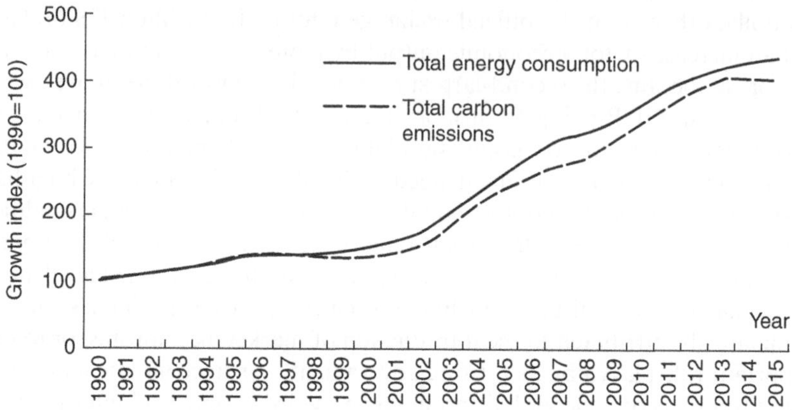

Figure 3.6 Growth trends of China's energy consumption and carbon emissions from 1990 to 2015

Source: China Statistical Yearbook – 2016; China Information Center for Global Change Studies.

model and establish a sustainable economic system in terms of both resources and environment.

From the perspective of the economic system itself, China has entered the "new normal". The so-called "new normal" is not merely a decline in the economic growth rate but more of a change in the development model, that is, a shift from high-input factors and export-oriented development models to a diversified development model relying on innovative activities with more emphasis on domestic consumption and global vision. During the nearly four decades of the reform and opening up, China first participated in the global division of labor by virtue of its comparative advantage in cheap labor, and established an export-oriented economic development model, driving economic growth by largely attracting FDI and promoting exports. Later, China developed large-scale capital-intensive industries, including steel, non-ferrous metallurgy, machinery and equipment, automobiles, high-speed rail and real estate, promoting its economic growth through investment. Since the global financial crisis in 2008, with the deterioration of international market conditions and overcapacity of domestic production, this economic development model driven by high-intensity factor input and large-scale exports has come to an end. And China, objectively, has to start an industrial transformation and upgrading to develop a diversified economy essentially driven by innovation with new markets to be opened.

However, whether an industrial transformation and upgrading or the implementation of innovation-driven development, this means the spatial restructuring of economic activities, especially spatial restructuring on a global scale. In other words, China's transformation of its development model may only be accomplished when its planning and resources allocation is made on global scale. As President Xi Jinping pointed out at a symposium on the promotion of BRI held by the central government on August 17, 2016, "only a strong country can confidently open up, and the openness in return will promote the prosperity of such a country . . . As China's economic development has entered an era of a new normality, in order to maintain a sustainable and sound development of economy, we must coordinate the overall domestic and international situation from a global perspective with our own initiative and to design the grand strategy of a full opening up from all perspectives, taking a more proactive approach to the world".[3]

In fact, such spatial restructuring has kicked off, manifested by the rapid growth of China's FDI since the 2008 financial crisis (Figure 3.7). Despite some fluctuations, China's outward FDI (OFDI), from only several billion US dollars per year before 2005, rose to 55.9 billion US dollars in 2008 and exceeded 100 billion US dollars in 2013. In 2015, China, with its OFDI reaching 145.6 billion US dollars, notably in excess of its foreign investment (135.6 billion US dollars), ranked only second to the United States in the world. This indicates that China, having evolved from a development stage emphasizing a "bring in" strategy to one stressing both a "bring in" and a "going global" strategy, will be integrated into the world economic system in a more active and deeper way. The growth trend of China's OFDI over the past decade actually is quite similar to that of developed economies in the 1980s and 1990s (Figure 3.8). If the dramatic increase in FDI in advanced economies back then gave rise to what Dicken called the global shift, the growth trend of China's OFDI might mean the arrival of the second round of a global shift.

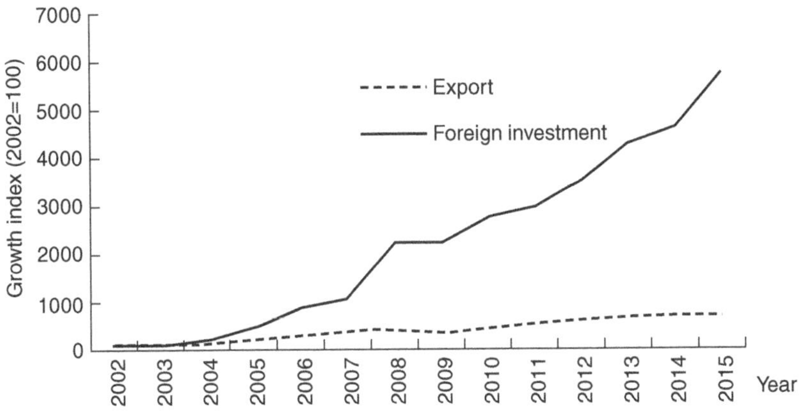

Figure 3.7 Export and foreign investment growth of China from 2002 to 2015
Source: China Statistical Yearbook – 2016.

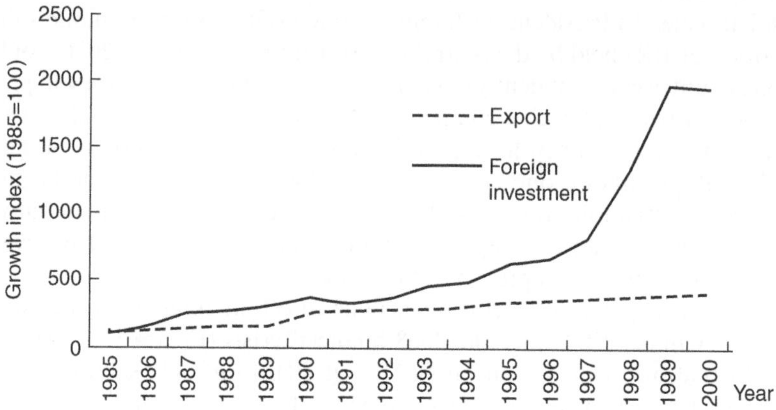

Figure 3.8 Export and foreign investment growth of advanced economies from 1985 to 2000

Source: UNTCAD database.

In brief, the dramatic increase in China's OFDI over the past decade may be largely driven by four factors. First, as labor costs rise, some of China's labor-intensive industries are losing their international competitiveness and having to move to lower-cost countries or regions. Since 2000, the average real wage index of urban employment in China has been rising fast, with a growth rate of more than 10 percent in most years and an increase by 4.8 times from 2000 to 2015. The cost of frontline workers in factories, including direct wages plus "social insurances and housing funds", today is already close to 5,000 yuan/month. The rapid increase in wages on the one hand allows workers to share the substantial benefits of economic growth, while on the other hand erodes the competitiveness of labor-intensive manufacturing industry. Research statistics show that labor costs in China's factories have already more than doubled that of countries such as India and Vietnam, and more than tripled that of countries such as Cambodia and Bangladesh, which is also close to that of South Korea and Taiwan if labor productivity factors are taken into account. Thus, a great number of labor-intensive industries invested in by MNCs have been transferred to other countries and regions such as South Asia, Southeast Asia, and Africa, while China's private labor-intensive industries, including textile and clothing, footwear, and toy assembly, have also begun such a transfer. This is the direct result of a new round of a global shift that will bring opportunities for the growth of less-developed countries.

Second, a prominent overcapacity makes China in urgent need of a "spatial fix". Though there is no doubt that the investment stimulus plan for the 2008 global financial crisis effectively helped China cope with the complicated international economic situation at that time, it also resulted in overcapacity in many sectors. Currently China's steel production capacity exceeds 1.2

billion tons, cement clinker production capacity 2 billion tons, electrolytic aluminum production capacity 40 million tons, automobile production capacity 31 million (with a capacity of 6 million under construction), and shipbuilding capacity 80 million DWT (almost the annual demand of the world today). Based on the need for a "spatial fix" for capital accumulation and the past experience of developed countries, China is in need of a spatial transfer in some capital-intensive industries, which is actually a normal phenomenon of a global shift and economic globalization as well as an opportunity for less-developed countries.

Third, a number of Chinese enterprises have grown into large companies with strength in international investment in the past two decades. A lot of Chinese companies, including both state-owned enterprises with a certain monopoly position and private enterprises that have grown up in the severe competition of market economy, have grown fast thanks to the policy of the reform and opening up and China's huge consumer market. One hundred ten Chinese companies were listed in the rankings of the Fortune Global 500 in 2016, of which 97 were from mainland China. This number was zero 30 years ago. These major companies have truly become multinational companies with the strength of transnational investment, whose expansion in global business in fact has led to most of the international mergers and acquisitions by China in recent years.

Fourth, China needs to secure a natural resources supply in the international market. It is difficult for China to meet the needs of multiple resources for economic development with its domestic reserves since the per capita resources in China are relatively low. With 60 percent external reliance on important resources, such as iron ore, bauxite, copper concentrate, and crude oil, China, following the path once taken by developed countries, has to continue to improve its security level in respect of the reserve or supply of its natural resources so as to meet its needs for sustainable economic development. Market-based approaches, such as purchase from the market, mergers and acquisitions of mines and oil fields, and joint venture mining, are all available to China for that purpose. As shown in the structure of China's foreign investment, the mining industry has remained at a high proportion of 15 percent since 2000.

Looking back over the past 30 years, it is clear that China's economic development and its participation in economic globalization have gone through three phases (Figures 3.9 and 3.10). In the 1990s, especially after Deng Xiaoping's Southern tour speech, China's FDI underwent a surge of growth. In 1991, China attracted only 4.37 billion US dollars in foreign capital, which however increased to 47.13 billion US dollars in 1996 with an average annual growth rate of 61 percent. Although it suffered in the Asian financial crisis in 1997, China still remained at a high level in attracting foreign investment. The average annual growth rate of FDI attracted by China reached 27.8 percent in general in the 1990s, while the average annual growth rate of exports was only 15.2 percent during the same time period. It was, therefore, a so-called

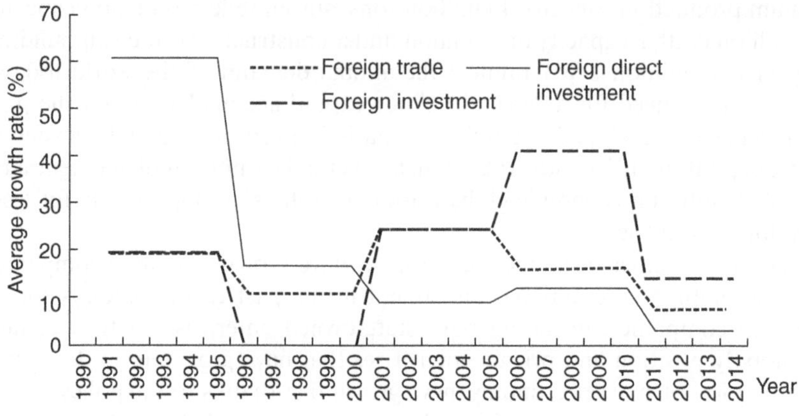

Figure 3.9 Growth rate of China's foreign trade, foreign investment, and foreign direct investment from 1990 to 2014

Source: China Statistical Yearbook – 2015.

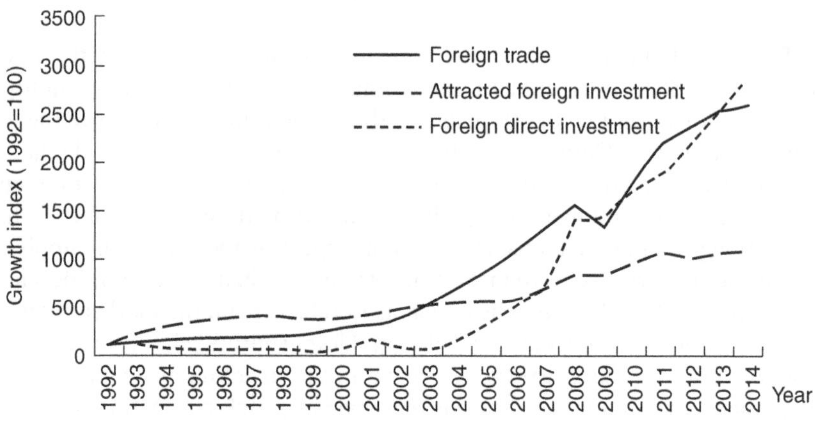

Figure 3.10 Growth index of China's foreign trade, attracted foreign investment, and foreign direct investment from 1990 to 2014

Source: China Statistical Yearbook – 2015.

stage of dependency globalization where challenging issues, such as lack of capital, technology and management experience for economic growth, were addressed by attracting foreign capital. From 1996 to 2000, foreign investment accounted for 8.4 percent of China's fixed asset investment, which was much higher than budgeted investment.

Since 2000, especially after joining the WTO at the end of 2001, China has experienced a period of rapid growth in foreign trade exports. From 2001 to

2008, China's exports expanded at an average annual rate of 23.5 percent, which means that it doubled in 3.3 years. Meanwhile, though the foreign investment attracted by China kept increasing rapidly, the average annual growth rate has dropped to 10.8 percent. This was the stage of the so-called globalization of trade. With the rapid expansion of trade scale, especially the growth of trade surplus, China's foreign investment has been increasing dramatically. For example, from 2006 to 2014, the average annual growth rate of China's FDI reached 23.7 percent, while the average annual growth rate of foreign trade and the foreign investment it attracted dropped to 11.8 percent and 8.3 percent respectively. Therefore, it is self-evident that China has entered the new stage of "capital globalization", where a new national initiative with a global orientation is urgently needed so as to safeguard the interests of China's large-scale overseas investment and ensure the country's capital globalization to benefit more developing countries and regions, achieving a win-win situation.

III. Other factors

As mentioned above, it is the profound development of economic globalization in the past three decades and the dramatic changes in the global context led by such development, as well as the inherent demands of China's own transformation of the development model, that are fundamentally attributable to the proposal of the BRI. Of course, other additional factors have also contributed to the emergence of the BRI, including management of a sound geopolitical relationship, creation of a peaceful and stable surrounding environment and promotion of the security level of the natural resources supply.

It is contrary to the basic idea of the BRI that some scholars have been describing it as a geostrategy of China since the proposal thereof. This so-called geostrategy is generally understood as a geopolitical strategy that entails the relationship between political acts of state and geographical location, and the political and military struggles between countries seeking living space. Traditionally, a geopolitical strategy is considered a speculative practice that explores foreign policy and acts of state mainly through binary spatial imaginations such as the East and the West, you and us. From Friedrich Ratzel's theory of "Staaten somLifsform" to Alfred Thayer Mahan's theory of "sea power", and to Halford Mackinder's "heartland theory", all the traditional geopolitical ideas that have been under discussion concern how to control the world and how to carry out the expansion of forces, especially control and expansion relying on military forces with the precondition of a "zero-sum game". After World War I, studies in geopolitics waned for a long time due to the notoriety of this subject since some geopolitical theories, especially Mackinder's "heartland theory", had been used to serve the expansion of Nazi Germany. Even today, as its reputation keeps being rebuilt to a large extent, studies in geopolitics are still mainly used by states as a reference to the formulation of offensive defense and foreign policies. The BRI, however, is aimed at promoting win-win cooperation, rather than worsening competition and conflicts. In other words, the BRI proposes, rather than playing a "zero-sum game" to gain from others' losses, to jointly make a bigger "cake" to share with each other, which is quite different from the core ideas that traditional geopolitics concerns.

Certainly, if geostrategy only refers to geoeconomic relations, it does have certain similarities with the BRI's ideas. However, the thing is that geostrategy has often been interpreted by the international community as having a traditional geopolitical meaning, which is offensive and belligerent. It has been manifested in historical experience that the world, fueled by different opinions and theories, has always advanced in the evolution of relations between competition and cooperation, and conflict and partnership. Some scholars and politicians may understand and shape the world as one with an absolute conflict and competitive relationship, advocating a "zero-sum game", while others still have reasons to advocate and promote cooperation and partnership, which is in fact more active and constructive in today's world since countries have been closely connected with each other during the process of economic globalization.

Though the BRI is not China's geopolitical strategy in the traditional sense, it does not mean that no geographical concern is involved in the proposal thereof. To a certain extent, the purposes of maintaining a sound geopolitical relationship and creating a peaceful and stable surrounding environment have been taken into account in the BRI. To achieve the "Chinese Dream", China, now at a critical stage of its growth, is in need of a peaceful and stable international environment, especially a surrounding environment, which, however, is indeed quite complicated. First, with 14 neighboring countries, China is one of the countries in the world with the most land-based neighboring countries, second only to Russia[4]. The complexity of the "neighborhood" is inevitable for China with such a number of "neighbors".[5] Furthermore, border issues between China and some of its neighboring countries (India and Bhutan) remain to be resolved, while some of the surrounding regions are still highly unstable, such as the Korean Peninsula and Afghanistan, or are struggling with terrorism. How to develop peaceful and amicable relationships with neighbors with diverse perspectives of development models, religious culture, political systems and ethnic structures, among others, achieving "harmony in diversity", is a major issue that China has to consider during the process of its future development. It is beneficial for China to develop a sound "neighborhood" and a peaceful and stable surrounding environment by sharing the spillover effects and real benefits from its economic growth with neighboring countries through the Belt and Road construction, as well as promoting its development and alleviating poverty.

Furthermore, with the Yellow Sea, the East China Sea, and the South China Sea in the east and south of China all being coastal waters that need to be delimited with neighboring countries, China is not a country that can directly embrace the ocean, and it still to some extent has maritime border disputes in respect of the aforesaid waters with the neighboring countries concerned. The existence of a complete island chain in the east and south of China is common knowledge. A flotilla voyaging north has to pass through the Korean Strait, the Sea of Japan, and the Sōya Strait, or, heading east, it passes through the Miyako Strait or the Balingtang Strait. If sailing southward, it needs to pass through the Straits of Malacca or the Sunda Strait and the Lombok Strait. Ocean shipping has become an organic part of China's social and economic system since China has assumed its responsibilities in the global division of labor as the factory of the world and formed an economic development pattern where raw materials and products, the two ends of production, either come from or are sold to international markets, resulting in a large volume of both export and import. Therefore, China needs a safer and more efficient marine transportation environment than those other countries that claim to maintain the safety of marine transportation.

In addition, the Belt and Road construction is also connected to China's need to strengthen the security of its natural resources supply. Corresponding material resources, especially the support and guarantee of crucial resources, is indispensable for the modernization of a country. These so-called crucial resources refer to those natural resources that provide basic support for social and economic activities, such as energy, water and land. From the perspective of history, the process of modernization of a major country is in fact a process of expanding its supply of crucial resources. Developed countries, in the process of their economic rise, have obtained important resources for economic development with such unjust methods as colonial systems or war. In today's world, however, economic globalization has made marketized approaches and win-win cooperation the mainstream to obtain natural resources. Undoubtedly, it is an important precondition of the achievement of the "Chinese Dream" to adopt reasonable marketized approaches to increase the security level of China's natural resources supply.

For large countries, their rise and modernization process depend on two types of crucial resources. One is phased crucial resources that are mainly related to infrastructure, such as iron ore, copper ore, and bauxite. The per capita demand for the aforesaid resources in the period of rapid industrialization and urbanization is large and growing fast, which, however, will gradually decrease and stabilize in a certain quantity thereafter. Moreover, as primary industries may shift overseas, their demand will further decline. For example, the per capita steel consumption of the United States during the peak period (early 1970s) was about 700 kg, which has now dropped to about 300 kg. That of Japan has dropped from about 800 kg during the peak period (in the early 1980s) to 500–600 kg today. The other is long-term crucial resources that are necessary for the operation of the social and economic system and the daily life of residents, especially energy. The per capita demand for these resources will continue to rise with the increase in the level of economic development until, after the completion of industrialization and urbanization, it reaches a certain quantity and remains basically stable in the long term. Since

China has entered the late stage of industrialization, the per capita consumption of various phased crucial resources has almost reached its peak, and will decline in the coming decades. It is thus significant for China to secure a crucial resources supply at a higher level since energy may be the most crucial resource that will affect the rise thereof in the future.

China, as already the second-largest economy in the world, is in increasing need of natural resources to secure its social and economic development. China now is not only the world's largest producer of raw materials for steel, aluminum, copper, cement, glass, and so on, but also the world's largest manufacturer of more than 20 categories of products, including electronics, communications, home appliances, textiles, clothing, automobiles, ships, and so on. In this context, China has heavily relied on the international market for various crucial resources. For example, China's dependence on foreign supply of iron ore, copper ore, and bauxite has exceeded 60 percent, and that of crude oil has also reached 60 percent. It is estimated that the total volume of primary energy consumption in China may reach 5.5 billion tons of standard coal in 2030, along with 700 million tons of crude oil and nearly 500 billion cubic meters of natural gas, under which circumstance China may have to import nearly 500 million tons of crude oil and 180 billion cubic meters of natural gas. How to steadily obtain these resources and safely ship them to the country has become a major issue that shall be carefully considered and planned for at a high level, and for this purpose, a diversity of supply resource and transportation channels is the key.

From the perspective of resources endowment, countries along the ancient Silk Road enjoy relatively good conditions of resources concentration. For example, Russia, Central Asia, and the Middle East all have abundant oil and gas resources. It is estimated that two-thirds of the recoverable oil and gas reserves that have been discovered in the world are located in countries along the ancient Silk Road, which provides a sound prerequisite for China to increase the security level of crucial resources supply through cooperative and win-win approaches. In recent years, China has signed large-scale oil and gas purchase agreements with countries such as Russia, Kazakhstan, and Turkmenistan, which has eased the situation such that China's oil and gas import is less dependent on the Middle East. Therefore, to strengthen economic and trade cooperation with countries along the ancient Silk Road, promoting the diversification of oil and gas resources imports will benefit the security level of China's energy supply.

From the perspective of ocean shipping, the following six sea lines are mainly involved in China's import of crucial resources and its export of merchandise: Middle East line, South America line, North Africa line, East Africa line, West Africa line, and North America line. All ocean transportation on the aforesaid sea lines other than the North American line passes through the Straits of Malacca. Of course, the Strait of Hormuz, the Mozambique Channel, and the Bab-el-Mandeb are also important strategic pivots. In particular, it has been heatedly discussed that 70 percent–80 percent of China's imported crude oil and more than 50 percent of other seaborne cargoes have to pass through the Straits of Malacca, which is so-called the Malacca dilemma. Therefore, the diversification of transportation channels has become an unavoidable issue for China.

Notes

1 Oxfam's Report on the Gap between Rich and Poor in the World (finance.chinanews.com/cj/2015/01-27/7009775.shtml).
2 Francis Fukuyama, Exporting the Chinese Model, Project Syndicate. Retrieved January12, 2016, from www.project-syndicate.org/commentary/china-one-belt-one-road-strategy-by-£rancis-fukuyama-2016-01.
3 Xi Jinping, Let the "Belt and Road" Construction Benefit the People of All Countries along the Line, news.china.com.cn/2016-08/17/content_39112444.htm, August 17, 2016.
4 Before the collapse of Soviet Union, China was the country with the most land-based neighboring countries in the world. Russia took the place of China thereafter.
5 By contrast, the United States enjoys a relatively luxurious neighborhood with only two neighbors, Canada and Mexico, and the Atlantic Ocean and the Pacific Ocean lying to the east and the west respectively.

4 Understanding the Belt and Road Initiative

I. Core connotation: Inclusive globalization

Though various interpretations of the BRI still exist, the argument of this volume is that, based on the above general context analysis and the *Vision and Actions*, the BRI is an initiative that will open up a new era of inclusive globalization.

The *Vision and Actions* explicitly states that "the initiative to jointly build the Belt and Road is designed to uphold the global free trade regime and the open world economy in the spirit of open regional cooperation", and that "it is aimed at promoting orderly and free flow of economic factors, highly efficient allocation of resources and deep integration of markets; encouraging the countries along the Belt and Road to achieve economic policy coordination and carry out broader regional cooperation of higher standards; and jointly creating an open, inclusive and balanced regional economic cooperation architecture that benefits all". This statement is actually a portrayal of economic globalization. However, the BRI is not a simple continuation of neoliberal economic globalization but a proposal, based on the cultural connotations of the Silk Road or "Silk Road Spirit", namely "peace and cooperation, openness and inclusiveness, mutual learning and mutual benefit" (see Chapter 1) and the principle of "achieving shared growth through discussion and cooperation", for connecting the development strategies of countries along the Belt and Road. The BRI aims to seek a conjunction of interests and the "biggest common denominator" for development so as to achieve a win-win cooperation that promotes common development and prosperity. From this perspective, it is an organic combination of the "Silk Road Spirit" and the idea of economic globalization and an attempt to open a new path toward inclusive globalization.

As noted above, globalization over the past three decades was a combined product of a "spatial fix" for capital accumulation and neoliberalism, the essence of which is, as advocated in the Washington Consensus, liberalization, market mechanism and full privatization with governments' power and role in national and world economic governance reduced. Of course, from the perspective of the results achieved, countries adopting the Washington

Consensus barely grew. Thus, on the one hand, economic globalization has promoted world economic growth, while on the other, it has also created imbalances and social problems at various scales, especially the continuous expansion of the gap between the rich and the poor. The biggest winner from neoliberal economic globalization, it may be argued, was capital, while society has paid a huge price, which is exactly the root cause of the questioning of economic globalization in recent years. Further promoting globalization requires a new model of global economic governance, under which it is essential that governments act to maintain social justice and market fairness, and combine their actions with the powerful forces of capital accumulation under market mechanisms, so that more areas and people will benefit from economic development and globalization.

Since the 1980s, China has continuously and deeply participated in the process of economic globalization through gradual reform and opening up. On the one hand, it has driven the growth of its own economy by introducing capital, technology, and management experience into the country. On the other, it has gradually established a governance mechanism basically adapted to economic globalization. Admittedly, China, whose rapid economic development has benefited from economic globalization, has also made tremendous contributions to world economic growth and changed the economic landscape of the world. Today, China's economy is so closely connected with the rest of the world that neither could develop without the other. Therefore, China needs to make greater contributions to safeguarding the achievements of economic globalization and developing the mechanisms of economic globalization, playing a greater role in promoting global economic growth. The BRI is precisely the effort China is making to promote inclusive economic globalization in this context.

Inclusive globalization is not the same as the neoliberal globalization of the past 30 years. Although there are links between them, there are also fundamental differences. Inclusive globalization is not a regression or reversal of globalization but the development and reform of it. Inclusive and neoliberal globalization are similar in that they are both driven by technology, and both are driven by the quest for a spatial fix for capital accumulation. The fundamental difference between them lies in the fact that globalization cannot only serve the spatial expansion and accumulation of capital but also has to meet the needs of living people, requiring the state to play a role as a regulator, addressing "term mismatch"[1] in capital markets, finding development paths suited to the national conditions, ensuring the equal participation of all parties and protecting cultural diversity in the process of economic globalization. These are the core connotations and main manifestations of inclusive globalization.

(1) **Inclusive growth**. The state has to play a greater role as a "regulator" so as to make economic growth more inclusive. The relationship between free markets and government intervention has always been the focus in research studies

and the practice of global development or national development. From the economic liberalism of the Cambridge School in the early twentieth century, to the government interventionism of the Keynesian school from the 1930s, to the neoliberalism that dominated in the 1980s, the focus of policy and practice has swung in a seesaw manner between completely free markets and government intervention. Harvey pointed out that in the era of neoliberalism, the main function of a state was to provide sound conditions and a good environment for the global expansion of capital, while solving the complicated problems accumulated by the practice of neoliberalism requires the reconstruction of state power. Of course, this does not necessarily mean a return to Keynesianism, but there is certainly a need for a certain form of interventionism. In particular, the state has to shift its focus from serving the accumulation and expansion of capital to improving social equity and governance capacities. First, governments need to strengthen cooperation in response to global challenges, such as the turmoil in financial markets and climate change. Second, the state has to protect the common people and the poor through reemployment training, innovation and entrepreneurship, poverty alleviation, and so forth. Third, countries need the ability to guide capital markets, allocate resources, and provide basic public services. The BRI, stressing the role of the government, first emphasizes policy communication and the connecting up of development strategies, planning, and projects, among countries along the Belt and Road, with the purpose of seeking a common interest. Under a development model of this kind, not only will capital's need for free spatial expansion be satisfied but so too will the needs of underdeveloped areas and ordinary people, making development more inclusive.

(2) **Inclusive infrastructure development**. The governments should address term mismatch in the capital market, and extend reliable and affordable infrastructures to less-developed regions. Many studies have shown that connectivity is a prerequisite for a region in securing development opportunities from economic globalization, while investing in infrastructure bottlenecks will also stimulate economic growth and bring social and financial returns. In practice, there are opportunities that are not realized. Although modern infrastructure connects many regions of the world into a networked "small world" and developed market system, many regions and billions of people have not been included into this modern system, while aging infrastructures in developed countries (such as the United States) have not been updated in a timely manner. These issues are to a large extent connected with changes in global capital markets in the past three decades. Traditional financial institutions, such as traditional savings and investment banks that once played a leading role in financial markets, have been in decline in the past 30 years and replaced by various new financial intermediaries, such as pension funds, hedge funds, sovereign funds and insurance company money. Gordon Clark's research shows that pension funds in OECD countries have become the largest savings and investment institutions. For instance, the size of pension funds in

the United Kingdom reached 3.5 trillion US dollars in 2016, which was more than seven times higher than in 1987. US pension funds reached 27 trillion US dollars. In addition, global sovereign funds reached 15 trillion US dollars. These new financial intermediaries are more inclined to allocate finance to speculative or short-term investments in financial markets, which are typically markets for "hot money". Stiglitz, the Nobel Prize winner in economics, once said that "for hedge funds, a quarter is almost an eternity". By contrast, the returns on infrastructure construction projects, characterized by a large scale, long cycles and high capital intensity, are long term and not attractive to "hot money". Therefore, the financing market for global infrastructures has been faced with a serious situation of term mismatch, and more "patient capital" is urgently needed, as argued by Justin Lin. One of the priority areas in the BRI proposed by the Chinese government is the connection of facilities and the provision of a large amount of finance for infrastructure construction, which can help give less-developed countries and regions access to modern infrastructure networks, thereby providing them with more development opportunities. This is one of the important reasons why the BRI has been welcomed by many developing countries.

(3) **Inclusive development paths**. The promotion of a single development model or best practice has to be abandoned. In other words, globalization does not require a single development model. With economic globalization, the United States and the United Kingdom, among others, continued to press other countries, and especially developing countries, to adopt neoliberal ideas. In the mid-1990s, the "Washington Consensus" led by the International Monetary Fund, the World Bank, and the United States Department of the Treasury became the standard prescription, setting standards and principles for the global economy. A country, once in need of financial assistance, had to adopt neoliberal economic policies in accordance with the "Washington Consensus" or it would never get such assistance and would face the risk of collapse. Until the global financial crisis of 2008, the World Bank sold its "best practices" to developing countries, the essence of which was privatization, marketization and liberalization. However, in the last two decades, countries forced to adopt the "Washington Consensus" fell into a financial dilemma and lost their economic independence and autonomy. China, instead of adopting this standard prescription, explored a suitable development path in relatively uncharted territory, achieving unprecedented economic growth. Thus the BRI, unlike neoliberal globalization, does not advocate one best development path for the world (i.e., the road taken by developed countries), but emphasizes that each country should select its own development path in the light of its own development conditions. Chinese president Xi Jinping pointed out at the Belt and Road Forum for International Cooperation that China does not intend to interfere in other countries' ideology or to export its own development model but rather focus on mutual benefit from a jointly developed bigger "cake".

(4) **Inclusive participation**. It is necessary to guarantee the equal participation of all parties in globalization. As contained within its concept, globalization is an enterprise of all the nations and people in the world. Each country should have the basic right to participate equally in globalization, of which, though, the world's powers are the driving forces. Previous phases of global economic expansion have been associated with the exercise of hegemony by leading powers. The trade expansion of British and French colonialism or the capital expansion associated with US imperialism were both extremely unequal forms of international economic exchange and trade. During the process of economic globalization in the last three decades or so, large multinational corporations were dominant players occupying hegemonic positions and possessing great power, leaving many countries with relatively weak negotiating positions. As demonstrated by the concept of "obligated embeddedness" of Weidong Liu and others, big countries do enjoy a natural advantage in globalization. How to take the "weak" into account has undoubtedly become a key issue for inclusiveness in the process of future globalization. The BRI, adhering to the ideas of "openness and inclusiveness" and "equality and mutual benefit", and the principle of "achieving shared growth through discussion and collaboration", has made seeking the "biggest common development denominator" the priority, stressing common development and prosperity. Furthermore, the BRI advocates that interested countries or regions equally participate in an appropriate manner and with an open attitude rather than build a small circle with only one voice. The joint communiqué of the Leaders Roundtable of the Belt and Road Forum for International Cooperation particularly emphasized that countries, such as the least-developed countries, landlocked developing countries, and small island developing states, deserve special attention, which is exactly a manifestation of the great inclusiveness of the BRI.

(5) **Cultural inclusiveness**. Cultural diversity should be protected in the process of economic globalization. Countries in Western Europe and North America have taken the lead, emerging as developed countries and dominating global economic expansion over the past three centuries, which, on the one hand, led to a self-centered ideology and notion of the absolute cultural superiority of these Western countries, and on the other hand, created a sense of cultural inferiority in many developing countries that found themselves under great pressure. Especially in recent decades, with the increasing power of economic globalization, the cultural independence of many countries has become precarious under the combined effect of subjective and objective factors. Various cultural conflicts brought by Hollywood movies, the McDonald's fast food culture, color revolutions, and so on that have swept over many countries and regions, and the consequences in terms of Western centralism and cultural superiority are not conducive to sustainable global development. By contrast, the spirit of "mutual learning" deriving from the ancient Silk Road reflects completely different cultural values. The BRI based on the "Silk Road Spirit" advocates the cultural values of "harmony in diversity", emphasizing common development, prosperity, and peace on the basis of maintaining

cultural diversity. This "harmony in diversity" refers to equal treatment, mutual learning, and the coexistence of diversity and unity. President Xi Jinping has repeatedly stressed that the BRI does not draw ideological lines or aim for political agendas, that no one civilization can be judged superior to another, and that human civilizations have become richer and more colorful and innovative with exchanges and mutual learning.

According to the *Vision and Actions*, the BRI might be simply summarized by "one core concept" (peace and cooperation, openness and inclusiveness, mutual learning, and mutual benefit, i.e., the Silk Road Spirit); "five cooperation priorities" (policy coordination, facilities connectivity, unimpeded trade, financial integration, and people-to-people bonds); and "three communities" (communities of shared interests, a shared future, and shared responsibility). Its core connotation is to promote international and regional economic cooperation with the Silk Road Spirit, not only satisfying the need for Chinese capital to "go global" but also benefiting local people.

At the Belt and Road Forum for International Cooperation held on May 14–15, 2017, many heads of states pointed out in their speeches that the Belt and Road construction, with its strong inclusiveness, will allow more regions to share the benefits brought by globalization. For example, then-Prime Minister Sharif of Pakistan noted that the BRI has demonstrated its great praise of cultural diversity and inclusiveness, providing development opportunities for people on the verge of globalization. Former French prime minister de Villepin stated that the Belt and Road construction is a bridge that connects the past, the present, and the future, aiming to "leave no one behind" on the path of development. President Bachelet of the Republic of Chile, President Erdoğan of the Republic of Turkey, President Zeman of the Czech Republic, and President Mulatu of Ethiopia, among others, expressed the same high expectations. Secretary General António Guterres of the United Nations pointed out in an interview with China Central Television (CCTV) on the eve of the Summit Forum that the BRI is significant and will unite the world, promoting a more equitable globalization path.

The joint communiqué proposed a "shared commitment to build open economy, ensure free and inclusive trade . . . joint endeavor on the Belt and Road Initiative and seeking complementarities with other connectivity initiatives to provide new opportunities and impetus for international cooperation, facilitating the achievement of a globalization that is open, inclusive and beneficial to all . . . achieving inclusive and sustainable growth and development". It might be said that promoting inclusive globalization is an important consensus reached by the heads of state at the Belt and Road Forum for International Cooperation.

II. Thinking of construction approaches

The BRI is a brand-new national strategy[2] proposed by China to respond and adapt to changes in the global context and in its own development model.

It is a leading strategy for all aspects of opening up and the major flag carrier for achieving "open development". China's "Thirteenth Five-Year Plan" proposed a new development philosophy with five elements, "innovation, coordination, green, opening up and sharing". In particular, the "opening up" therein is significantly different from the one in the earlier "reform and opening up". Unlike the mostly one-way "opening up" of the past three decades, that is, actively responding to trends in the global transfer of industrial activities and attracting foreign capital to participate in China's economic construction, the "opening up" marked by the BRI is a two-way approach organically combining a "bringing in" strategy with a "going global" strategy, and an overall plan for China to truly consider its development path and resources allocation on a global scale. Therefore, this new national strategy needs new perspectives and new ideas that differ from those underpinning previous phases of domestic development.

It should be clearly understood that BRI is a cause closely connected with both domestic and international situations, rather than with just one of them, and involves their comprehensive coordination. It means balancing the deepening of reform at home, and a full opening up and "going global" strategy, enabling domestic reform to support the Belt and Road construction and in return to promote domestic reform through the BRI. Meanwhile, since the cooperation with neighboring countries is indispensable in the construction of an economic belt, it is not only the interests of China but also those of relevant cooperating countries that should be taken into account, that is, to seek a conjunction of interests and the "biggest common denominator" for development, deepening pragmatic cooperation across all issues and creating a community of shared interests.

First, the BRI is indeed a strategy to go global for China, the deep promotion and long-term implementation of which requires further institutional and structural reforms. Over the past 30 years, China's opening up has mainly focused on a "bringing in" strategy, with its core mechanism the attraction of investment, mainly driven by active sectors and local actors, each of which have their own advantages. However, the exploration of a "going global" strategy, like "being a guest" in other people's homes, needs a different institutional mechanism. China should make full use of the enthusiasm at all levels in the country, strengthening the coordination and integration of social, economic, and cultural resources with elaborate organization, scientific arrangements, a reasonable pace, and high efficiency, so as to promote the Belt and Road construction powerfully, in an orderly way and effectively. Furthermore, China has to follow the trend of the modernization of the national governance system, distinguishing different functions and responsibilities of governments, enterprises, institutions, and nongovernmental organizations. The Chinese government should not undertake everything, which will allow enterprises, institutions, and nongovernmental organizations to have the space to play their roles to the greatest extent. In addition, it is necessary for China to familiarize itself with international rules and practices, and to strengthen its cooperation with international agencies, as sometimes what concerns China is also worth international attention. It also might be better for Chinese enterprises, when investing overseas, to cooperate with stakeholders in different countries through joint investment to mitigate risks.

Objectively speaking, China's current institutional mechanisms have yet to meet the needs of going global. Though foreign-related departments have been established in many government sectors, such as the departments for international cooperation, the international exchanges that many government departments are engaged in are still limited to their respective traditional businesses and are notably lacking coordination. Their tendency to maintain their respective traditional resource allocation fields and rights is also obvious. Therefore, what is needed to promote the BRI is a coordination body, and not just a leading group. International experience shows that major developed countries all have agencies leading foreign-related development, such as the UK Department for International Development (DFID), the German International Cooperation Agency (GIZ, i.e., Die Deutsche Gesellschaft für Internationale Zusammenarbeit), the Japan International Cooperation Agency (JICA), and France's Ubifrance. The US Department of State is that country's leading agency for global affairs, with the United States Agency for International Development (USAID) coming under it, which is quite different from China's State Council. China, however, does at present have a mechanism for coordinating overseas development and foreign aid work, a situation that might adversely affect the integration of resources for this purpose. Therefore, there is an urgent need for China to establish its own "agency of international development" or a similar institution as a major measure to further promote the Belt and Road construction.

Second, the BRI is a platform of inclusive globalization rather than a Chinese government project. In the first three years since the BRI was proposed, the Chinese government has been vigorously promoting the Belt and Road construction, signing cooperation memoranda focused on jointly building the Belt and Road with more than 30 countries[3] and cooperation agreements on production capacity with more than 20 countries, and establishing the Silk Road Fund especially for the Belt and Road construction. China has also made great efforts to establish the Asian Infrastructure Investment Bank (AIIB) to support the Belt and Road construction. Along with a large number of news reports largely focusing on governmental cooperation, the BRI, for outsiders, still feels more like a Chinese government project. However, the BRI is actually a public service platform that China is providing to the world aimed at global capital flow and inclusive development. Therefore, in the process of furthering the Belt and Road construction, it is necessary to stress the important functional roles of capital markets and enterprises, that is, to attract not only Chinese enterprises but also international capital to participate in the BRI.

Third, the BRI is a significant long-term, strategic cause, which cannot be achieved overnight. There is an urgent need for top-level design, taking overall state interests as the priority with as few "segmentations" as practical for every key task to be properly done. China should first commence from the easiest part to consolidate a foothold in surrounding areas, taking the neighboring regions and bilateral cooperation as breakthrough points. Projects with clear intentions for cooperation and common interests, especially strategic ones, would be a great start, setting an example of amicable cooperation and laying a solid foundation for the Belt and Road construction. Over the past 30 years, China's rapid economic growth path has cultivated a popular psychology of "pursuing speed", particularly with some grassroots officials seeking great political results in only one or two years. This attitude will adversely affect the Belt and Road construction. An orderly promotion of the BRI requires China to get rid of the expectation of "speed first", which has existed for a long time during the process of domestic construction. It should be kept in mind that the BRI, rather being than a one-time plan, is indeed a long-term and major strategy to coordinate China's opening up in all aspects. Moreover, with considerable construction work to be done with countries along the Belt and Road, it is actually impossible for everything to proceed as China expects. Faced with a complicated international environment, China needs long-term and systematic plans made with strategic determination to implement the BRI. And China must do its best to avoid making mistakes caused by impatience

Fourth, for the purpose of the BRI, an organic integration of a "bringing in" and a "going global" strategy is significant for China's industrial upgrading and the transformation of its development model. Though the export of capital constitutes an important part of the Belt and Road construction, it does not necessarily mean a one-directional change. With the large technology gap between China and developed countries, the "bringing in" strategy warrants great attention for a long time to come. Economic globalization indeed is a process of mutual investment and complementarities between countries. Over the last three decades, developed European and American countries have been both major investors in foreign countries and major destinations for foreign capital. Therefore, to advance the Belt and Road construction, China should not only encourage domestic capital to "go global" but also attach great importance to attracting FDI. Only with an organic combination of these two strategies will international economic cooperation and trade facilitate the transformation and upgrading of Chinese industries and sustainable and sound economic development. Since not all regions within China's vast territory have entered the "going global" stage on a large-scale due to great differences in regional development levels, each region, instead of blindly following others' steps, needs to scientifically determine its priorities for participating in the BRI based on its own characteristics. Unnecessary investment risks would be inevitable in an excessive pursuit of "going global". A top-level design formulating differentiated policies to encourage various companies to "go global" with an approach that respectively suits them is urgently needed. Moreover, a core consideration of such a design is how to achieve industrial transformation and upgrading as well as create employment, rather than whether capital is "going global" and what is its amount. China, when carrying out the "going global" strategy, not only needs to prevent its manufacturing industry from "hollowing out" but also needs to mitigate various investment risks.

Fifth, cultural cooperation, including exchanges in the fields of culture, education, science and technology, sports, and so on, as well as livelihood assistance, should be government priorities in the Belt and Road construction. Paying full attention to cultural connotations of the Silk Road is of significance for China, in order to make relevant countries understand that the BRI aims to promote inclusive globalization, share a bigger "cake" and advance common prosperity. At the same time, China could gradually eliminate the effects of negative opinions, such as the idea that China is "resource predator", the "China threat theory", and the like through practical actions. In recent years, however, China's positive image in neighboring countries has been compromised to some extent since some Chinese companies have failed to fully consider local social and cultural traditions and to appropriately fulfill their social responsibilities due to a lack of experience in respect of "going global". At the same time, China has also suffered from surreptitious insinuations that have been advanced out of ulterior motives by some countries. Meanwhile, due to the huge size of China's economy, many neighboring countries have ambivalent attitudes toward cooperating with China: on the one hand, they want to promote their own economic development through working with China, but on the other are concerned about being swallowed up in the wake of China's economic expansion. To promote the smooth and long-term development of the BRI, China must therefore strengthen people-to-people communication with countries along the route since only the emergence of common interests and goals among people can eliminate the misgivings and concerns of neighboring countries.

III. Spatial connotations

The BRI is on the face of it a spatially highly selective strategic concept. As "Belt" and "Road" literally refers to economies located along certain axes, notions of spatial exclusivity have emerged, leading to some misunderstandings of the BRI. For example, some provinces believe they have a special and exclusive status in the "Belt and Road", while others consider themselves irrelevant to the Belt and Road construction. However, the truth is that the BRI is a multiscalar concept with multiple spatial connotations.

First, with no boundaries the BRI is not a closed system, which means it is impossible to accurately plot its spatial scope on the map. The BRI is fundamentally an open and inclusive international economic cooperation network that countries can participate in as they see fit. That is, it is not an exclusive platform. Therefore, although the Ministry of Foreign Affairs once mentioned there are more than 60 countries and more than four billion people along the

Belt and Road, the *Vision and Actions* points out that the BRI crosses Afro-Eurasia, and does not define its geographical scope or provide a list of countries included in it. President Xi Jinping noted at the Belt and Road Summit Forum for International Cooperation that the BRI is rooted in the ancient Silk Road. It focuses on the Asian, European and African continents, but is also open to all other countries.

Second, as an international economic cooperation network, undoubtedly the BRI stresses cooperation between countries rather than subnational cooperation with neighboring countries. From a domestic perspective, the *Vision and Actions* mentioned some provinces and cities, for example, referring to making Xinjiang and Fujian core areas of the "Silk Road Economic Belt" and the "21st Century Maritime Silk Road", respectively, to making Xi'an a new focus of reform and opening up in China's interior, to supporting Chongqing, Chengdu, Zhengzhou, Wuhan, Changsha, Nanchang, Hefei and other cities as leading areas of opening up in inland regions, and to strengthening the construction of cities such as Shanghai, Tianjin, Ningbo, Guangzhou and Shenzhen, and so on. However, these statements do not necessarily grant exclusive status to these provinces and cities. In fact, all regions can participate in the Belt and Road construction, especially as the co-construction of economic and trade cooperation, cultural cooperation, financial cooperation, and so forth will by no means be the "exclusive" tasks of the provinces and regions mentioned in the *Vision and Actions*. Provinces such as Jiangsu and Shandong that are not mentioned are actually more involved in trade and cultural exchanges with countries along the Belt and Road. The references to the roles of certain provinces and regions in the *Vision and Actions* was designed to combine the Belt and Road construction with existing regional development strategies in the country, to strengthen interaction and cooperation among the eastern, western and central regions, to promote relatively balanced development and to maximize the degree of opening up. These references were not meant to specify that certain areas are within or outside of the BRI.

Last, the co-construction of the BRI involves facilities connectivity, especially the construction of international land and maritime transport corridors. These corridors do refer to specific spatial orientations and do have a specific spatial scope. For example, the *Vision and Actions* proposes that the Silk Road Economic Belt focus on bringing together China, Central Asia, Russia, and Europe (the Baltic); linking China with the Persian Gulf and the Mediterranean Sea through Central Asia and West Asia; and connecting China with Southeast Asia, South Asia and the Indian Ocean. The 21st-Century Maritime Silk Road is designed to extend from China's coastal ports to Europe through the South China Sea and the Indian Ocean along one route, and from China's coastal ports through the South China Sea to the South Pacific on the other. The *Vision and Actions* also mentioned the focus on jointly building a new Eurasian Land Bridge and developing the China-Mongolia-Russia, China-Central Asia-West Asia, and China-Indochina

Peninsula economic cooperation corridors and further promoting the construction of the China-Pakistan Economic Corridor and the Bangladesh-China-India-Myanmar Economic Corridor. Along these routes and corridors with their clear spatial directions there will be more co-construction of infrastructures. In other words, of the "five connectivities", facilities connectivity has stronger subnational features. The other connectivities are more matters of cooperation between countries.

Some domestic officials, scholars, and the media are accustomed to considering the BRI as China's regional development strategy due to their insufficient understanding of its multiple spatial and multiscalar nature. This lack of understanding has caused a certain degree of confusion. The BRI is a long-term top-level strategy that coordinates all aspects of China's opening up, as well as an initiative to create jointly with other countries an open and inclusive international economic cooperation network. Thus, it is undoubtedly a national rather than a regional strategy. Certainly, this national strategy has significant regional impacts due to the existence of multiple spatialities. However, to call it China's regional strategy just because of its regional impacts would not only undermine its status and effect but also be a cause of concern in participating countries along the Belt and Road. Therefore, it is inappropriate to refer to the BRI along with "the coordinated development of Beijing-Tianjin-Hebei" and "the construction of the Yangtze River Economic Belt" collectively as China's three major regional strategies in the new era.

Although the BRI is an open system in which interested countries are able to participate, a spatial focus on practical work is still necessary. According to the construction vision proposed by China, this spatial focus is the "Six Corridors and Six Ways, Multiple Countries, and Multiple Ports"[4]. The specific countries and regions prioritized in carrying out the Belt and Road construction will depend entirely on the strategic connectivity between China and countries along the Belt and Road, and the results of joint consultations on common interests. For instance, China has already coordinated with Kazakhstan's "Bright Road" strategy, with Mongolia's "Prairie Road" strategy, with Russia's" Trans-Eurasian Transport Corridors" strategy, and with Pakistan's "2025 Vision", leading to the development of the China-Mongolia-Russia Economic Corridor and the China-Pakistan Economic Corridor, as well as the Sino-Kazakhstan capacity cooperation process.

Notes

1 Translator's Note: it refers to mismatch between the long-term orientation of infrastructure development and the short-term orientation of hot money.

2 "战略" ("strategy" in English) is an ambiguous word. In the Chinese context, it refers more to a scheme or the long-term planning of a task, such as the main functional area strategy, new urbanization strategy, innovation-driven development strategy, etc. In some foreign language contexts, however, it is more of a military term and literally translating it as "strategy" might sometimes cause misunderstanding. Since

this book was originally published in Chinese, the phrase "Belt and Road strategy" is used in some contexts, while the terms "Belt and Road construction" and "Belt and Road Initiative" are used more often.

3 By the time of this volume's publication, over 100 countries have signed memoranda of understanding with China on jointly building the Belt and Road.

4 "Six Corridors" refer to six major international economic cooperation corridors. "Six Roads" refer to the promotion of connectivity of railways, highways, waterways, airways, passageways and information highways. "Multiple Countries" refer to certain countries to be developed as anchors in the "Belt and Road Initiative". "Multiple ports" refers to certain ports to be developed as maritime anchors in the "Belt and Road Initiative".

5 Issues on how to build the Belt and Road

I. Distinguishing the BRI from China's regional development strategies

The BRI, though not a regional development strategy itself, will no doubt have a significant impact on China's regional development strategies. How to connect the BRI and the four traditional regional strategies of China (i.e., the Western Region Development Strategy, Rejuvenating the Old Industrial Bases in the Northeast, the Rise of Central China, and coastal regions as pioneers in achieving modernization) and the two newly added strategies (the coordinated development of Beijing-Tianjin- Hebei and the construction of the Yangtze River Economic Belt) has become an essential task for government and its leadership at all levels and a confusing topic for the public. It is not easy to clarify the relationship between these strategies, but the distinction between the BRI and the other strategies seems quite simple. That is, the former is a proposal to jointly create an open, inclusive, and balanced international economic cooperation architecture that benefits all and focuses on cooperation between countries, while the latter are institutional arrangements to address certain regional development issues inside China. Therefore, the BRI is more like a general top-level strategy, which can act as a guideline for regional development strategies.

Such a directive role for the BRI embodies various opportunities brought by a two-way opening up and the construction of major economic corridors. There is no doubt that opening up in all aspects, especially in the improvement of transport accessibility and trade convenience inside Eurasia, will bring new development opportunities for the western and northeastern regions of China, with many former "peripheral" regions becoming the forefront of opening up, promoting the concentration of elements therein. However, it is not only these enormous opportunities but also the differences between coastal and interior opening up that should be clearly noted. The coastal area can achieve a "1+N" version of opening up, that is, getting access to all coastal regions and cities in the world through maritime transportation, while the interior area can directly open up to neighboring countries or indirectly to other countries via a third-party port. After all, there is no public land in the world, except on the Antarctic continent, that can be shared by countries, while the oceans are mainly high seas.

Specifically speaking, the Belt and Road construction will help China achieve a more balanced territorial development pattern. The construction of the New Eurasian Land Bridge and the China-Central Asia-Western Asia Economic Corridor and the China-Pakistan Economic Corridor will change the location disadvantages of northwest China that have existed for a long time in opening up, promoting the development of this region, especially Xinjiang. The construction of the China-Indochina Peninsula Economic Corridor and the Bangladesh-China-India-Myanmar Economic Corridor will facilitate the opening up of southwest China, which is particularly important in promoting the development of Yunnan and Guangxi provinces. The China-Mongolia-Russia Economic Corridor may give new impetus to the revival of Northeast China by deepening the level of opening up in this region. In addition, the Belt and Road construction will provide the coastal regions with a much broader market, which is conducive to the region's industrial transformation and upgrading and its status in the global division of labor. The development of closer economic and trade ties and cultural exchanges will drive cities like Beijing, Shanghai, Guangzhou, and Shenzhen to become cosmopolitan, with more international influence, and cities like Chongqing, Xi'an, Chengdu, Zhengzhou, Urumqi, and Wuhan to become new foci of reform and opening up in China's interior. The construction of open platforms, such as national key ports and cross-border economic cooperation zones, will shape some new economic growth poles in the border regions such as the Dongxing, Ruili, Erenhot, Manzhouli, and Suifenhe.

In general, the Belt and Road construction, unlike the coastal opening-up strategy in the 1980s with its clear regional direction, is a strategy for an all-around opening up and international cooperation initiative that various regions can participate in. From this perspective, it is an inclusive strategy that brings almost the same development opportunities to different regions. As to which of them will seize such opportunities, it depends both on the right strategy for engagement, and their foundations and strengths. A single focus may end up achieving nothing.

II. Building cross-border transport corridors as a priority

The construction of transport infrastructure in advance is one of the successful experiences of China's economic development, and the idea that road construction leads to prosperity has been deeply rooted in people's minds. Modern transport systems (air, rail, highways, ocean shipping, etc.) have significantly reduced the time and cost of overcoming distance, forming the modern world system that links many regions in the world much more closely. In this system, the increasing breadth and depth of commodity trade, personnel exchange, and information dissemination have driven globalization. When people were cheering the "flat world", many regions in the world remained outside of this modern world system, due to the lack of modern transport infrastructure and short of accessibility. Therefore, facilities connectivity is one of the essential tasks of the BRI. In fact, it is linear infrastructures that may first come to people's mind when the BRI is mentioned.

Internal transport connectivity on the Eurasian continent is still comparatively poor. Although the eastern and central regions of China on the eastern side and Europe on the western side have developed high-density traffic networks, inland, South Asia, and Southeast Asia are still extremely in demand of modern transport infrastructures. And along with the various technical standards of different countries, further development of trade and economic exchanges between countries along the Belt and Road has been restrained to a large extent. As far as China's westbound cross-border railway transport routes are concerned, there are only the New Eurasian Land Bridge corridors that exit China from Korgas or Alashankou, and the China-Mongolia-Russia corridor that travels northward along the Russian Siberian Railway to Europe. In respect of roads, most of the inland countries are faced with such issues as a comparatively low technical level (with few lanes), congestion on arterial roads and poor road conditions (cracking and aging of roads) due to disrepair. At the same time, they lack high-grade highways that could connect each other. Thus, improving connectivity within the Eurasian continent is, with a broad basis and a great conjunction of interests, not only an important objective of the BRI but also a major focus of international organizations and institutions like the Asian Development Bank, the United Nations Economic and Social Commission for Asia and the Pacific, and the European Bank for Reconstruction and Development.

In respect of cross-border transport links, the BRI mainly focuses on those associated with the six major economic corridors. The new Eurasian Land Bridge Economic Corridor includes two major transport links, both of whose domestic parts start from the east coast and pass through the Lanzhou-Xinjiang railway or Linhe-Hami railway to Xinjiang. Then one of them enters Kazakhstan through Alashankou, passing Aktogay, Balkhash, Karaganda, and Astana, to Russia and arrives in Europe. The other enters Kazakhstan through Korgas port, passing through Almaty, Shymkent, Kandyagash, and the Urals, to Russia before ending in Europe.

The transport routes envisaged in the China-Mongolia-Russia corridor include the China-Russia route (Moscow-Chita-Manzhouli-Suifenhe-Vladivostok/Nakhodka/Vostochny or Manzhouli-Harbin-Dalian/Yingkou); the China-Mongolian-East Russia route (Moscow-Ulan-Ude-Ulaanbaatar-Choibalsan-Arxan-Hunchun-Zarubino); the China-Mongolia-Middle Russia route (Moscow-Ulan-Ude-Ulaanbaatar-ZamynUeued-Erenhot-Beijing-Tianjing); and the China-Mongolia-West Russia route (Moscow-Tashangta-Tsagaannuur-Hovd-Bulgan-Taykexkin-Urumqi).

By contrast, the cross-border transport links in the China-Central Asia–Western Asia Economic Corridor remain unclear. One possible route may commence form Korgas, entering Kazakhstan, passing through Almaty and

Shymkent to Uzbekistan, and Tashkent and Samarkand to Turkmenistan, and Merv and Ashgabat to Turkmenbashi. Then it crosses the Caspian Sea by waterway to the Caucasus, passing through the Black Sea by waterway before arriving in Central and Eastern Europe. Another potential path depends on the construction of the China-Kyrgyzstan-Uzbekistan railway, which starts from Kashgar, Xinjiang, passing through Osh and Samarkand of Kyrgyzstan before entering Turkmenistan.

The transport links in the China-Pakistan economic corridor are relatively simple, starting from the Khunjerab Pass to Pakistan and passing through Islamabad to Karachi port or Gwadar port. The China-Indochina Peninsula economic corridor mainly consists of three possible cross-border transport routes, including the China-Laos-Thailand line starting from Boten, that is, the middle route; the China-Myanmar line starting from Ruili, that is, the western route; and the China-Vietnam-Cambodia- Thailand line starting from Hekou, that is, the eastern route. The construction of the China-Laos railway, that is, the middle route, has already begun and is scheduled to be completed in 2020, while the construction of the China-Thailand line will commence soon, with negotiations almost completed. The transport links initially envisaged in the Bangladesh-China-India-Myanmar economic corridor start from Kunming in the east, passing through Ruili westward before entering Myanmar, and then cross Mandalay and Sittwe port (Kyaukpyu port) to Bangladesh, passing through Chattogram and Dhaka before its arrival in India.

III. Making the China-Europe Railway Express an innovative transport platform

The so-called China-Europe Railway Expresses refer to fast cargo expresses from China to countries along the Silk Road Economic Belt mainly in Europe and Central Asia, which are "designated trains" as a new form of overland transport (established routes, stations, train numbers, times, and prices). These designated trains first traveled on the "Chongqing-Xingjiang-Europe line" from Chongqing to Duisburg, Germany, and then followed the "Sichuan-Xingjiang-Europe line", the "Xi'an-Xingjiang-Europe line", the "Zhengzhou-Xingjiang-Europe line", the "Wuhan-Xingjiang-Europe line", and so on, respectively, starting from Chengdu, Xi'an, Zhengzhou, Wuhan, and so on. By the middle of 2016, China had opened 39 operational "China-Europe Railway Express" lines, involving 31 cities and five border crossings (Alashankou, Erenhot, Manzhouli, Suifenhe, and Korgas), leading to 28 foreign cities such as Moscow, St. Petersburg, Hamburg, Duisburg, Lodz (Poland), Tehran, and Madrid. These lines have become a landmark transport cooperation platform of the BRI.

There is no doubt that the opening of the China-Europe Railway Expresses, with improved convenience and efficiency compared with previous cross-border trains, has provided a new channel for cargo transport on the Eurasian continent and has also established a great example of the transport cooperation among countries along the Belt. However, it has left a false impression that trade between countries in Eurasia will return to the railway era. As a matter of fact, the operation of China-Europe Railway Expresses largely depends on government subsidies due to the much higher cost of land transport compared with maritime transport. Taking Chongqing as an example, the cost of shipping a container to Duisburg, Germany, via the "Chongqing-Xingjiang-Europe line" is more than US$ 9,000 (the lowest cost of "the five designated trains" in China, in 2016) per container, while the cost of shipping a container to Europe using river-ocean or railway-ocean multimodal transport via Shanghai or Shenzhen port is below US$5,000. Although it will only take two weeks if such a container is transported by designated trains (five or six weeks by ocean transport), the cost gap is still too enormous to be ignored. Therefore, objectively speaking, China-Europe Railway Expresses are only profitable for the transport of certain goods such as high-value-added products or time-sensitive fresh goods, or within appropriate geographical ranges, such as to areas that lie inland and far away from the coast. That is, this form of transport can only complement and not replace maritime transport. In fact, in 2016, the number of containers transported by railway accounted for less than 1 percent of the total volume in China's export. Other than for certain types of goods transported and for certain destinations, the running of China-Europe Railway Expresses would be unsustainable without government subsidies.

A quantitative analysis of economically suitable regions for international container overland transport, which takes Chongqing and Xi'an as a starting point and is based on parameters collected from investigations and surveys, indicates that, competing with sea freight, Central Asia, Mongolia, and Russia's Siberian, Ural, Volga, and the Central Federal Districts are the comparative advantage regions for railway transport along the Belt, with countries and regions such as Ukraine, Belarus, Poland, and Russia's Northwestern and Southern Federal Districts being extended advantage regions. As for most regions in Europe, maritime transport (land-ocean transport) is much more advantageous than railway transport. To take full account of factors of railway crossings, national railway container terminals, marshaling stations, national integrated transportation hubs, national-level logistics parks, national highway hubs, local supply, hinterland scope and distance, traffic of main railways, distance from crossings, and the operational status of China-Europe Railway Expresses, it might be advisable to build Harbin, Xi'an, and Urumqi into main operation hubs for the China-Europe Railway Expresses.

IV. Choosing appropriate modes of "Going Global"

The essential experience China has gained in promoting high-speed economic development since the reform and opening up is the establishment of various special economic zones, the exploration of pilot economic policies and management tools, and the active attraction of external production factors. With the increasing scale of FDI from China, many host countries and even some Chinese enterprises wish to replicate the Chinese experience of industrial parks. Indeed, in recent years, Chinese enterprises have already established industrial cooperation zones with various functions and of different sizes in countries along the Belt and Road. These zones, including processing zones, industrial parks, science and technology industrial parks, and economic and trade cooperation zones, have both achieved successes and generated disputes. How to correctly understand this new phenomenon and to properly lead the construction of industrial cooperation zones have become significant issues in the Belt and Road construction.

From a global perspective, China's promotion of industrial cooperation along the Belt and Road by establishing industrial parks abroad is not only in line with new trends in international cooperation but also meets the development needs of countries along the Belt and Road. With the deepening of economic globalization, international economic cooperation is undergoing a transformation from past practices of simply introducing a project and attracting foreign investment to the co-development of industrial cooperation parks. Singapore and Japan as well as the United Kingdom, Germany, and other European countries have all begun to explore the construction of industrial parks overseas. Most countries along the Belt and Road are emerging or developing countries in the early stages of industrialization. Some of them, inspired by China's experience in the construction of development zones and parks, have started to create export processing zones, free trade zones and special economic zones of various sizes, and expressed a willingness to co-build industrial parks with China and learn from China's experience.

In essence, China's establishment of industrial cooperation zones in countries along the Belt and Road is an economic action designed to help Chinese enterprises meet challenges and mitigate the risks of investment overseas, which is a new platform of industrial cooperation aligned with market principles but with the guidance of the government. Countries along the Belt and Road have increasingly become significant destinations for China's FDI. Connection to the national development strategies of these countries, and active participation in the construction of industrial cooperation zones with comparatively improved infrastructures and matching legal policies, will enable Chinese enterprises to "go global" in groups. This will not only facilitate China's industrial transformation and upgrading, but also contribute to local development, benefiting local people. Stability and sustainability should be a priority principle in the construction of industrial cooperation zones, which means factors like appropriate positioning and specialization-based host country condition, step-by-step development, and risk control are key considerations. Chinese companies should adhere to the principle of joint construction through consultation to meet the interests of all parties, which involves negotiating with the host countries on the location of parks, jointly creating a suitable business environment and addressing development problems, and sharing development interests.

In addition, China should coordinate the resources of the National Development and Reform Commission, the Ministry of Commerce, the Ministry of Science and Technology, and financial institutions to form a joint force to promote the Belt and Road construction in key areas and key countries. The key countries and areas should in the first stage involve neighboring countries as well as pivot cities and transportation in other countries. The Chinese government should also establish sound assessment criteria based on the different types of industrial cooperation zones and their different functions, and accordingly give these parks differentiated supports. These zones may include trade, commerce, and logistics parks in cities acting as transport hubs along the Belt and Road; high-tech parks in major science, technology, and cultural centers; energy- and resources-processing parks in important port cities and resources-abundant regions; and manufacturing and agro-processing parks in regions with a sound basis.

V. Developing and consolidating opening-up platforms

The Belt and Road construction fundamentally aims to improve trade facilitation and to deepen economic cooperation, while opening-up platforms are carriers of economic and trade cooperation between China and countries along the Belt and Road. The so-called opening-up platforms include various trading ports (road, railway, inland rivers, harbors, airports, etc.); special customs supervision zones (bonded zones, bonded warehouses, export processing zones, bonded port zones, bonded logistics parks, comprehensive bonded zones, etc.); border cooperation zones; cross-border cooperation zones, and so on, in which most cross-border trade takes place. In more than 30 years of reform and opening up, the hard and soft conditions for opening up in China's coastal regions have been increasingly improved so that all harbor and air ports, special customs supervision zones and free trade zones have been able to meet the needs of international economic and trade activities. In contrast, the construction of opening-up platforms inland and in border areas has fallen behind, and still does not satisfy the needs of opening up. Tremendous room for improvement also exists in inland border ports in terms of hardware facilities, digitalization of customs clearance and mutual recognition of inspection and quarantine. In addition, most of China's border ports are connected to less-developed neighbors with lower-quality port facilities and "gray" customs clearance[1]. Therefore, an important task in the Belt and Road construction is to further improve both the hard and the soft environment of opening up, that is, various platforms.

In the framework of the Belt and Road construction, existing ports, special customs supervision zones, and border economic cooperation zones should be fully integrated based on the location characteristics, industrial structures, and foreign trade patterns of each province, city, and district to optimize the function of coastal opening-up platforms and build new platforms in boundary regions and inland, so as to develop a multilevel, prioritized, and coordinated opening-up system in the six economic corridors as aforementioned. The specific plan is as follows: first, to promote the upgrading of railway stations such as Manzhouli, Alashankou, Suifenhe, and Erenhot, so as to enhance the customs clearance capacity and cargo handling capacity at these railway ports; to actively connect to neighboring countries, for example, effectively connecting broad- and narrow-gauge rail systems in the corresponding ports of the two countries, so as to improve the reloading capacity of railway ports and the functions of customs clearance services, and to achieve joint inspection and mutual recognition. Second, to consolidate and develop the construction of infrastructures in highway ports such as Korgas, Alashankou, Ganqimaodu, Mohan, and Tengchong, and to build port-bonded storage and transportation warehouses and logistics parks in these places, so as to improve customs clearance capacity, personnel circulation and cargo handling capacity; to facilitate the construction of digital ports on the Chinese side and offer assistance to neighboring countries on the construction of digital ports so as to digitalize customs clearance and joint inspection management. Third, to expand and improve the comprehensive service functions of river ports such as Heihe, Tongjiang, and Fuyuan and to support the construction of related complementary infrastructures such as port terminals and freight yards, so as to improve passenger and cargo traffic capacity and promote the development of border trade, international logistics, and tourism. Fourth, to further construct such border ports as Dongning, Arihashate, Baketu, Jeminay, Takeshken, Karasu, Tuernate, Khunjerab, and Jilong.

Key border economic zones that meet certain conditions, such as Ruili, Wanding, Lincang, Hekou, Pingxiang, and Dongxing, should be supported to expand in scale and adjust their position, applying to the State Council following existing procedures to establish special customs supervision zones, such as export processing zones and border export processing zones, in order to develop vigorously export processing trade. The further construction of cross-border economic cooperation zones will deepen cross-nation cooperation. China should make a great effort to develop export-oriented industries in cross-border economic zones and improve related industrial chains, exploring and establishing industrial development coordination mechanisms with neighboring countries. China needs to deploy improved investment promotion policies to make the Dongxing (Guangxi, China)-Mong Cai (Vietnam) cross-border economic zone into border import and export resources processing bases, trade centers, modern logistics centers, and information exchange centers. Furthermore, it is necessary to accelerate infrastructure construction in cross-border economic cooperation zones such as Mohan (China)-Boten (Laos), Ruili (China)-Muse (Myanmar), Pingxiang (China)-DongDang (Vietnam), and Longbang (China)-Tralinh (Vietnam), and to develop new cooperation zones, according to a suitable schedule, in places such as Erenhot (China)-ZamynUeued (Mongol), Manzhouli (China)-Zabaikalsk (Russia),

Heihe (China)-Blagoveshchensk (Russia), Suifenhe (China)-Пограничный (Russia), and Honghe (China)-Lao Cai (Vietnam).

VI. Promoting people-to-people exchanges

People-to-people exchange is not only the foundation of a pervasive concept of the BRI but also a significant way of deepening mutual understanding between the peoples along the Belt and Road. It is also conducive to the identification of joint interests and mutually beneficial economic cooperation projects. It should be a priority for the governments that are taking part in the BRI to promote and for all sectors of society to participate in the Belt and Road construction, the key areas of which include culture, education, science and technology, health, tourism, and poverty alleviation.

In recent years, the content of people-to-people exchange between China and countries along the Belt and Road has been enhanced and the areas of cooperation have been continuously expanded in the framework of multilateral platforms such as the Shanghai Cooperation Organization (SCO), the China-ASEAN cooperation framework, the cooperation framework between China and Central and Eastern European Countries, the East Asia Summit, the Asia-Europe Meeting, the BRICS (Brazil, Russia, India, China and South Africa), and the Greater Mekong subregional mechanism. For example, as a result of the joint efforts of China, Kazakhstan, and Kyrgyzstan, the World Heritage Conference in June 2014 decided to formally include "Silk Roads: the Chang'an-Tianshan Corridor Route Network" in the World Heritage List. Cultural weeks, exhibitions, forums, and other activities jointly held by countries along the route are enriched in this way. However, due to factors like lack of funds, interference from external forces, and lack of long-term cooperation mechanisms, nongovernmental exchanges between China and the countries along the Belt and Road are still insufficient, and the forms of communication are unattractive, so that current arrangements are far from meeting the needs of the Belt and Road construction.

First, extensive cultural exchanges are required in the form of special festivals, cultural weeks and other events reflecting cultural traditions of countries along the Belt and Road. It is advisable to enhance the cooperation of culture industries in such areas as film and television, publishing, printing, performance arts, and cultural services to create a four-in-one cultural exchange system for newspapers, radio, film and television, and to develop the BRI satellite channels, making full use of multimedia channels such as the Internet to expand publicity of the BRI. China and other countries along the Silk Road should collectively protect and make good use of the cultural heritage of the Silk Road on the basis of respecting cultural traditions and cultural diversity, and to co-build a grand cultural brand of Silk Road with international influence by taking the good opportunity of the inclusion of the Silk Road in the World Heritage List to enhance its promotion.

Second, there is a need to expand the scale of student exchange between China and countries along the Belt and Road. This requires both an increase in scholarships for international students to come to China and the other participating countries, and the sending of more Chinese students to the other participating countries. Meanwhile, it is also necessary for China to help train talented technical and managerial staff in developing countries along the Belt and Road, and to encourage and support universities and relevant ministries and commissions to provide short-term training opportunities to government officials in these countries.

Third, there is a need to coordinate funds and projects in R & D in various sectors, integrating different funding resources to carry out science and technology cooperation in an orderly manner. Science and technology cooperation and services in areas relating to people's livelihoods should in particular be strengthened to help improve the distribution of benefits to people in all of the relevant countries, covering economizing on water, irrigation, improved livestock varieties, high-yield cotton, the processing of agricultural products, prevention and control of diseases, prevention and control of desertification, environmental protection, and disaster prevention and reduction. In addition, it is important to guide the establishment of bilateral or multilateral science and technology parks, and R & D centers, strengthening cooperation in scientific research projects and high-tech industries, so as to build a "Silk Road of Science and Technology".

Fourth, there is a need to actively develop tourism cooperation, promoting cross-border tourism and featured border tourism products, and to jointly build border tourism cooperation zones. These zones may focus on the Altai Mountain International Ecotourism Hotline, the China-Kazakhstan-Kyrgyzstan Transnational Tourism Line and the China-Kyrgyzstan-Uzbekistan Corridor Tourism Line. Furthermore, China should make full use of the opportunities brought by the inclusion of the Silk Road in the World Heritage List to carry out a Silk Road rally, and to create a Silk Road international tourism brand by drawing on the cultural heritage of the Silk Road, so as to create high-end Silk Road tourism routes, such as the Baoshan (China)-Myitkyina (Myanmar)-Imphal (India)-Dhaka (Bangladesh)–Kolkata (India) route.

Fifth, there is a need to promote cooperation on poverty alleviation, helping less-developed countries along the Belt and Road achieve poverty reduction goals. It is necessary not only to integrate government resources to form joint forces but also to make full use of the capabilities of nongovernmental organizations and enterprises, so that assistance will have substantial and long-term impacts in benefiting local people. China should also share its experience in poverty reduction with countries along the Belt and Road through existing mechanisms such as the "10·17 Poverty Alleviation and Development Forum", the "China-ASEAN Poverty Alleviation and Development Forum", and the "China-Africa Poverty Alleviation and Development Conference". In addition, China could establish joint centers for poverty alleviation in relevant countries.

VII. Enhancing risk control

Since the Belt and Road construction involves a large number of Chinese overseas investments, issues of risk prevention and control require attention. On the one hand, Chinese companies, having only started to "go global" recently, lack international experience and risk control capabilities. On the other hand, potential geopolitical and nontraditional security issues as well as economic, operational, and natural disaster risks are prominent in regions along the Belt and Road. The conjunction of these factors increases the risks confronting China's overseas investment and construction projects. At the same time, the diversity, complexity, and long-term nature of many projects have made risk prevention and control an issue that needs to be dealt with jointly by participating entities in regions along the Belt and Road, rather than something that just one country or government should handle. Therefore, it is essential to emphasize risk identification, prevention, and control in promoting the Belt and Road construction.

In order to cope with possible risks, it is urgent that China conduct detailed research on the development conditions and key issues of countries along the Belt and Road. Macroeconomic risks might be assessed from the four perspectives of geopolitical risks, nontraditional security risk, economic risk, and operational risk. Currently, geopolitical risks in the Belt and Road construction are associated with the overall challenges brought about by the containment strategies of major Western powers, multiple forms of resistance from regional powers in the neighborhood, and the potential risks of political instability and the escalation of military conflicts in neighboring countries. Nontraditional security risks are mainly threats associated with China's borderland security and hostile overseas forces as well as natural hazard risks. Economic risks largely consist of the economic instability of some countries along the Belt and Road, risks of debtor countries' breach of repayment terms, project bubbles, and global economic and trade change that may hinder Chinese capital "going global". Operational risks are mostly attributable to the inferior operating environment of countries along the Belt and Road and to Chinese companies having less experience in doing international business.

First, China should promote the construction of bilateral and multilateral cooperation mechanisms under the Belt and Road framework, and strengthen diversified dialogue and consultation mechanisms and regional co-development mechanisms. Second, it is necessary to publish regularly country investment risk reports by combining research resources at home and abroad and conducting specialized research. Third, China needs to establish an early warning and emergency response mechanism for overseas investment risks and to improve the effectiveness of emergency response by properly coordinating with countries along the Belt and Road. Fourth, the Chinese government should boost the policy support for its "going global" strategy, enhancing the ability of enterprises to resist risks and ensuring that various financial institutions and credit insurance agencies give full support to the strategy. Fifth, Chinese enterprises must also strengthen their own response capability, clarifying their strategic positioning; ensuring the soundness of information management, risk assessment, risk prevention, and emergency response; and accelerating the construction of their own organization to enhance the awareness of corporate risk and to regulate their own corporate actions.

Note

1 Translator's note: "gray" customs clearance refers to illicit customs clearance.

Appendix 1: Relevant essays

Scientific connotations and scientific issues relating to the Belt and Road Initiative[1]

Liu Weidong

I. Introduction

At the Boao Forum for Asia in Hainan on March 27, 2015, the *Vision and Actions* was jointly issued by the National Development and Reform Commission, the Ministry of Foreign Affairs, and the Ministry of Commerce of the People's Republic of China, with State Council authorization, marking the start of fully promoting Belt and Road construction, which will certainly have a historic impact on China's development. If the three decades since the reform and opening up have been a process in which China has been deeply involved in economic globalization actively under a "bringing in" strategy, then the BRI marks the arrival of the new stage of globalization in which China will proceed with the distinctive features of a "going global" strategy. Since President Xi Jinping proposed in Kazakhstan on September 7, 2013, to jointly build the "Silk Road Economic Belt", and the "Maritime Silk Road" in Indonesia on October 2 in the same year, all sectors at home and abroad have been paying close attention to the Belt and Road strategy, including the academic community. However, since the Chinese government did not issue an official document to specifically elaborate on this strategy, various sectors of the community had to more or less rely on conjecture to understand the "Belt and Road". The issuance of the *Vision and Actions* has made the Belt and Road strategy more open and transparent. Moreover, it has made it possible to scientifically interpret the strategy and understand the scientific problems it brings.

According to *Vision and Actions*, the BRI is aimed at promoting the orderly and free flow of economic factors, the highly efficient allocation of resources, and the deep integration of markets; encouraging a broader, deeper, and higher standard of regional cooperation; and jointly creating an open, inclusive, and balanced regional economic cooperation architecture that benefits all. It suggests that China expects to, in line with current world development mechanisms and trends, integrate into the global economic system to a deeper extent and play a more active role in leading world economic development. However, the Belt and Road framework contains a completely different concept from previous efforts at economic globalization, that is, "peace and cooperation, openness and inclusiveness, mutual learning, and mutual benefit", with the principle of jointly building the Belt and Road through consultation to meet the interests of all. The BRI might be simply summarized by "one core concept" (peace, cooperation, development and mutual benefit); "five cooperation priorities" (policy coordination, facilities connectivity, unimpeded trade, financial integration, and people-to-people bonds); and "three communities" (communities of shared interests, destiny, and responsibility). The BRI is not an accidental move, but an inevitable result of changes in the world economic landscape and the in-depth development of economic globalization. The scientific connotations and issues involved remain to be answered by the academic community.

II. The cultural connotations of the Silk Road

Though the term "Silk Road" is referred to in both the Silk Road Economic Belt and the 21st-Century Maritime Silk Road, the BRI, rather than proposing to rebuild past international trade routes, is built upon the cultural connotations of the "Silk Road", namely peace, friendship, exchange, and prosperity, which are precisely the core ideas advocated by *Vision and Actions*.

The deep integration of the economies of different countries and the advanced trade system are two of the prominent features of today's world economy. It can be said that the economic activities and lives of people in all countries of the world have become inseparable from trade exchanges. However, people are so familiar with today's manner of trade that they often forget there was a relatively developed trade in ancient times. In fact, as early as the Spring and Autumn period and the Warring States period (dating back to the Shang and Zhou dynasties), ancient China carried out trade activities with other countries in Eurasia. Since the Han dynasty, these trade activities have been gradually dominated and even monopolized by the government, and in its heyday even expanded throughout Eurasia, stretching as far as North and East Africa. Historically, there was no proper term to describe these transnational and long-distance trade exchanges until the German geographer Richthofen first used the term *Seidenstraße(n)* ("Silk Road(s)" or "Silk Route(s)") in 1877 in his book entitled *China: Ergebnisseeigner Reisen und daraufgegründeter Studien* (China: The results of my travels and the studies based thereon). The term "Silk Road" used by Richthofen refers only to the trade route from the Central Plains through the Hexi corridor and the Tarim Basin to Central Asia and the Mediterranean, and this is called a silk road as silk was one of the major bulk commodities traded on this route from the Han dynasty to the Tang dynasty. The term Silk Road, embodying such strong historical and cultural connotations, had been widely recognized and used in practice. The long-established "Southern Tea Route" and northern grassland trade routes, as well as the maritime trade routes from the time of the Song and Yuan dynasties, were often referred to as the "Silk Road" too. The dominant goods traded, certainly not always silk, changed in different historical periods. For example, during the Song, Yuan and Ming dynasties, the goods traded along the Maritime Silk Road were mainly silk, porcelain, tea, and spices. In addition, "Silk Road" was not only synonymous with ancient trade but also a historical "symbol" of cultural exchanges between China and Eurasian countries. Along with the trade in goods and the exchange of personnel, splendid civilizations emerged during the process and were mutually enriched.

Discussions of and the focus on the "Silk Road" in the past were mainly limited to the history and cultural relics of communities without utilitarian purposes. However, since the proposal of the BRI, the degree of exploration of historical and cultural relics of the "Silk Road" has risen since most regions and countries along the Belt and Road intend to establish their positions in relation to it. Although it is hard to completely deny the significance of approaches that involve learning from the ancients in studying contemporary issues, this is clearly a misunderstanding of the underlying meaning of the reference to the "Silk Road" in the BRI. Historically, the specific routes and spatial orientation of the Silk Road constantly changed along with changes in the geographical environment, the state of economic development and the evolution of politics and religions. The Silk Road that people are trying to outline today is a picture that has been created through observing thousands of years of history. Therefore, the "Silk Road", semantically speaking, cannot be understood as a spatial phenomenon with fixed lines. Rather than as a spatial phenomenon, it should be viewed as more of a cultural symbol with abstract meanings for today's society. In addition, historically the Silk Road mainly existed in peacetime (often interrupted during wartime) when the exchange of goods and knowledge brought common prosperity. Therefore, the connotations of the Silk Road as a cultural symbol may be summarized as peace, friendship, exchange, and prosperity, which, from this perspective, are the ideas of "peace, cooperation, development, and mutual benefit" that the Chinese government has sought to deliver to the world through the use of this cultural symbol.

III. The BRI and economic globalization

According to the *Vision and Actions*, the co-construction of the Belt and Road is not aimed at making a fresh start but rather making a great effort "to uphold the global free trade regime and the open world economy". In other words, the BRI, emerging in the context of major adjustments in the world structure and economic globalization, is a significant framework for promoting the in-depth development of economic globalization. However, instead of simply being a continuation of past economic globalization, it is a new manifestation of globalization with the integration of the cultural connotations of the "Silk Road" as its prominent feature. To put it simply, the BRI is an embodiment of inclusive globalization within the basic mechanism of economic globalization, namely investment and trade liberalization.

It is well known that the emergence and development of economic globalization are inseparable from the prevalence of neoliberalism. Marked by the two global oil crises in the 1970s, the Western developed countries entered an era of severe stagflation as a 20-year postwar economic boom ended. In order to address stagflation, countries such as the United Kingdom and the United States switched from welfare state policies to neoliberal ones that reduced government intervention and implemented full privatization. At the same time, Western corporations started to export capital on a large scale and to transfer industries overseas. The world thus entered the stage of the global expansion of capitalism. Neoliberalism is regarded as the theoretical basis for the promotion of investment and trade liberalization. The "Washington Consensus" is a typical "prescription" that at that time was designed by the United States for Latin American and Eastern European countries in transition, the core of which was trade and capital liberalization, comprehensive market liberalization, and full privatization. However, from the perspective of the results, the economic growth rates of countries adopting the "Washington Consensus" stagnated, while China, which organically combined government intervention and market mechanisms, grew rapidly. It might be said that economic globalization based on neoliberalism has shaped the world of the past three decades, and that the neoliberal regulatory approach to financial markets led to the global financial crisis of 2008. Therefore, in the process of economic globalization based on neoliberalism, capital was the biggest winner, while the rest of society paid a huge price. In this context, developed countries such as the United States and the United Kingdom, and developing countries, as represented by China, all have been considering reform of the governance model to promote the further spread of economic globalization. The BRI might be a promising effort in this respect.

Since the 1980s, China has continuously and deeply participated in the process of economic globalization through gradual reform and opening up. China, on the one hand, has driven the rise of its own economy by introducing capital, technologies, and management experience into the country, and on the other hand, has gradually established a governance mechanism adapted to economic globalization. Admittedly, China, whose rapid economic development has benefited from economic globalization, has also made tremendous contributions to world economic growth and changed the economic landscape of the world. At the beginning of the reform and opening up, China's GDP only accounted for 5 percent of the world's share, while its exports accounted for less than 1.5 percent of the world's total exports. By 2013, the share of China's GDP in the world had risen to 12.3 percent and its share of exports had also risen, in this case to 12 percent. Correspondingly, China became the second-largest economy in the world in 2010, and the world's largest country for trade in goods in 2013. Moreover, since the global financial crisis in 2008, China's contribution to world economic growth, equal to 27.8 percent in 2014, has remained around 30 percent on average. China, whose economy, though remaining large but not strong, has become one of the major forces shaping

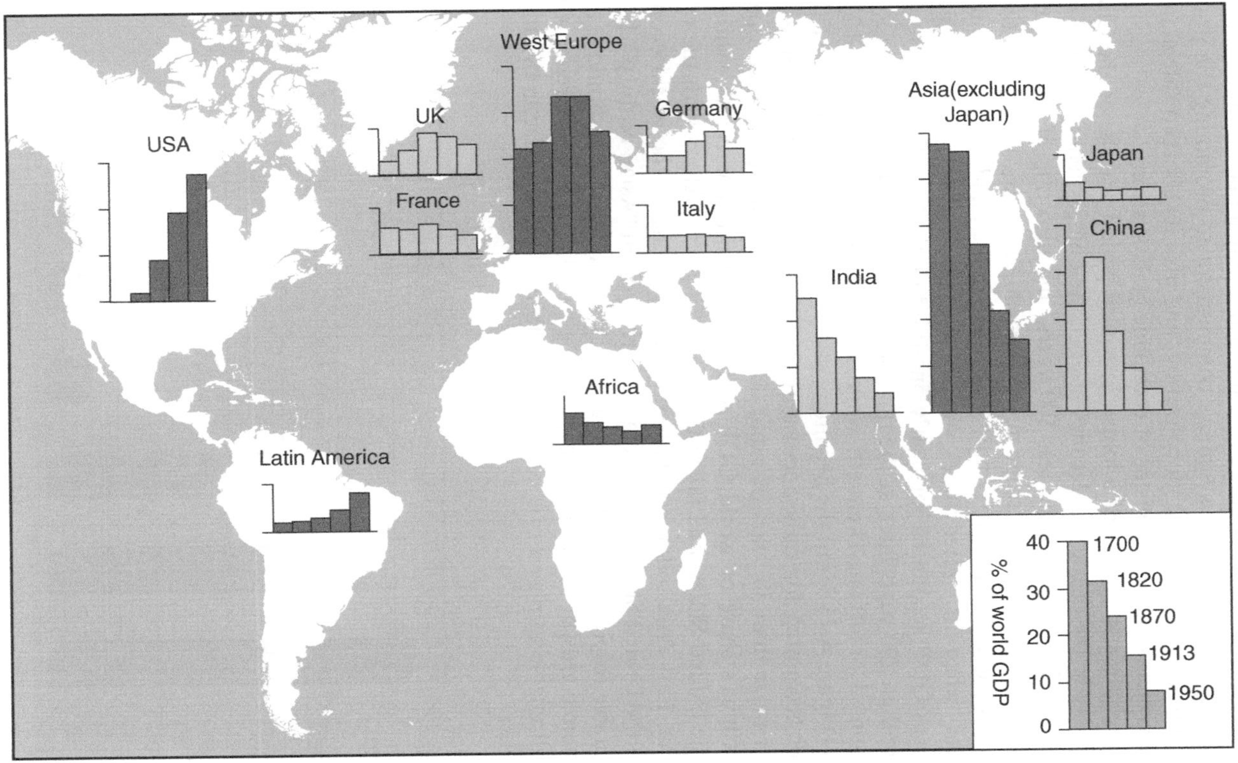

Figure A.1 Changes in the world economic landscape (1700–1950)

Source: cited from Dicken (2010).

the global context due to the size of its economy (10 trillion US dollars in 2014). Furthermore, under the trend of increasingly close economic linkages among countries in the world, it is inevitable that the development of and changes in such a large economy will substantially influence other countries. In this context, the BRI is China's commitment to promoting the in-depth development of economic globalization, and also its effort to safeguard the achievements and mechanisms of economic globalization.

From the perspective of a longer historical period, the rise of the Chinese economy in the past three decades has been the biggest change in the world economic landscape in the last 100 years, and also one of the few major changes in the world landscape in the past 300 years. According to estimates by an economic historian, Angus Maddison, in the middle of the eighteenth century when the United States' share of the world's economy was negligible, China's GDP accounted for nearly one-third of the world's total. However, more than 200 years later, at the time of the founding of New China, China accounted for just one-twentieth, while the United States' share reached 27 percent (Figure A.1). Until the beginning of the reform and opening up, China's GDP accounted for only one-twentieth of the world's total (Figure A.2). After more than 30 years of rapid development in the reform and opening up, China's share of world GDP returned to nearly one-eighth, while that of the United States' had fallen to about 22 percent. Along with the rise of China, East Asia today accounts for a larger share in the world economy than the United States, suggesting the arrival of an "Asian century". It is an inevitable responsibility of China as a major country that it should lead the economic growth of Asia and even of the world. However, currently China is still unable to play a role compatible with its economic size in driving the

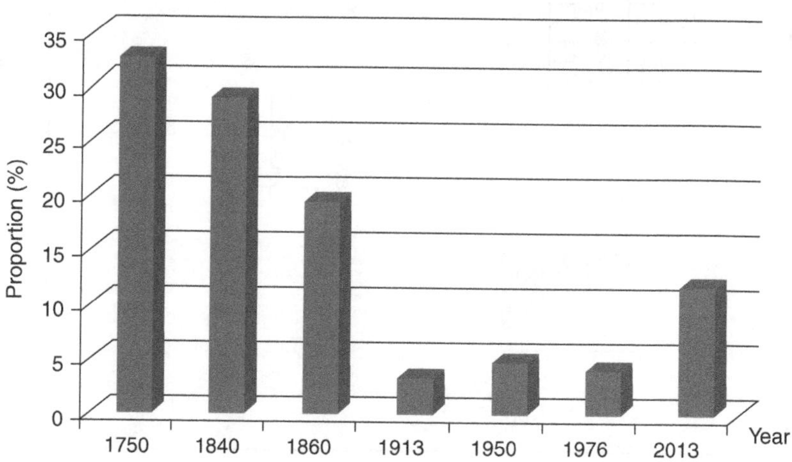

Figure A.2 Changes in the proportion of China's total economic output (GDP) accounting for the world's total from 1750 to 2013

Source: Maddison (2007).

economic growth of the world since its share in multiple international financial institutions remains at a low level. For example, it has only 5.17 percent, 3.81 percent and 6.47 percent of the voting rights in the World Bank, the International Monetary Fund and the Asian Development Bank respectively. Therefore, in order to change this unreasonable situation, Belt and Road construction is of great importance.

From the perspective of its own development stage, China's economic growth is entering a stage of "new normal". On the one hand, with the "demographic dividend" that has lasted for more than three decades fading away, and labor costs rapidly increasing, some labor-intensive industries have been losing their competitive advantage, which is actually in line with the basic cyclical law of economic globalization, that is, that a round of large-scale industrial transfer occurs every 30 to 40 years. On the other hand, due to over-optimistic capacity expansion in the past decade or so, the production capacity of some raw material industries in China has experienced a serious surplus as economic growth has slowed down. However, this overcapacity is not backward technologically. It just needs to be transferred outward because of over-supply. In addition, China's huge consumer market has led to the emergence of a number of large companies, which have been transforming themselves into multinational companies with capabilities to invest multinationally and engage in global operations. Due to these particular factors, China is walking into an era of "going global" on a large scale. As reflected in Figure A.3, since 2004, and especially after 2008, China's FDI surged. China's FDI was only 5.5 billion US dollars in 2004, reached 55.9 billion US dollars in 2008 and rose to 140 billion US dollars in 2014, increasing nearly 25 times in ten years (Figure A.3). This growth trend is quite similar to those of developed countries in Europe and the United States in the 1980s and 1990s (Figure A.4). Therefore, the mechanism that China employs to "go global", whether a

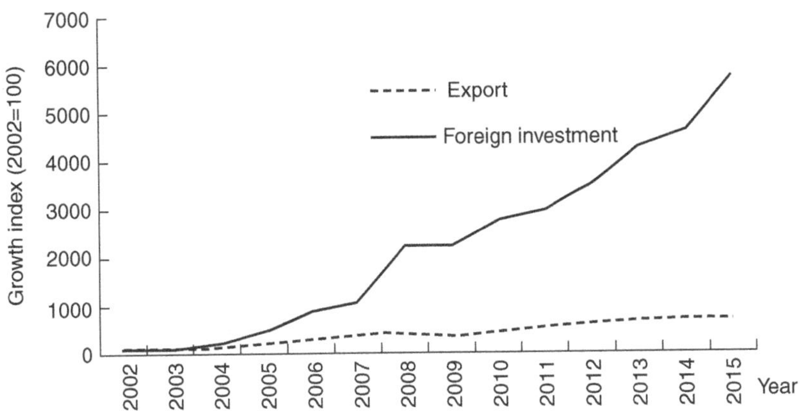

Figure A.3 Export and foreign investment growth of China
Source: China Statistical Yearbook of relevant years

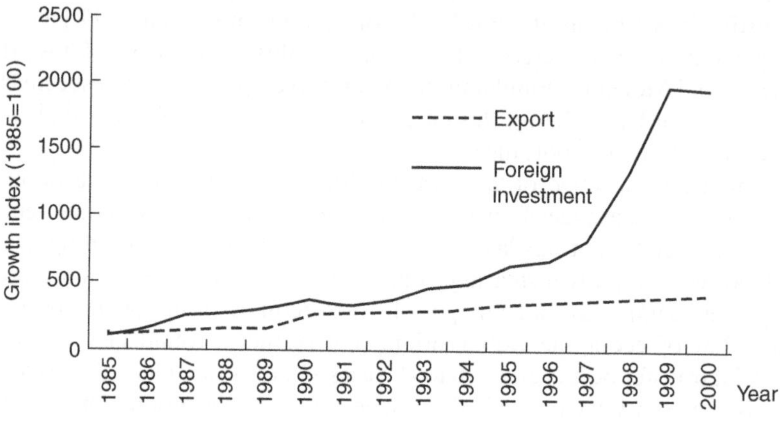

Figure A.4 Export and foreign investment growth of advanced economies
Source: UNTCAD database (www.untcad.org).

neoliberal one or an inclusive one, will influence a large number of countries. To improve the mechanisms of economic globalization through Belt and Road co-construction, avoiding as much as possible negative impacts, will meet not only China's need to "go global" but also the need of more countries to benefit from globalization.

Therefore, the BRI in general is a Chinese version of economic globalization and an exploration in promoting the healthy development of globalization. It is not a "maverick" move by China or the Chinese version of "Marshall aid" but rather an international cooperation platform to promote regional development that benefits all under the economic globalization mechanism.

IV. Spatial connotations of the BRI

The BRI is on the face of it a strategic concept with high spatial selectivity. As "Belt" and "Road" literally refer to economies located along certain axes, the consequent spatial exclusivity has led to some misunderstandings of the Belt and Road strategy. For example, some provinces believe they have a special and exclusive status in the "Belt and Road" project, while others consider themselves irrelevant to "Belt and Road" construction. However, the truth is that the "Belt and Road" is a cross-scale concept with multiple spatial connotations.

First, with no absolute boundary, the BRI is not a closed system, which means it is impossible to accurately draw its spatial scope on a map. The BRI is fundamentally an open and inclusive international regional economic cooperation network in which others can choose to participate. That is, it is not an exclusive platform. Therefore, though the Ministry of Foreign Affairs once mentioned more than 60 countries and more than four billion people along the Belt and Road, the *Vision and Actions* simply points out that the BRI crosses Afro-Eurasia, rather than defining a specific scope and list of countries.

Second, as an international regional economic cooperation network, undoubtedly the BRI stresses cooperation between whole countries rather than subregional cooperation with neighboring countries. From the domestic perspective, although the *Vision and Actions* mentions some provinces and cities, for example, making Xinjiang and Fujian the core areas of the "Silk Road Economic Belt" and the "21st-Century Maritime Silk Road" respectively; focusing on Xi'an as a new site of reform and the opening up of China's interior, supporting Chongqing, Chengdu, Zhengzhou, Wuhan, Changsha, Nanchang, Hefei, and other cities as leading areas of opening up in the inland regions; and strengthening the construction of cities such as Shanghai, Tianjin, Ningbo, Guangzhou, and Shenzhen, it does not necessarily grant an exclusive status to these provinces and cities. In fact, all regions may participate in Belt and Road construction, especially in the co-construction of economic and trade cooperation, cultural cooperation, financial cooperation and so on. The project is by no means the "exclusive" task of the provinces and regions mentioned in the *Vision and Actions*. Provinces such as Jiangsu and Shandong that are not mentioned are actually more connected with the trade and cultural exchanges with countries along the Road. The reason for the references to the positioning of certain provinces and regions in the *Vision and Actions* was to combine Belt and Road construction with existing regional development strategies in the country, so as to strengthen interaction and cooperation among the eastern, western and central regions, and promote a relatively balanced development of opening up. It was not meant to specify that certain areas were included and others not included in the BRI.

Furthermore, the co-construction of the BRI involves facilities connectivity, especially the construction of international land and maritime transport corridors, which does entail a specific spatial orientation and spatial scope. For example, the *Vision and Actions* proposes that the Silk Road Economic Belt focuses on bringing together China, Central Asia, Russia, and Europe; linking China with the Persian Gulf and the Mediterranean Sea through Central Asia and West Asia; and connecting China with Southeast Asia, South Asia, and the Indian Ocean. The 21st-Century Maritime Silk Road is designed to run from China's coastal ports to Europe through the South China Sea and the Indian Ocean along one route, and from China's coastal ports through the South China Sea to the South Pacific along the other. Mention was also made of the focus on jointly building a new Eurasian Land Bridge and developing the China-Mongolia-Russia, the China-Central Asia-West Asia, and the China-Indochina Peninsula economic cooperation corridors and so on, and further promoting the construction of the China-Pakistan Economic Corridor and the Bangladesh-China-India-Myanmar Economic Corridor. Along these routes and corridors with their clear spatial directions there will be co-construction of infrastructures. In other words, of the "five connectivities", facilities connectivity has more small-scale and sub-regional features, while the other four are much more matters of cooperation between countries.

Some domestic officials, scholars, and the media are accustomed to considering the BRI as China's regional development strategy due to their insufficient understanding of its multiple spatial and cross-scale features, which has led to a certain degree of confusion. The BRI is a long-term, top-level strategy that coordinates China's opening up from all aspects, as well as an initiative to create an open and inclusive international regional economic cooperation network by China and the countries along the Road. Thus, it is undoubtedly a national strategy rather than a regional one. Certainly, this national strategy has significant regional impacts due to its multiple spatialities. However, to call it a Chinese regional strategy just because of its regional influences not only undermines its status and effects but may also cause concern among the participating countries along the Road. Therefore, it is inappropriate to refer collectively to the BRI, "the coordinated development of Beijing-Tianjin-Hebei" and "the construction of the Yangtze River Economic Belt" as China's three major regional strategies in the new era.

V. Geographic study issues in respect of the Belt and Road

The BRI is a new development concept and international regional cooperation model proposed by China for the further in-depth development of economic globalization. Belt and Road co-construction has raised many scientific issues for the academic community, of which those worth deeper study by the geography academic community include: the core elements and driving mechanisms of geopolitical relations in the era of globalization; geographic studies of individual countries along the Road; the theory of FDI within the framework of the Belt and Road; the spatial organization of land and ocean transportation and so forth.

Geopolitics is a traditional area of geography. Fundamentally speaking, geopolitics explores the relationship between geographic factors, such as location, ethnicity, and economic strength, and the political actions of states, especially the role of geographic factors in the protection of national interests. In modern history, rising powers have always attached great importance to geopolitical studies. In the past there were a number of leading geopolitical scientists, including Ratzel from Germany, Mahan from the United States, and Mackinder from the United Kingdom. However, geopolitical studies in China, by contrast, remain quite weak for various reasons. With only a handful of scholarly research teams and a limited published literature, it is hard for China to meet its needs for its rising international status. Without a doubt, Belt and Road construction will involve the coordination of the interests of participating countries along the Road, and also lead to changes in the global context, inevitably changing geopolitical structures. Therefore, the geography academic community cannot avoid analyzing the geopolitical basis of the BRI and its impact on geopolitical patterns, and must seek to develop geopolitical theories consistent with the ideas of the BRI.

The *Vision and Actions* has proposed basic principles of jointly building the Belt and Road through consultation to meet the interests of all. The key to effectively promoting Belt and Road construction is to find common interests and mutually beneficial construction projects with countries along the Belt and Road. These choices must connect with the policies and construction plans of the countries concerned. Consultation and connectivities require a deepening of mutual understanding, including political, legal, administrative, cultural, religious, demographic, economic, social, and resources environments, and differences in national governance structures. For this purpose, national geographical studies are required. Over the past three decades, owing to value orientations and the strong demand for domestic construction, studies of world geography or the geography of foreign countries by China's scholars of geography have declined. The systematic understanding of many countries along the Belt and Road remains at the same level that it was ten years ago. This situation will, to a certain extent, adversely affect the consultations and connectivities between China and the countries along the Road, and it is also not conducive to avoiding unnecessary risks. It is thus urgent to carry out national geographic studies in respect of countries along the Belt and Road.

The co-construction of the Belt and Road will be a process of in-depth development of globalization notably associated with China's "going global" strategy, requiring the support of suitable theories of FDI. Since Western developed countries started to "go global" with large-scale outward direct capital investment in the 1970s, theories of FDI have been an important topic of study in the international geography and business communities. Theories of the "new international geographical division of labor" at an early stage, then Dunning's Eclectic Theory and, later, network theory in the 1990s all played a significant role in guiding developed countries' FDI. However, since the existing FDI theories are mainly based on the experience of these countries, especially in neoliberal contexts, it remains to be seen whether such theories will be effective in guiding Belt and Road construction. Therefore, a cutting-edge academic topic in the geography field involves using Belt and Road construction as a case for examining existing FDI theories, and discovering new key variables, so as to modify or reconstruct them.

The optimization of transport organization for trade in goods is another prominent feature of Belt and Road construction. In the past century, international trade has mainly involved maritime transport thanks to the continuous development of maritime transport technology. Though with unparalleled convenience and cost advantages compared with other modes of transportation, the time cost of maritime transport is still too high. For instance, shipping from China's coastal ports to Europe generally takes more than 30 days. By contrast, though land (railway) transport has a moderate price and time cost, existing between those of sea and air transport, international rail transport is too cumbersome since it has to pass through the customs systems of multiple sovereign countries. Joint construction of facilities connectivity and trade facilitation in the context of Belt and Road construction will help improve the comparative advantage of land (railway) transport. In fact, China has already started preliminary exploration in this respect by opening several "designated train" lines in recent years, such as the Chongqing-Xingjiang-Europe line, the Sichuan-Xingjiang-Europe line, and the Xi'an-Xingjiang-Europe line. Therefore, with the deepening of Belt and Road construction, the question of the further optimization of goods transport organization is also an issue worthy of further study by the geography community.

VI. Conclusion

The BRI is a new model of international regional economic cooperation proposed by China to advance the in-depth development of economic globalization. It will not only have a profound historical impact on China's social and economic development and all-around opening up but also actively drive economic development for countries along the Road, and change international economic structures. It is a national strategy on the part of China to coordinate its all-around opening up to the world, and should not be considered a regional strategy, despite its significant regional impacts. A correct understanding of this strategy requires not only a deep understanding of the cultural connotations of the Silk Road and the general trend of economic globalization but also a scientific understanding of the spatial connotations, especially the spatial multiplicity, of the BRI.

A major national strategic need now and for a long period in the future is to provide scientific support for Belt and Road construction. As it has rich geographical connotations, the BRI opens up significant opportunities for the development of geography in China, promoting studies and innovations in such areas as geopolitics, world geography, theories of foreign capital investment, and transport organization.

Discussion of misunderstandings about the BRI[2]

Liu Weidong

I. Introduction

In September and October 2013, President Xi Jinping, during his visit to Central Asian and Southeast Asian countries, proposed a major initiative to jointly build the "Silk Road Economic Belt" and the "21st-Century Maritime Silk Road", and he received positive responses from relevant countries. In November of the same year, the *Decision of the Central Committee of the*

Communist Party of China on Some Major Issues Concerning Comprehensively Deepening Reform proposed to "build a Silk Road Economic Belt and a Maritime Silk Road, so as to form a new pattern of all-around opening up". The Belt and Road, specifically referred to the "Silk Road Economic Belt" and the "21st-Century Maritime Silk Road" at the Central Economic Work Conference that year, and has now gradually become a long-term and major national strategy for coordinating China's all-around opening up. For more than two years, especially since the publication of the *Vision and Actions on Jointly Building Silk Road Economic Belt and 21st-Century Maritime Silk Road* (hereafter "*Vision and Actions*") in March 2015, this strategy has been assigned to various departments. The Belt and Road strategy has received a warm response from all sectors, regions, and communities of society, the whole country having participated in the Belt and Road construction.

The *Vision and Actions* states that "the initiative to jointly build the Belt and Road is aimed at promoting an orderly and free flow of economic factors, highly efficient allocation of resources, and the deep integration of markets; encouraging the countries along the Belt and Road to achieve economic policy coordination and carry out broader and deeper regional cooperation; and jointly creating an open, inclusive, and balanced regional economic cooperation architecture that benefits all". Based on the principle to jointly build the Belt and Road through consultation to meet the interests of all, China has launched various connectivity projects with countries along the Road for the purpose of the Belt and Road construction, especially cooperative planning of major economic corridors, to further broaden and deepen economic and trade cooperation. With such a sound start, the BRI thus has been widely recognized by the international community.

In the meantime, however, since the BRI is an overarching strategy that involves many issues, there are still different was of understanding it, and even biased perspectives, among various sectors of the society. These misunderstandings may have a negative impact on the promotion of Belt and Road construction. This essay is aimed at attracting some revealing academic discussion by illustrating some of the debatable opinions and by proposing the writer's own understanding in respect of the BRI.

II. Several misunderstandings

1. The BRI is not aimed at rebuilding ancient international trade routes

Some scholars and local officials have misunderstood "Belt and Road" construction as rebuilding ancient international trade routes because the concept of the "Silk Road" is used in the BRI. It is notable that some regions have been keen to explore their own roles in the ancient Silk Road, such as starting points, passages, and links, in order to establish their special position in the current Belt and Road. Although it is hard to completely deny the practical meaning of such opinions, especially due to the significance of such an approach for learning from the past in order to deal with current issues, it is clearly a misunderstanding of the underlying meaning of the reference to the "Silk Road" in the BRI as it reduces the enormous historical and cultural value of the Silk Road.

The Silk Road is a general term for long-distance commercial trade and cultural exchange routes that gradually developed from ancient times, starting from China and stretching through Eurasia and even North Africa and East Africa. However, the concept itself was not established by Chinese scholars but by the German geographer Richthofen in 1877 in his book entitled *China: Ergebnisseeigner Reisen und daraufgegründeter Studien* (China: The results of my travels and the studies based thereon) in which he introduced the term *Seidenstraße(n)* ("Silk Road(s)" or "Silk Route(s)"). The term "Silk Road" was used by Richthofen at that time to refer only to the multiple trade routes from the Central Plains through the Hexi Corridor and the Tarim Basin to Central Asia, West Asia, and the Mediterranean. French Sinologist Édouard Chavannes later in 1903 in his work *Documents sur les Tou-kiue (Turks) occidentaux* (Documents on the Western Turks) first included former maritime trade routes from China within the realm of the Silk Road. Fundamentally speaking, though the Silk Road is largely about historical trade relations between China and other countries in the world, it is indeed not exclusively owned by China. Instead it is a historical and cultural heritage shared by countries along the Road. For example, "Silk Roads: The Routes Network of the Chang'an-Tianshan Corridor" was formally included on the World Heritage List in 2014, as a result of the joint efforts of China, Kazakhstan, and Kyrgyzstan.

In addition, the Silk Road that people are trying to outline today is a picture that was created when observing 2,000 years of history. Historically, the specific routes and spatial orientation of the Silk Road have constantly changed along with changes in the geographical environment, the state of economic development and the evolution of politics and religion. The "Silk Road" that people observe today from the perspective of history is actually a quite dense trade network rather than some fixed routes. Therefore, when we try to understand its meaning, the Silk Road should be deemed a historical and cultural symbol commonly recognized by countries along the Road, with connotations of peace, friendship, exchange, and prosperity, rather than a specific spatial phenomenon.

Therefore, it is the ideas of "peace, cooperation, development, and mutual benefit" referred in the *Vision and Actions* that the BRI has presented to the world using the Silk Road as a cultural symbol. Although the spatial orientation of the "Silk Road" in history has some symbolic significance, the BRI is meant neither to restore these ancient trade routes nor to raise the threshold for participating in such a major project or to confine it to regions along the ancient Silk Road. Instead, it is aimed at building an international regional cooperation platform for China and the countries along the Road to achieve common development and shared prosperity. It is the "Silk Road" as a historical and cultural heritage that laid the cultural foundations for this international regional cooperation.

2. *The BRI is not a regional development strategy*

It has been a widely argued since the BRI was proposed that it is a regional development strategy of China, especially a development strategy for regions along the ancient Silk Road. Moreover, the BRI, together with "the coordinated development of Beijing-Tianjin-Hebei" and "the construction of the Yangtze River Economic Belt", have been collectively referred to as China's three major regional strategies in the new era. Such opinions have caused quite a lot of misunderstanding about the Belt and Road. For example, some provinces believe in their special and exclusive status in the "Belt and Road", while others consider themselves irrelevant to "Belt and Road" construction.

Regional development strategies are special institutional arrangements that deal with the development relations between regions within a country and the relationship between regional development and the overall development of the country, and are internal affairs of the country. Generally speaking, the core purposes include cultivating regional competitiveness, promoting the development of less-developed regions, and supporting the revitalization of "problem regions". For example, the Western Development Strategy, the rejuvenation of the old industrial bases in the Northeast and support for the rise of Central China are all typical regional development strategies. According to *Vision and Actions*, the BRI is a long-term top-level strategy that coordinates China's opening up from all aspects, as well as an initiative to create an open and inclusive international regional economic cooperation network involving China and countries along the Belt and Road. In other words, its construction is based on cooperation between countries rather than between a few neighboring regions. Therefore, the BRI is a national strategy involving international cooperation, and is the main banner and platform for China's opening up and development. It is in no way a regional development strategy, whether from the perspective of its attributes or scope.

Belt and Road construction, even only from a domestic perspective, should also be a nationwide strategy rather than a specific cause of certain regions. With regard to the five cooperation priorities (i.e., the "five connectivities"), policy coordination, unimpeded trade, financial integration, and people-to-people bonds are national tasks that all regions in the country can and should participate in. Facilities connectivity does surely have specific spatial directions that will benefit certain areas more than others. Therefore, the BRI is a grand and long-term design and a top-level national strategy, and should not be deemed a regional development strategy of China. To do so would undermine its status and function, causing doubt among participating countries along the Road. *The Suggestions of the CPC Central Committee on the Thirteenth Five-Year Plan for National Economic and Social Development* (hereafter "*Suggestions*") adopted in November 2015 further clarified that advancing Belt and Road construction is an important aspect of China's opening up and development.

Certainly, the Belt and Road strategy does have significant regional impacts or certain regional attributes. For example, on the one hand, the building of the six major economic corridors and economic leading areas of opening up in the inland regions (see *Vision and Actions*) will drive the development of certain areas in the central and western regions, forming new growth poles, while, on the other hand, the deepening and expanding of economic and trade exchanges with countries along the Belt and Road will promote the sustainable development of coastal economic centers, improving their international competitiveness. That is why the *Suggestions* stated in the elaborations on how to expand the space of regional development, indicate that China will form vertical and horizontal economic axes mainly comprised of economic belts along its coastline, major rivers, and the Belt and Road, based on its overall strategy on regional development and guided by such development plans as the "Belt and Road" initiatives; the integrated development of Beijing, Tianjin, and Hebei; and the Yangtze River Economic Belt.

In general, the Belt and Road strategy does have multiple spatial attributes, including, from top to bottom, international regional cooperation networks, major economic corridors, node cities, and concentrated industrial areas. However, even with such regional attributes, the BRI is fundamentally a major national strategy that coordinates China's all-around opening up, so its regional attributes should be subordinated to its national attributes, rather than replacing them.

3. The BRI is not a one-way "going global" strategy

Going Global is not only an important part in the Belt and Road construction but also its strategic foundation. As a result, there has been a misunderstanding in Chinese society that Belt and Road construction is all about "going global". Correspondingly, the expectation of accelerating "going global" has been noted in some local government circles, while some enterprises have become eager to "go global" as soon as possible, and a few local governments have even considered the results of "going global" as a political achievement. This is a quite risky misunderstanding.

China is entering a new stage of capital "going global" on a large scale. From 2004 to 2014, China's foreign investment increased more than 20 times. In 2014, China's outward and inward FDIs were basically equal to one another. And this growth trend was quite similar to that of North American and European developed countries in the 1980s and 1990s. The main reasons are the following: labor-intensive industries need to shift to countries with lower labor costs as they are losing competitiveness in China; some industries need to shift overseas due to problems of overcapacity; China's huge consumer market has fostered a number of large enterprises with international investment capabilities; China needs to establish strategic resource support bases overseas. The new stage marks the beginning of the second global industrial shift characterized by the "going global" of China's capital, and will open a new era of economic globalization.

Though in the above context the export of capital constitutes an important part of "Belt and Road" construction, it does not necessarily mean a simple one way out. With a large technology gap between China and developed countries, the "bringing in" strategy is still worthy of great attention on the part of China for a long time to come. Economic globalization indeed is a deepening process of mutual investment between countries. Over the past three decades, European and American developed countries have been both major investors in foreign countries and major destinations for foreign capital. Therefore, to advance "Belt and Road" construction, China should not only attach great importance to "bringing in capital" but also encourage domestic capital to "go global". Only with an organic combination of these two international economic and trade cooperation strategies will the transformation and upgrading of Chinese industries and sustainable and sound economic development be facilitated.

In addition, since not all regions within China's vast territory have entered the "going global" development stage on a large scale due to great differences in regional development levels, each region, instead of blindly following others' steps, needs to analytically determine its priorities for participating in the "BRI" based on its own characteristics. Unnecessary investment risks would be inevitable in the excessive pursuit of "going global".

In Belt and Road construction, enterprises in different categories should be encouraged accordingly to "go global" in an appropriate manner rather than just to rush to set up factories overseas. A top-layer design formulating differentiated policies to encourage various companies to "go global" with an approach that suits them in particular is urgently needed during the process of "going global". And it is China's industrial transformation and upgrading and employment, rather than whether capital is "going global" and on what scale, that are essential for such a top-level design. China, when carrying out the "going global" strategy, not only needs to prevent its manufacturing industry from "hollowing out" but also to mitigate various investment risks. Mitigation of risk especially requires government support and services, in which regard China may learn from the Singapore government's experience in establishing overseas industrial parks, such as Singapore's Suzhou Industrial Park. For instance, China may negotiate and cooperate with some countries that are relatively developed in economy or advanced in technology to establish a number of industrial parks supported by the governments of such countries, so as to create more stable conditions for Chinese enterprises, especially private enterprises, to "go global".

4. The BRI is not a traditional geostrategy

The emergence of the BRI can be attributed to changes in China's development stage and to changes in international economic structures in the past three decades. Among other factors, China has become the second-largest economy in the world, the largest manufacturing country, the largest commodity trading country and a significant capital exporting country, which are important foundations for Belt and Road construction. In this context, some scholars tend to interpret the BRI as a geostrategy employed by China. However, this interpretation is far from the fundamental idea of the BRI.

A so-called geostrategy is generally understood as a geopolitical strategy involving the relationship between the political acts of states and geographical location. From Ratzel's theory of "Staaten somLifsform" (National Organism), to Mahan's theory of "sea power", to Mackinder's "heartland theory", all these traditional geopolitical ideas concern how to control the world and carry out an expansion of forces, especially control and expansion relying on military forces. After World War I, studies in geopolitics waned for a longtime due to the ill use of some geopolitical theories to serve the expansionist goals of Nazi Germany. Even today, with the reputation of geopolitics rebuilt to a large extent, studies in geopolitics are still mainly used by states in reference to the formulation of offensive defense and foreign policies. The BRI, in contrast, advocates promoting a deepening of international economic and trade cooperation among countries along the Belt and Road, an issue that is different from the core issues with which traditional geopolitical strategies are concerned. Geostrategy does have certain similarities with the BRI, but only if it refers to geoeconomic relations. However, the point is that geostrategy has often been understood as a traditional geopolitical strategy, which is offensive and belligerent.

According to the *Vision and Actions*, the BRI is a way to achieve win-win cooperation that promotes common development and prosperity and a road toward peace and friendship by enhancing mutual understanding and trust, and strengthening all-around exchanges. The Belt and Road should be jointly built through consultation to meet the interests of all, and efforts should be made to integrate the development strategies of the countries along the Belt and Road.

It can be said that the two terms "joint" and "cooperation" occur the most frequently in *Visions and Actions*. Therefore, the BRI is an attempt to explore new ways of bringing about international cooperation such as integrated development and win-win cooperation as well as a new model of global economic governance that is completely different from the self-interested expansion discussed in the traditional geopolitical strategy. To some extent, a distortion and interpretation of the BRI as China's geostrategy will undermine the concept of "integration" and "cooperation" advocated in it and adversely affect the smooth construction of the BRI.

5. *The Belt and Road is not a simple linear economy*

Almost everyone who reads the term "Belt and Road" will unconsciously keep asking the question "Where are the Belt and the Road?" This is actually another misunderstanding. The term "Belt and Road", though it includes the direct meaning of linear economies, is an abstract and metaphorical concept, whose core connotation is not just building a few roads but also creating a platform for international regional economic cooperation by employing the cultural connotations of the "Silk Road". Linear economies, such as economic corridors and economic belts, are just important elements of this platform, or in other words, its representation.

In this regard, it is essential to appropriately handle the relationship between "the abstract" and "the concrete". The so-called "the abstract" refers to the concept of Belt and Road construction and the cooperation platform it is aimed at building. In other words, the "Belt and Road" is first and foremost a link for the strategic integration of China and other countries. It is a "stage" for cooperation that allows China to go out into the larger world arena, permits a common discourse with others and is in this way conducive to cooperation. "Concrete" means various concrete-based construction projects for the Belt and Road construction, including many linear infrastructures.

The *Vision and Actions* proposes six major economic corridors for international cooperation, namely the new Eurasian Land Bridge; the China-Mongolia-Russia, the China-Central Asia-West Asia, and the China-Indochina Peninsula Economic Corridors; the China-Pakistan Economic Corridor; and the Bangladesh-China-India-Myanmar Economic Corridor, which are the important carriers of a more ambitious economic vision of cooperation among the countries along the Belt and Road, but not the whole, which instead is an open, inclusive, and balanced regional economic cooperation architecture that benefits all. Therefore, to correctly understand the "BRI", it first should be regarded as a platform for development, integration, and cooperation between China and the countries along the Belt and Road, and then as a carrier of various linear economies. Otherwise, it might be difficult for the BRI to fully play its role as a connecting platform, which is also inconsistent with its open and inclusive nature.

III. The BRI: opening a new era of inclusive globalization

The academic community has not yet established a corresponding academic discourse for supporting the implementation of the Belt and Road strategy since it was proposed more than two years ago. There have been many interpretations, yet no consensus has been reached. And, as mentioned above, some readings are biased, while others involve misunderstanding. For the purpose of correctly comprehending the emergence of the BRI, the in-depth development of economic globalization needs to be recognized.

Over the past 30 to 40 years, the mechanisms and processes of economic globalization have profoundly changed the world economic landscape and have also led to changes in the social structure worldwide. On the one hand, the economies of developed countries have been being constantly "financialized" and shifted to high-tech industries, "hollowing out" their manufacturing industries. On the other hand, some developing countries, as represented by China, have risen to become major manufacturing powers. It can be said that the first global industrial transfer since the 1970s has changed the traditional binary structure of "core (developed countries) and periphery (less-developed countries)" to a ternary structure of "developed countries (finance, technology) – emerging countries (manufacturing) and less-developed countries (primary products)". In addition, the gap between the rich and the poor in the world has widened dramatically at various scales to a certain degree due to the inherent contradiction of economic globalization mechanisms. That is, capital may freely flow among countries to seek production locations with the lowest cost, while it is difficult for the labor force to migrate across countries. According to studies by Oxfam (a charity for the alleviation of poverty), the 1 percent rich of the global population in 2016 had more wealth than the remaining 99 percent. How to avoid the deepening gap between the rich and the poor (between countries, regions, and income classes), while promoting the in-depth development of economic globalization, is a prominent issue in achieving sustainable development of the world.

With Chinese capital "going global" on a large scale, the world now is undergoing a second global industrial shift. Due to the changes in economic structures (from "binary" to "ternary ") and prominent social conflicts (the widening gap between the rich and the poor), there is a need for new governance mechanisms to promote and protect a new round of economic globalization. In this regard, China, at the heart of a second round of global industrial shifts, needs to make a greater effort to promote the further development of economic globalization.

Through gradual reform and opening up since 1978, China has continuously and deeply participated in the process of economic globalization. On the one hand, it has driven the rise of its own economy by introducing capital, technology, and management experience into the country. On the other hand, it has gradually established a governance mechanism basically adapted to economic globalization. Admittedly, China, whose rapid economic development has benefited from economic globalization, has also made tremendous contributions to world economic growth, especially since 2008, as from that year onward China's contribution to world economic growth has exceeded 30 percent. Today, China's economy is so closely connected with the world that neither China nor the rest of the world can develop without the other's involvement. Therefore, China needs to make greater contributions to safeguarding the achievements of economic globalization and developing the mechanisms of economic globalization, and to integrate the country into the global economic system to a deeper extent in line with current development mechanisms and trends.

The "Belt Road Initiative" is precisely the effort made by China to promote inclusive development of economic globalization at home and abroad. According to *Vision and Actions*, the BRI is designed to support a global free trade regime and the open world economy. It is not a simple continuation of the economic globalization of the past but a new manifestation of globalization that notably features integration with the cultural connotations of the "Silk Road". That is, it advocates inclusive globalization. Such inclusiveness is mainly reflected in the following points: first, the ideas of "openness and inclusiveness" and "equality and mutual benefit" are highlighted, which advocate that willing countries or regions equally participate in an appropriate manner and with an open attitude, rather than building a small circle with only one voice. Second, the principle of "achieving shared growth through discussion and collaboration", as common development and common prosperity, are particularly emphasized in the BRI. Third, the cultural values of "harmony in diversity" seek common development, prosperity and peace on the basis of maintaining cultural diversity and the shared wishes of most countries.

Therefore, the co-construction of the BRI in general is a proposal for inclusive globalization and an exploration in promoting the healthy development of globalization. It is neither a "maverick" move by China nor the Chinese version of "Marshall Aid" but rather an international cooperation platform to promote regional development that benefits all under the economic globalization mechanism. To improve the mechanism of economic globalization through Belt and Road construction meets not only China's need to "go global" but also the need for more countries and regions to benefit from globalization. The BRI is going to open a new era of inclusive economic globalization!

IV. Conclusion

The BRI is a major proposal by China to cope with changes in the world economic structure and economic globalization, and promote a new stage of development, which will have a lasting impact on the development of China and the world. For China itself, it is a leading strategy for all-around opening up and the major flag and carrier for achieving "open development" that will decide the development path and model of China in the coming decades. As for the rest of the world, it is an attempt to reform the existing mode of international economic governance and to achieve inclusive development, an effort to change the world development mode from a binary division to a ternary integration, which may change the global economic landscape in the next few decades.

It should be kept in mind that the BRI, rather than being a one-time plan, is indeed a long-term and major strategy to coordinate China's opening up from all aspects. Moreover, with considerable work to be done in connection with countries along the Road, it is actually impossible for everything to proceed as China hopes and expects. Faced with rather a complicated international environment, China needs long-term and systematic plans made with strategic determination to implement the BRI, rather than expecting it to be achieved just overnight. Therefore, during the implementation process, while some key issues may proceed at a comparatively fast speed in order to set an example, overall construction should steadily advance with a systematic plan as China tries its best to avoid mistakes caused by impatience

In general, the BRI is not an internal strategy that concerns China's own development but a global strategy of China that should first be considered, observed and understood from the perspective of the world, especially from the viewpoint of economic globalization. Only with a correct understanding of its starting point and connotations in macroscopic terms will the BRI realize its potential and play a more active and effective role. The writer discusses several misunderstandings of the BRI in this essay with the aim of helping make its strategic connotations better understood in practice. However, it should be emphasized that these misunderstandings are not 100 percent wrong but involve the lack of a macroscopic perspective.

Inclusive globalization: New philosophy of China's BRI[3]

Weidong Liu

Introduction

The BRI is the banner and main carrier of China's all-around opening up in the new era, and also an attempt to promote the reform of the world economic governance. It derives from two proposals made by President Xi Jinping during his visits to the countries in Central Asia and Southeast Asia in September and October 2013. In a speech at Nazarbayev University in Kazakhstan on September 7, 2013, the general secretary proposed to jointly build an "'economic belt along the Silk Road' with the countries in Central Asia". In his speech before the People's Representative Council of Indonesia on October 3, he indicated that China is willing to "jointly build the 21st-Century Maritime Silk Road" with Association of Southeast Asian Nations countries. At the Central Economic Work Conference held in December of the same year, Belt and Road became a term specifically referring to the "Silk Road Economic Belt" and the "21st-Century Maritime Silk Road". At the Boao Forum for Asia, held in Hainan on March 28, 2015, the *Vision and Actions* was jointly issued by the National Development and Reform Commission, the Ministry of Foreign Affairs, and the Ministry of Commerce of the People's Republic of China, with State Council authorization. At a symposium on the promotion of the Belt and Road held by the central government on August 17, 2016, President Xi Jinping delivered an important speech, stressing the solid promotion of Belt and Road construction step by step from eight perspectives.

Over the past three years, Belt and Road construction has entered a stage of full implementation, having had an extensive impact on the international arena, while much important progress has been made. The BRI has not only gained wide support from the countries along the Belt and Road but also begun to be reexamined by some developed countries that formerly displayed a wait-and-see attitude or just turned a blind eye to it. The international context today is undergoing drastic changes, as the rise of protectionism and populism has generated many destabilizing factors affecting global economic growth. In particular, the withdrawal of the United States from the Trans-Pacific Partnership Agreement (TPP) by the Trump administration and its plans to tear up multilateral trade agreements have to some extent caused retrogressive trends in economic globalization. In this context, the co-construction of the BRI will certainly assume a more significant historical role, becoming a stabilizer and driver of global economic growth as well as a banner in promoting the reform and development of economic globalization. This essay will analyze the macro background of the Belt and Road construction, discuss the mechanisms of economic globalization and its limitations and explore the connotations of the BRI from the perspective of promoting the reform and development of economic globalization. The writer argues that the BRI reflects advocacy of inclusive globalization, which will bring new philosophical thinking, contribute to world peace and development in the twenty-first century, and become a navigation light in promoting the world economy in the current downturn.

The general context of the BRI

The Belt and Road construction is a long-term and major strategy of the Chinese Communist Party Central Committee and the State Council to coordinate changes in the domestic and international situations, which are the inevitable result of China's specific development stage and shifts in the world economic structure. In general, it is urgent for China to change its attitude in a timely manner so as to consider problems and plan resource allocation more from a global perspective, whether for transforming and upgrading its huge economy or for assuming greater international responsibilities in the current global context and situation. Only in this way will China promote the sustained and healthy development of its social economy, build a strong country and realize the "Chinese dream". Furthermore, it will also benefit China's participation in international economic governance, allowing it to make greater contributions to global sustainable development.

The past 40 years have witnessed major changes in the global socioeconomic context that are largely driven by economic globalization. Though globalization seems to be all-encompassing, its core phenomenon is an increasingly close world socioeconomic space jointly driven by institutional, economic, and technological forces, with interactions and mutual influence between various entities becoming ever stronger. Prominently driven by investment and trade liberalization, globalization is particularly manifested in the following outcomes. Global trade has been growing faster than production, and FDI has grown faster than trade; multinational enterprises have been rising both in number and strength; and changes in production organization (especially the prevalence of parts and components "outsourcing") have led to closely connected global production networks. From the perspective of results, on the one hand, economic globalization played a positive role in promoting global economic growth. From 1970 to 2010, the average annual growth rate of the world economy reached 3.16 percent, and the total size increased 3.47 times. On the other hand, economic globalization has intensified the uneven development of countries (regions) in the world, leading to increasingly prominent social inequality worldwide as, in particular, a large number of developing countries gained little, while even within the developed countries, large companies and their executives have benefited the most, and ordinary people less. According to studies by Oxfam, in 2016 the richest 1 percent of the global population had more wealth than the remaining 99 percent. Therefore, how to avoid the deepening of the gap between the rich and the poor (between countries, regions, and income classes) while promoting the in-depth development of economic globalization is a prominent issue in achieving sustainable global development.

Moreover, China, benefiting from economic globalization, has made remarkable economic progress over the past four decades and changed the world economic landscape (Figure A.5). In 1978, China's GDP only accounted for 1.8 percent of the world total (4.9 percent if estimated on the basis of PPP), while its exports accounted for less than 1.5 percent of world exports. Nevertheless, by 2015, the aforementioned figures had risen to 15.0 percent (20 percent if estimated on the basis of PPP) and 13.8 percent, respectively. Correspondingly, China became the second-largest economy in the world in 2010, the world's largest country for trade in goods in 2013 and the second-largest foreign investor in the world in 2015. At the same time, China is currently the world's largest manufacturing country, accounting for 24 percent of the world's manufacturing output. Moreover, since the global financial crisis in 2008, China's contribution to world economic growth has remained around 30 percent on average. Such a large economy (11 trillion US dollars in 2016) has inevitably made China one of the major forces in shaping global economic structures. Recently, claims such as "China will lead the world" and "China will lead globalization" have been exaggerated by many domestic and foreign commentators. Under the current world structure, China needs to carry out careful research studies and take proper approaches, as well as develop innovative ideas and implementation platforms, regarding how to deepen its participation in the governance of the world economy and to better undertake the responsibilities that it should bear.

Although China is the second-largest economy in the world and an upper-middle-income country, it is still in the process of realizing the "Chinese Dream", and there is still a long way to go for it to achieve industrial transformation and upgrading and become a strong country in the world. From a historical perspective, the rise of the Chinese economy in the past four decades has been the biggest change in the world economic landscape for the past 100 years, and also one of the few major changes in the world landscape in

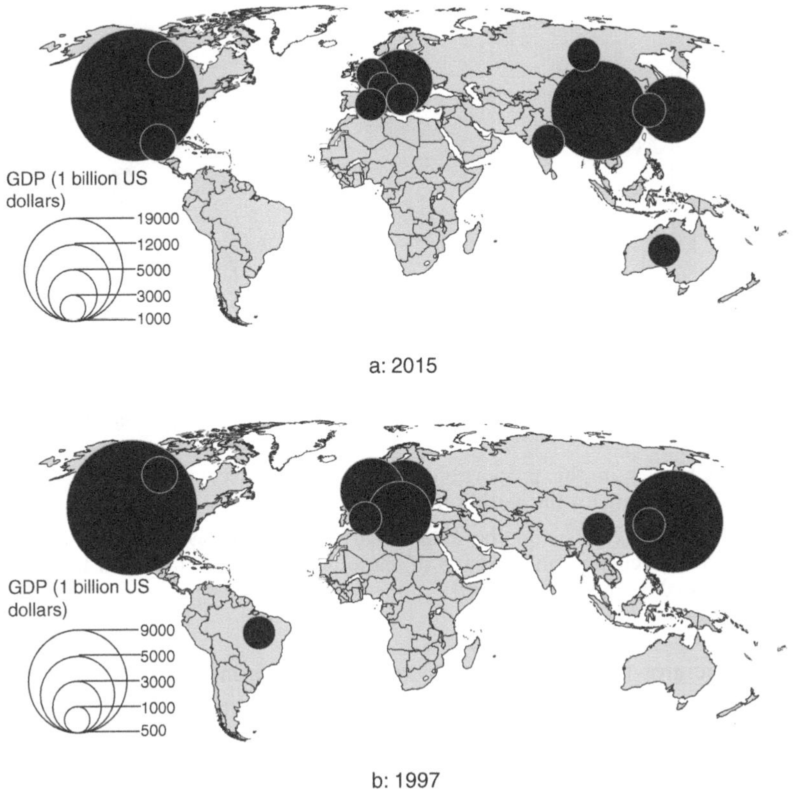

Figure A.5 Distribution of GDP in major countries
Source: World Bank Database.

the past 300 years. According to estimates by Angus Maddison, former chief economist of the OECD, at the beginning of the eighteenth century China's GDP accounted for nearly one-third of the world total, but had fallen to 4.6 percent by the time of the founding of the New China, and had recovered to only 4.9 percent at the beginning of the reform and opening up (Figure A.6). After engaging in great endeavors for more than 40 years, China's share of world GDP has recovered to 20 percent or so based on the estimates of Angus Maddison, or 15 percent according to the current exchange rate. As far as rejoining the great powers of the world, China has so far only moved halfway to this goal. As every step up is very difficult, no slackening can be allowed. At the same time, China needs a broader perspective on the world.

In addition, after nearly four decades of rapid growth, China's economic system is now faced with huge pressure to transform itself. First, China has paid a large price in terms of resources and the environment for its achievements

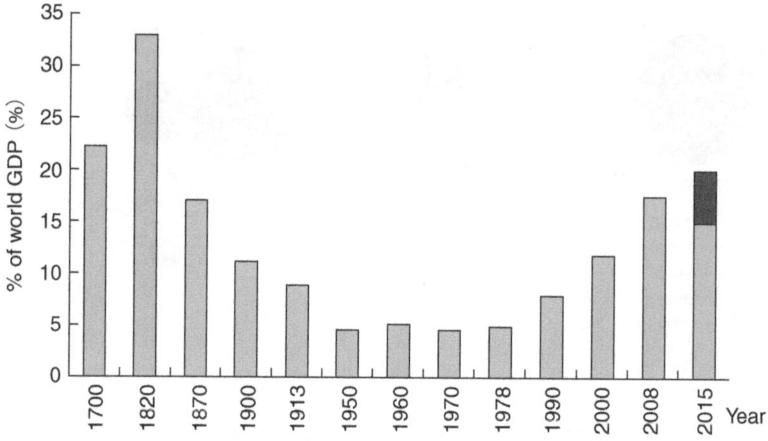

Figure A.6 Changes in the proportion of China's total economic output (GDP) accounting for the world's total

Source: Maddison (2009), and the data of 2015 are estimates by the author (the hatched part is calculated on the basis of the official exchange rate, and the dotted part is calculated on the basis of PPP).

in economic growth. A series of ecological and environmental issues such as atmospheric pollution (especially smog), water pollution, soil pollution, the disappearance of wetlands, and the degradation of grasslands have seriously threatened the sustainable development of China. Moreover, since China has entered a "new normal" stage from the perspective of its economic system, it is in need of a shift from a high-factor input and export-oriented development model to a diversified development model relying on innovative activities with more emphasis on domestic consumption. However, industrial transformation and upgrading and the implementation of innovation-driven development both involve a spatial restructuring of economic activities, especially spatial restructuring on a global scale. In other words, China's transformation of its development model cannot be accomplished without a global outlook. In fact, such spatial restructuring has already begun. From 2006 to 2016, China's FDI rose rapidly from several billion US dollars to more than 170 billion US dollars (excluding financial investments). A new national strategy with a global orientation is thus urgently needed so as to safeguard the interests of China's large-scale overseas investment and to ensure that China's capital globalization benefits more developing countries and regions, achieving a win-win situation.

The mechanism of economic globalization and its limitations

The BRI was proposed in the macro context of economic globalization. Correctly understanding the significance and role of this initiative requires a deep understanding of the mechanisms of economic globalization and its limitations. As mentioned above, economic globalization is a historical phenomenon that emerged from the combined effects of institutional, economic, and technological forces, involving both objective motivations and institutional factors. In terms of objective motivations, on the one hand, endless spatial expansion and spatial restructuring are inherent needs of capital accumulation, and, on the other hand, the shift of production organization from Fordism to post-Fordism has led to the increasing prevalence of parts and components "outsourcing", making many regions in the world closely interconnected through supply chain relationships, and leading to the formation of global production networks. In addition, advances in technology over the past half-century have led to a significant drop in transportation and communications costs, resulting in so-called time-space compression. However, all of these factors only create possibilities. The decisive factor lies in investment and trade liberalization policies embraced by most countries in the world, including developed and developing countries, which were convinced of the benefits of free trade.

Though the term "economic globalization" was not widely used until the 1990s, the process of global expansion of economy has existed for several centuries. The first wave of globalization emerged from the late eighteenth century to the mid-nineteenth century, largely manifested by trade expansion in a colonial context. At that time, developed industrial countries represented by Great Britain and France, backed by military force, forced colonial and semicolonial countries to reduce or even eliminate tariffs, turning the latter into raw materials suppliers, dumping products in their markets and exporting capital, leading to an international division of the world into a core-periphery structure. So-called "free trade" at that time was deeply based on colonialism. That is, developing countries were forced to adopt free trade policies and open their markets. The second wave occurred from the late nineteenth century to the early twentieth century, and was mainly reflected in the global expansion of capital driven by technological progress. On the one hand, advances in electricity, communications and transportation technologies led to a significant drop in the costs for people to cross space. On the other hand, technological innovation saw the emergence of monopoly capitalism, resulting in a dramatic increase in global FDI. For example, the total foreign investment in the world almost doubled to 43 billion US dollars from 1900 to 1914. However, the global expansion of capital during this period, still notably associated with colonialism, stopped abruptly due to the two World Wars.

After World War II, the global expansion of economy reached its third climax, and was associated with the establishment of a series of international economic cooperation mechanisms and international organizations led by the United States. Referred to as the Bretton Woods system, it included the International Monetary Fund, the World Bank, and the GATT, and involved the development of exchange rate mechanisms and movement in the direction of free trade. Although the postwar colonial system gradually collapsed, the unequal global division of labor remained unchanged as the previous core-periphery model still functioned. In the postwar boom period, major Western countries, considering government regulation and interventionist measures necessary, adopted Keynesian economic policies. At the same time, due to the economic prosperity of the times (i.e., high profitability), there was not much pressure on capital accumulation. Furthermore, there were also capital controls in major Western countries. These two factors together led to very limited capital export. In addition, since the expansion of trade played a far greater role than that of capital in global economic expansion under the Cold War structure, economic globalization in the true sense had not yet started.

In the 1970s, after the postwar boom period, serious issues of stagflation emerged in major Western developed countries. In order to get out of this crisis, Western countries represented by the Reagan and Thatcher governments shifted from Keynesian polices to neoliberalism, largely reducing government intervention, privatizing state-owned enterprises, and taking measures to promote the liberalization of investment and trade. Under such circumstances, the capital of developed countries began to flow to developing countries on a large scale. Dicken called this movement a "global shift". In particular, after the end of Cold War in the early 1990s, the foreign investment of developed countries grew explosively. In the meantime, the economic crisis forced Western enterprises to continuously adjust their production organization, from the vertical integration and mass production of the earlier Fordist model, to components and parts outsourcing and flexible production of post-Fordist model. This kind of shift caused a gradual extension of the supply chain and increasingly specialized division of labor in regions producing parts and components, bringing substantial growth in supply chain trade. For example, despite the growing popularity of industrial clusters, more than 70 percent of internal trade in East Asia today is trade of intermediate products. In short, large-scale foreign investment by developed countries, changes in mode of production organization, advances in information technology, and the prevalence of neoliberalism have jointly driven the world to become an increasingly close socioeconomic space. This historical phenomenon is called "economic globalization", and it has coincided with the fourth peak of global economic expansion.

Throughout history, capital's spatial expansion has been the fundamental driving force for global economic expansion, while technological progress was the "catalyst", and national controls and interventions were the "gates". Marx offered an inspiring discussion in *Das Kapital*, stating that the capitalist production mode always results in the overaccumulation of capital, causing cyclical economic crises, the occurrence of which, however, can be delayed by technological progress and spatial transfer. In the 1970s, David Harvey, a well-known American geographer, based on Marx's thinking, developed a full set of theories explaining the geographical mechanism of capital accumulation, the core concept of which was the "spatial fix" of capital. Harvey notes that since it is difficult to maintain the accumulation of capital without spatial expansion and restructuring, it is necessary to constantly seek a spatial fix. As the progress of transportation and communication technologies has reduced the costs of spatial displacement, it has provided necessary conditions for the spatial expansion of capital. Therefore, restless movement is a prominent feature of capital accumulation. It is a perfect combination of the "spatial fix" of capital accumulation and the trend toward neoliberalism that were the prelude to large-scale spatial expansion of capital on a global scale, and that gave rise to the emergence of economic globalization.

Therefore, economic globalization over the past three decades has comprised a set of international economic governance mechanisms developed on the foundations of neoliberalism by developed countries in Europe and America to address the crisis they encountered in the 1980s. In the process of promoting economic globalization, developed countries, convinced that market liberalization was a one-size-fits-all solution to all problems, and that the development path they had taken was the "best" in the world, continuously exported these ideas to developing countries. It was the "Washington Consensus" policies of the 1990s (a product of neoliberal policy) that caused the Soviet Union and Eastern European countries to suffer from economic recessions. Moreover, mainstream Western economics and development economics argued, based on their mathematical models, that free trade would enable countries to achieve balanced development. The reality, however, was quite the opposite at many spatial scales. The reason is that free trade theory is based on epistemological individualism, and all people in a country are averaged. The lack of attention paid to social and regional differentiation, which is associated with significant variations around average outcomes, is an important reason why developed countries have gained huge benefits from globalization while their ordinary people have lost out.

Therefore, neoliberal economic globalization is a set of mechanisms that mainly meet the needs of capital's spatial expansion or spatial fix, and from which capital and large companies have gained enormous benefits, while society, especially many ordinary people, has paid a huge price. Moreover, neoliberal globalization results in the coexistence of prosperity and precarity because capital can flow freely across countries while labor cannot. If such a mechanism continues to dominate, social conflicts around the world may become more and more apparent, and global sustainable development goals will become hard to achieve. In fact, a series of "black swan events", including the election of Donald Trump as the president of the United States and the issue of Brexit, have manifested the need to reform the current economic globalization mechanism.

The essence of the BRI: Inclusive globalization

Economic globalization is a "double-edged sword", which not only has promoted global economic growth but also brought serious social problems. Recently, the withdrawal of the Trump administration from the TPP and its plans to tear up multilateral trade agreements seem to have to some extent caused a retrogressive trend in economic globalization. However, due to modern production organization, global production networks (especially global supply chains) and modern communications technologies, most countries in the world are so closely interconnected that each has a stake in the well-being of the others. It is impossible for the world to return to complete isolationism. Therefore, at this historical juncture, what the world needs is to reform the mechanism of economic globalization rather than start all over again.

It is notable that in the world today there are voices seeking reform, and reforms in particular require new thinking and new models. As the world's second-largest economy, and a big country with a successful development experience, China should put forward Chinese proposals as a contribution to the reform and development of economic globalization. From the perspective of addressing the negative effects of globalization, the interests of ordinary people should be taken into account in the new international economic governance model. It is necessary to extend modern infrastructures to more regions, allowing economic growth to benefit more people. The practices of the past three decades have proved that it is difficult to achieve such a goal by relying entirely on market mechanisms, requiring a suitable role for the state. It is thus necessary to carry out reforms while preserving the beneficial side of economic globalization. Fundamentally speaking, neoliberal thinking should be abandoned, while the banner of "inclusive globalization" should be adopted, which is precisely the core connotation and essence of the BRI proposed by President Xi Jinping. The BRI may become a banner for leading inclusive globalization.

According to an important speech delivered by the President Xi Jinping, the BRI is aimed at promoting cooperation among countries along the Belt and Road in the Spirit of the Silk Road, so as to achieve mutual benefit. The so-called Spirit of the Silk Road refers to the spirit that has been passed from generation to generation on the Silk Road, namely, "peace and cooperation, openness and inclusiveness, mutual learning, and mutual benefit". The *Vision and Actions* explicitly states that "the initiative to jointly build the Belt and Road is designed to uphold the global free trade regime and the open world economy in the spirit of open regional cooperation", and that "it is aimed at promoting orderly and free flow of economic factors, highly efficient allocation of resources and deep integration of markets; encouraging the countries along the Belt and Road to achieve economic policy coordination and carry out broader and deeper regional cooperation of higher standards; and jointly creating an open, inclusive and balanced regional economic cooperation architecture that benefits all". The BRI is indeed an organic combination of the "Spirit of the Silk Road" and the idea of economic globalization in an attempt to open a new path toward inclusive globalization.

The BRI advocates inclusive globalization that can be understood based on at least the following points. First, governments should play an important role especially in maintaining social equity and reducing poverty as it is impracticable just to rely on market mechanisms to solve all problems. Second, the diversity of development paths chosen should be respected, and each country should explore suitable development paths based on its own characteristics. (Neoliberal globalization only promotes the one path that at present is pursued by developed countries.) Third, the BRI emphasizes the interconnectedness of the development strategies of the countries involved with the purpose of seeking a common interest, which not only meets capital's need for free spatial expansion but also will benefit more regions. Fourth, it should make the pursuit of the "biggest common denominator" for development the top priority in promoting common development and prosperity while adhering to the principles of "openness and inclusiveness", "equality and mutual benefit", and "achievement of shared growth through discussion and collaboration". Fifth, it stresses the search for common development, prosperity, and peace on the basis of maintaining cultural diversity with respect for the cultural values of "harmony in diversity".

Therefore, the BRI has provided new thinking about promoting a deep development of economic globalization, that is, inclusive globalization. From the perspective of historical trends, inclusive globalization might be regarded as the second version of economic globalization that will contribute Chinese wisdom and a plan by China for world peace and development. Perhaps it will be the new governance model after Keynesianism and neoliberalism.

Conclusion

After more than 200 years of global economic expansion, the world has entered the era of economic globalization under the combined effects of institutional, economic, and technological factors. However, following more than three decades of development, economic globalization has arrived at a "crossroads", and how and where it will proceed is essential for sustainable development of the world. Today, economic globalization is a topic extensively debated with both strong advocates and sharp critics. China, having largely benefited from economic globalization in terms of economic growth, has been called upon by many scholars and commentators at home and abroad to lead in the process of globalization. Though such opinions might be correct in general, China cannot take the old path in order to promote globalization. First, the problems brought about by economic globalization should be taken seriously during the process of solution seeking. Second, it is the organic integration of market forces and government forces in China, led by a strong government, rather than Western development models, that enabled China to benefit from economic globalization. To continuously promote neoliberal globalization that mainly met capital's needs of spatial expansion, is not only unfavorable to the sustainable development of the world but also incompatible with China's social system. Therefore, China should make full use of its own development experience to lead the reform of the economic globalization mechanism and provide a Chinese solution for international economic governance.

The BRI, proposed by President Xi Jinping based on the historical and cultural connotations of the Silk Road, affords a new concept and model of international cooperation. Its essence lies in the organic combination of the Spirit of the Silk Road and globalization, while its meaning is inclusive globalization. More than three years ago, when China proposed and began the Belt and Road construction, no one could foresee such a precipitous decline in the globalization situation. At that time, China was only trying to make a greater contribution to global economic governance through Belt and Road construction. Now, however, since economic globalization has arrived at a "crossroads" and entered a vast and hazy period, the BRI has accordingly become a banner for countries in the world in promoting a deepening development of economic globalization and institutional reforms, which will lead to inclusive globalization.

A discursive construction of the BRI: From neoliberal to inclusive globalization[4]

Weidong Liu, Michael Dunford, and Boyang Gao

Introduction

In May 2017, the BRI entered a new historical stage, marked by the Chinese government's holding of the Belt and Road International Cooperation Forum in Beijing. The forum attracted 1,500 participants from more than 130 countries and 70 international organizations, including 29 foreign heads of state or government; nearly 100 foreign government ministers or top officials; and the heads of 60 international organizations, and it established a broad international consensus about China's initiative. On the second day of the forum, 30 heads of State, the United Nations, the World Bank, and the International Monetary Fund signed a joint communiqué at the conclusion of a round-table summit on international cooperation. The joint communiqué noted that the BRI afforded opportunities to deepen international cooperation and jointly address global challenges, affirmed a commitment to "free and inclusive trade" and noted that the BRI provided important opportunities for countries to deepen their cooperation and for a globalization path that is "open, inclusive, and beneficial to all". At the forum, a number of heads of state pointed out that the BRI has a strongly inclusive nature and will allow more regions to share the benefits of globalization. It can be argued that promoting inclusive globalization is one of the important understandings reached by the heads of state at this forum. Given this consensus, an understanding of inclusive globalization and its relationship with the construction of the BRI requires more in-depth discussion and discursive elaboration.

Inclusive globalization is a new concept developed in response to the ills of economic globalization as practiced over the last 30 years, and an important theoretical perspective for understanding the BRI (Liu Weidong, 2015; Liu Weidong and Dunford, 2015). In the past, "inclusive growth" and "inclusive development" were popular concepts. The discussion of "inclusive growth" dates back to the formulation in 2008 of the official 2020 Strategy of the Asian Development Bank (ADB, 2008). Since then, the concept of "inclusive development" has been accepted by the Chinese government as an important concept guiding macro policy (Li Shenping, 2012; Wang Yi, 2012) and was reflected in the Twelfth and Thirteenth Five Year Planning. As early as the opening ceremony of the fifth APEC Human Resources Development Ministerial Meeting in 2010, then-President Hu Jintao of China pointed out that achieving inclusive growth was a fundamental objective that would enable economic globalization and economic development to benefit all countries and regions, and reach all groups. After the eighteenth National Congress of the Communist Party of China in 2012, General Secretary Xi Jinping also spoke about inclusive development in important speeches and foreign visits.

Although inclusive development is directed at the salient problems related to the development of today's world, and is a core concept guiding global sustainable development, this concept is not geographically specified. The concept can refer to regional, national and international scales, and is not specifically targeted at global economic governance and international economic cooperation. From the specific perspective of global economic governance, Liu Weidong (2015) argues that "the BRI . . . is an important framework for promoting the deep development of economic globalization . . . is not simply a continuation of past economic globalization, but involves a new type of globalization, whose salient features are integrated into the cultural meaning of the Silk Road . . . [,] are the expression of inclusive globalization", and will usher in a new era of inclusive globalization (see also Liu Weidong et al., 2016; Liu Weidong, 2016, 2017a, 2017b; Liu Weidong, Tian Jinchen and Ou Xiaoli, 2017; Liu Weidong and Liu Zhigao, 2016). Over the past three years, the concept has received more and more attention and recognition from scholars (such as Xie Danyang and Cheng Qun, 2017; Wang Yiwei, 2017a, 2017b; Zhao Baige, 2017) as well as at the BRI International Cooperation Forum, the BRICS summit in Xiamen and the World Economic Forum in Davos, resulting in the emergence of a consensus among political leaders.

Although the concept of "inclusive globalization" has gained in popularity, it lacks rigorous academic analysis. In "Inclusive Globalization: New Philosophy of China's Belt and Road Initiative", Liu Weidong (2017b) identified five core characteristics of inclusive globalization. However, the analysis needs to be broadened, deepened and integrated more closely with existing theories of globalization and global governance. It is for this reason that this paper draws on exiting research to develop a concept of inclusive globalization and provide a more solid theoretical basis for promoting the construction of the BRI. To this end, what follows is a brief review of the course of global economic expansion, the limitations of neoliberal globalization, and the contribution of the BRI to the new type of globalization, along with an outline of some of the main dimensions of inclusive globalization.

Global economic expansion: From colonial trade to the global organization of production

At present, a consensus in academic circles is that the BRI represents a new type of globalization. Therefore, the establishment of a discursive basis for the BRI must start with a thorough understanding of economic globalization. Although the phenomenon is much older, the use of a concept of economic globalization dates from the 1980s and became popular in the 1990s. At that time, the concept was used to refer to historical phenomena deriving from the accumulation of capital on a global scale and underlying technological progress and institutional conditions, and to identify the main mechanisms governing world economic governance over the past three decades. In recent years, the use of the concept has widened. For example, some scholars trace the origins of globalization back to the development of cross-border trade in the ancient world. Others date it from the European Age of Discovery and European colonial expansion. Yet others focus on the international flows of capital and labor in the nineteenth and early twentieth centuries (Zhao Baige, 2017; Harod, 2001). In considering earlier eras, these generalizations deal, however, with phenomena that significantly differ from those that marked out the last 30 years, namely revolutionary changes in the organization of production and in particular the formation of global production networks (Dicken, 2010) along with the globalization of financial activities. In this paper, economic globalization is used in its original meaning to refer to the new stage of economic global expansion dating from the 1970s and 1980s.

Although globalization is a new phenomenon, economic global expansion has existed for centuries (Taylor, 2005). Due to low levels of productivity and transport constraints, in the ancient world trade was confined to regional and long-distance luxury goods trade. A typical trade route was the Silk Road. Starting in the latter part of the fifteenth and into the sixteenth century, European explorers discovered a new route to India and East Asia and the American continent. After that, European countries started to develop transoceanic colonial trade with Asia and the Americas. Until 1820, however, as a share of GDP, trade was persistently low: 99 percent of the world's manufactured goods had not yet entered international trade (Taylor, 2005).

If the Age of Discovery initiated global economic expansion, the Industrial Revolution saw the emergence of a high degree of economic interdependence and integration. From the end of eighteenth to the middle of the nineteenth century, the first industrial revolution unfolded mainly in Great Britain: factories gradually replaced artisanal workshops, large-scale production became a reality, productivity increased, and the types and quantities of goods that could be traded expanded significantly. Needing to export a large volume of

Table A.1 Share of major industrialized countries in world industrial production and trade, 1820–1870 (%)

Year	*Great Britain*		*France*		*Germany*		*United States*	
	Industrial output (%)	*Trade (%)*	*Industrial output (%)*	*Trade (%)*	*Industrial output (%)*	*Trade (%)*	*Industrial output (%)*	*Trade (%)*
1820	50	27	15–20	9	-	-	10	6
1840	45	25	-	9	12	8	11	7
1850	39	22	-	11	15	8	15	7
1870	32	25	10	10	13	10	23	8

Source: Kuklinski, 1955; Rostow, 1978.

industrial products and to import raw materials, Great Britain emerged as the world factory, catalyzing global economic expansion (see Table A). In order to expand their markets, the British, French and other developed industrial countries used their military and political power to force colonial countries to reduce or even abolish tariffs, opening up their markets for the dumping of Western commodities, turning their economies into suppliers of raw materials and resources and forming a "core-periphery" international division of labor. A consequence was economic dependency as many colonial economies gradually came to specialize almost entirely in agriculture and mineral products. The global trade of this period has often been characterized as free trade, with "free trade" used as a slogan to impose unequal trade relationships on countries the European powers colonized. In the case of Algeria, for example, the import of French goods was exempt from tariffs from 1835 on. Beginning in 1851, some Algerian goods were admitted duty-free into France. In 1867, tariff exemption was extended to all Algerian (and French settler) exports to France (Issawi, 1982).

The second wave of global economic expansion occurred in the second half of the nineteenth century and the early twentieth century and was closely linked with the second industrial revolution. Its main form was the global expansion of capital and finance promoted by technological progress. On the one hand, advances in power, communications, and transportation technologies have led to a significant reduction in the cost of distance, such as a 70 percent drop in world transport costs in 1840–1901 (O'Rourke and Williamson, 2001); on the other hand, the development in the late nineteenth century of monopoly capitalism, with the emergence of large cartels, syndicates and trusts in Europe and the United States (which saw the establishment from 1890 in the United States of antitrust (competition) law. In order to secure high rates of returns, these large monopolies started to invest and acquire assets in other countries, generating a sharp rise in world FDI. From 1900 to 1914, the total foreign investment almost doubled to reach 43 billion US

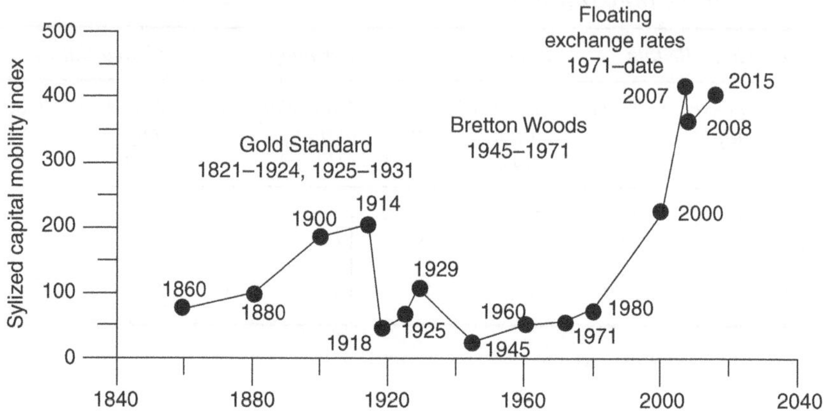

Figure A.7 Evolution of capital mobility
Source: Dunford and Liu Weidong, 2017.

dollars as part of a major upturn in the international expansion of capital (see Figure A.7). At the same time, large numbers of people migrated to the Americas and other white-settler countries (as Europe exported its surplus population). Between 1870 and 1910, the United States accepted 20.4 million immigrants from around the world. Comparable figures are 3.5 million for Argentina, 3.1 million for Canada, and 2.6 million for Brazil (Ferenczi and Willcox, 1929). The coexistence of high rates of capital and labor mobility has led some scholars to consider this phase the real stage of globalization. In this phase of global expansion, the United States replaced Great Britain as the world's main industrial nation. By 1913, Great Britain's share of world industrial output dropped to 14 percent, while the share of the United States rose to 36 percent (Dicken, 2010). In this phase, however, FDI came from relatively few countries and was mainly designed to acquire resources or sell into local markets.

From 1914 to 1945, two World Wars and the Great Depression of 1929–1933 had a severe impact on the international economic order, with global economic expansion going into reverse gear. For example, World War I alone reduced international trade by 40 percent, while international trade in the World War II period was mainly in armaments and strategic resources. The end of World War II ushered in a new phase of global economic expansion. This era was underpinned by the United States-led establishment at Bretton Woods in 1944 of a series of international economic cooperation mechanisms and institutions designed to move in the direction of free trade (via multilateral tariff reductions) and manage exchange rates and financial flows, namely the International Monetary Fund, the World Bank, and GATT. By the end of World War II, the United States was the largest economy in the world, while the European continent was greatly weakened. In 1945, the GDP of the United States accounted for around one-half of the world total, while in 1950, with European recovery well underway, the United States still accounted for 27 percent of the world GDP and nearly 60 percent of the world's gold reserves. In these circumstances, it was the United States that led the establishment of the new international cooperation and financial rules, but this system was confined to the capitalist part of the world. In 1949, after deciding not to participate in the US-controlled Marshall Plan, the Soviet Union established the Comecon: a socialist system of international economic relations in which general multilateral accords were implemented through more detailed, bilateral agreements. Whereas earlier economic expansion followed from developments in transport technology, industrial capacity, and national politics, as already mentioned, the years after World War II saw the establishment of international organizations to oversee and manage trade and international payments. International economic expansion occurred, but it was not global in that the world was divided into capitalist and socialist spheres.

Although the colonial system gradually disintegrated as former colonies secured independence after World War II, the core-periphery model did not disappear, and an unequal division of labor persisted. In the postwar period of prosperity, the major Western countries adopted Keynesian policies. Government regulation and interventionist measures were once again popular. At the same time, when the economies were growing rapidly and companies were able to maintain a high level of profitability, there was little pressure on capital accumulation and no large-scale flow of investment overseas (Hudson, 2016). Coupled with the domestic orientation of growth, the Cold War division of the world and the development of trade within the capitalist and socialist spheres of influence, capital mobility was much lower than in the wave of global expansion at the end of the nineteenth and the start of the twentieth century (see Figure A.7). As economic globalization in a real sense was not taking place, this phase can only be called one of economic internationalization.

In the 1970s, a serious stagflation and profitability crisis occurred in major Western developed countries. In response, Keynesian policies were largely abandoned in favor of a neoliberal model (an updated version of classical liberal economic thought that was dominant in the United States and Great Britain up to the Great Depression of the 1930s), especially in the United States and United Kingdom. State-owned enterprises and assets were privatized, government intervention was reduced, markets for goods, services and money were liberalized, and international investment and (managed) trade liberalization were actively promoted (Harvey, 2007; Hudson, 2016). These institutional changes along with a decline in profitability led to a large-scale offshore movement of the capital of developed countries to developing countries, generating the phenomenon Dicken (2010) called a global shift. At the same time, Western companies adapted to the economic crisis by reorganizing production, moving away from Fordist vertical integration and mass production to post-Fordist models, characterized by outsourcing of component manufacture and flexible production. Regional specialization in parts and components production expanded, resulting in a large increase in supply chain trade and the formation of global production networks. For example, more than 70 percent of current intra-East Asian trade is trade in intermediate products. Another factor that cannot be overlooked is that container technology, which spread in the 1970s, further reduced intercontinental transport costs, improved logistics, and stimulated global trade. Since 2000, the rapid progress of Internet technology facilitated the management of enterprises' transnational operations. In short, large-scale foreign investment by developed countries, the transformation of production organization, the progress in transport and information technology, and national and international neoliberal policies jointly promoted an era of economic globalization and a fourth upturn in global economic expansion. As these processes unfolded, the structure of the world economy evolved from a granular structure centered on national production systems to a variety of global production network structures, realizing the globalization of the organization of production.

Throughout the capitalist phases of these historical waves of global economic expansion, capital's quest for profit, and what Harvey (1975, 1981) calls "spatial fixes", were fundamental driving forces, while technological progress was a catalyst and national government policy acted as a gatekeeper. Harvey (1975; 1981) argues that the accumulation of capital comes up against internal limits. Capital, he contends, seeks to resolve these problems through, among other ways, geographical expansion and restructuring and the creation of new geographies of fixed investment, while the diffusion of major innovations in transportation and communication technology provide necessary conditions for geographical expansion/displacement by reducing the costs of distance. However, state intervention also shapes the friction of distance (what Marx called the "annihilation of space through time") and the spatial scope and direction of the spatial fix. As a result, capital, technology, and the state play different roles in the global expansion of the economy. The first two are the driving forces, while the third acts as a facilitator and is alone capable of adjusting the pace and direction of globalization. In the last three decades, the main aim of governments that chose or were made to choose neoliberal paths was to create a favorable political and economic environment for the global flow of capital (Harvey, 2007). In addition, this historical experience summarized above shows that only world powers can direct global economic expansion or globalization.

3 The limitations of neoliberal globalization

Economic globalization plays a positive role in promoting world economic growth. In 1980–2015, the world economy grew at an average annual rate of 2.86 percent and world GDP increased 5.2 times. Although the pace was

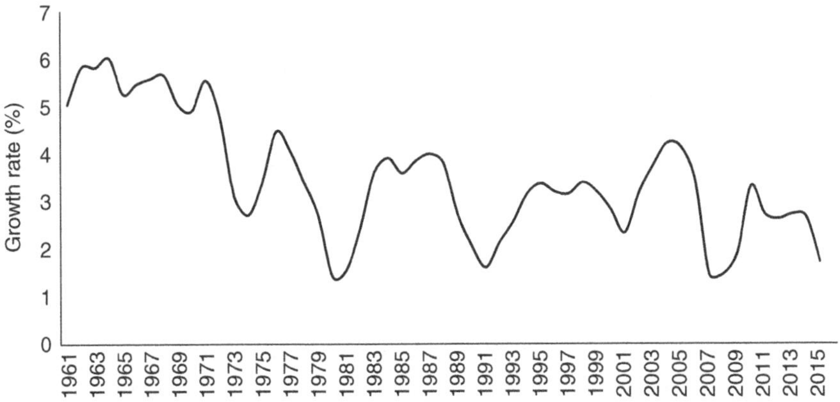

Figure A.8 World economic growth (three-year moving averages, 1961–2016)
Source: elaborated from World Bank data.

far below that of the earlier postwar boom (see Figure A.8), investment and trade liberalization helped overcome stagflation in developed countries from the early 1980s. In the same period, the volume of world merchandise imports and exports increased 7.3 times to 33.3 trillion US dollars/year, while outward direct investment increased 40 times to reach 2.1 trillion US dollars/year, and capital mobility soared to a new peak (Figure A.7). However, during this period, the world economy also experienced a number of financial crises, including those that occurred in 1997 and 2008. To date, it has not yet completely recovered from the 2008 financial crisis. In 2009–2015 the average annual growth rate of the world economy was just 2.24 percent, with negative growth at nominal prices occurring in 2009 and 2015.

As a result of the global shift of industry, global economic growth was associated with a certain degree of convergence at a continental scale. In 1980–2016, the economies of Asia, Africa, and Oceania grew at higher average annual rates than those of Europe and the Americas. The latter grew at less than the world average rate. Asia's average annual growth rate of 3.86 percent saw GDP increase 4.91 times to $26.9 trillion US dollars. Among the five continents, Europe with 41.9 percent accounted for the highest proportion of world GDP in 1980, the Americas accounted for 32.1 percent, and Asia, Africa, and Oceania for 20.6 percent, 3.7 percent, and 1.7 percent, respectively. By 2016, the Asian economies had leaped into first position, accounting for 35.5 percent of world GDP, followed by the Americas, which accounted for 32.8 percent, while Europe had fallen to 26.2 percent.

However, contrary to the claims of a large number of academic institutes dealing with free trade and globalization, globalization has led to increasingly serious development imbalances and social polarization at many spatial scales. According to World Bank data, in 1982 the ratio of the per capita GDP of the richest country in the world to that of the poorest country stood at 272:1. By 2015, it had increased to 336:1: the richest country was Luxembourg with an annual per capita GDP of $102,000 compared with just $303.7 for Burundi in Africa. This imbalance is not only manifested in the gap between developed European and North American countries and the developing countries in Africa, Asia, and Latin America, but also within developed countries. In recent years, in Japan, Germany, the United States, and other countries the share of the population living in poverty has increased, reaching about 15 percent. A recent study shows that the proportion of US workers in their thirties (30–39 years old) earning more than their parents fell from 90 percent in 1970 to 41 percent in 2014, with the most dramatic declines occurring for middle-class groups (Chetty et al., 2017). In other words, since the 1970s, US income growth has mainly benefited high-income families, while middle- and low-income families have found it increasingly difficult to raise their incomes. The main reason for this is the continued loss of stable manufacturing jobs in a country in which manufacturing jobs fell by 40 percent, from 19.43 million in 1979 to 11.53 in million in 2010 (Tong Jiadong and Liu Cheng, 2017) and the deprofessionalization of some service sector jobs. By 2016, the US middle class had fallen to 40 percent of the total population.

Worldwide, the gap between the rich and the poor is widening, as wealth is concentrated in the hands of a small global elite. Although the global Gini income coefficient has declined in the last 20 years as a result of a sharp rise in per capita income in emerging markets such as China and India, overall income growth has been concentrated in the hands of middle- and high-income groups, with hardly any of the fruits of the economic growth brought about by globalization accruing to low-income groups. Xie Danyang and Cheng Kun (2017) found that in 1978 to 2016, China's per capita income growth was the fastest, but its Gini coefficient also rose the fastest, from an extremely low 0.15 in the early days of the reform and opening up to 0.47 in 2016, while the richest 10 percent of the population saw its share of total income increase from 15 percent of the total in 1978 to 41 percent in 2015. Meanwhile, Oxfam (2016) reported that the wealth of the richest 62 people in the world was equal to that of the poorest one-half of the world's population, and identified an "economy for the 1 percent", in which the wealth of the richest 1 percent of the world's population was expected to exceed that of the remaining 99 percent by 2016. Moreover, the wealth of the world's poor did not increase in the five years from 2011 to 2015.

The negative effects and economic instability of the above-mentioned processes of economic globalization and the wave of deglobalization to which they gave rise have been widely discussed in academic circles (such as Tong Jiadong and Liu Cheng, 2017; Xie Danyang and Cheng Kun, 2017; Bao Qun, 2017; Henderson and Jepson, 2017; Piketty, 2014; Streeck, 2014). Neoliberalism assumed a variety of forms (Brenner, Peck and Theodore, 2010). In general however, the neoliberal theories that underpinned economic globalization, and especially their promotion of privatization, marketization and liberalization along with reduced government intervention, while solving the stagnation crisis faced by developed countries in the 1970s, generated new contradictions that have made further world economic development unsustainable.

Harvey (2007) has argued that neoliberalism was a political project of corporate capital. Designed to alter ways of thinking and create conditions for capital accumulation, offshoring some jobs to low-wage countries, automating others and promoting privatization and deregulation, it ultimately led to a serious polarization of wealth and income. Early advocates of neoliberal globalization argued that capital should be free from regional and national restrictions and able to flow freely. In *When Corporations Rule the World*, Korten (1995) described the ideology of corporate libertarians and their "dreams of global empires": money, technology, and the production of goods and services of all kinds are controlled and managed by huge global corporations; consumption increases endlessly with a unified consumption culture at each average level of material satisfaction; companies are free to act, externalizing costs in whatever ways increase their profitability; and all relationships are entirely determined by market relations and the competitive pursuit of individual self-interest. Korten's portrayal of a world in which corporate capital and finance reign supreme, although slightly extreme as a description of current reality, accurately expresses the direction of the deregulated rule of mobile corporate capital and global finance. Compared however with its reality, advocates of neoliberal globalization themselves inhabit an imaginary world, dreaming dreams of an idealized globalization, while ignoring its inner contradictions. At present, capital is relatively free to seek out the places in the world whose markets, resources, and cheap labor afford the highest rates of return, helping satisfy capital's quest for a "spatial fix". The mobility of people (and especially of blue-collar workers and low-income groups) is however restricted, although some neoliberal thinkers also insist that people should also be free to move. In the European Union, however, where labor is relatively free to move, some aspects of population mobility have themselves generated serious social tensions (as have the movements of refugees).

The limitations of this economic globalization are related to misleading economic studies (Sheppard, 2016). Mainstream economic models seek to demonstrate that free trade and free markets benefit all the parties involved and drive in the direction of even development. In practice, the opposite is true (at least at many spatial scales). In fact, as early as the mid-nineteenth century, by abolishing its own Corn Laws, Great Britain enticed other West European countries to move in the direction of free trade. Within a short space of time, other countries came to the conclusion that free trade was damaging their interests and they all adopted protectionist measures. As Sheppard (2016) argued, the mainstream economic theory of trade is based on the average individualism rather than on all individual cases. The extent to which different regions can benefit from globalization varies greatly, due to connectivity constraints and differences in the "socio-spatial positionality" of different regions. In particular, many developing countries have not yet been able to participate deeply in and benefit from the globalization process.

Therefore, neoliberal economic globalization has involved a set of mechanisms that have mainly served the needs of capital and its geographical expansion, while increases in the mobility of labor occurred, but were limited. The outcome is the coexistence of precarity and prosperity (Sheppard, 2016). Capital and large corporations have benefited enormously, while very many people, especially at the grassroots level, have paid a huge price, leading to serious social problems. If neoliberal mechanisms are allowed to dominate future world economic governance, global social contradictions will become increasingly prominent, and global sustainable development goals will be difficult to achieve.

The BRI and inclusive globalization

The problems generated by neoliberal globalization have resulted in constant academic criticism and social protest, especially since the global financial crisis of 2008. The recent election of Trump as president of the United States and Britain's decision to leave the European Union may be seen as responses leading in the direction of deglobalization. However, mainstream academic voices are attempting to rethink globalization, seeking new or alternative globalization paths. After revealing and criticizing the limits to globalization, Sheppard (2016), for example, did not advocate a revolutionary antiglobalization politics. Instead he called for more attention to, and research into, other forms of organization of international trade and investment, and for serious consideration of the possibility of alternative globalization paths. At present there is no academic consensus as to what this new type of globalization or alternative globalization is and what paths are available. However, increasing numbers of scholars believe that China's BRI is worthy of attention as a possible new globalization path (such as Wang Yiwei, 2017b; Zhao Baige, 2017; Braun et al., 2017).

In many debates, Liu Weidong (2017a) has argued, "modern production methods, global production networks and modern communication technologies have already created inseparably close links between many countries in the world, i.e. You are tied to me and I am tied to you. The world cannot return to isolationism and a closed era". At this time, the world needs to reform the mechanisms of economic globalization, and not to overturn and reinvent them. In order to tackle the negative effects of neoliberal globalization, a new global economic governance model needs to take into account the social interests of ordinary people, to extend modern infrastructure to more areas and to ensure that economic growth benefits more people. Neoliberal globalization has demonstrated that it is incapable of achieving these goals. The world should seek to preserve the beneficial side of economic globalization, introducing reforms to overcome the limitations of the neoliberal model. The BRI provides one platform and direction for reform.

From a macro perspective, the BRI is a result of the combined effect of the deepening of globalization, changes in the structure of the world economy and transformation of China's own development model. The core factor is the globalization of Chinese capital (Liu Weidong, 2017). As the earlier discussion of global economic expansion suggested, the way in which a country's capital is globalized affects not only its strategic interests but also the direction of globalization. China can neither invest abroad in a colonial manner nor can it adopt an imperialist path or a path consistent with currently dominant ideologies. Nor can China on its own establish a new international economic order. China can only operate within existing international economic governance conditions, while seeking new ways of strengthening international cooperation to generate mutual benefits and win-win solutions. To this end China can draw on the cultural connotations of the Silk Road and make the Silk Road Spirit the essence of the BRI.

According to the Chinese government's *Vision and Actions* and the 21st-Century Maritime Silk Road, the BRI is "designed to uphold the global free trade regime and the open world economy in the spirit of open regional cooperation. It is aimed at promoting [an] orderly and free flow of economic factors, highly efficient allocation of resources and deep integration of markets; encouraging the countries along the Belt and Road to achieve economic policy coordination and carry out broader and more in-depth regional cooperation of higher standards; and jointly creating an open, inclusive, and balanced regional economic cooperation architecture that benefits all". China's president, Xi Jinping, has repeatedly stressed that the BRI embodies the Silk Road Spirit, variously defined as "the aspiration for inter-civilization exchanges, the yearning for peace and stability, the pursuit of common development and the shared dream for a better life" and as "peaceful cooperation, openness, inclusion, mutual learning and mutual benefit". The BRI is therefore an organic combination of the "Silk Road Spirit" and economic globalization, pointing the way to a new, inclusive globalization path.

Designed as an immanent critique of the neoliberal globalization of the last 30 to 40 years, inclusive globalization embodies fundamental similarities and fundamental differences with the former. Inclusive globalization does not involve deglobalization or a reversal of globalization but rather a fundamental development and reform of globalization. As far as technology-driven globalization is concerned, inclusive, and neoliberal globalization drive in the same direction. A quest for a spatial fix is also an important mechanism in both cases. The fundamental difference between the two is that inclusive globalization is designed first and foremost to improve people's livelihoods rather than only serve the interests of capital. To this end, the state must first play an effective regulatory role to ensure economic growth is inclusive. Second, capital markets require reform in order to direct investment to infrastructure and productive activities. Third, instead of a neoliberal path imposed from above, countries should choose development paths that suit their own national conditions. Fourth, participation should be open to all and should generate mutual benefits. Finally, cultural diversity (and the environment) should be protected.

Inclusive growth

In both global and national development research and policy, the relationship between markets and government intervention has been a focus of attention (Henderson and Jepson, 2017). From nineteenth- and early twentieth-century economic liberalism to the rise of Keynesian government interventionism in the 1930s and the rise of neoliberalism from the 1970s, policy orientation has witnessed a seesaw motion, with the roles of free markets and government intervention rising and falling (Wei Weiqiang, 2006). In a neoliberal order, the role of the state is limited to provision of good conditions for the accumulation of capital by defining and protecting property rights, enforcing contracts, regulating money markets, and helping finance infrastructure and skills. To perform these roles, the state itself is reconfigured (Harvey, 2007).

An inclusive growth model requires a more active state, no longer subservient to the needs of capital accumulation, with greater emphasis on social equity and environmental sustainability and improved governance capacity, although it does not necessarily mean that there has to be a return to Keynesianism. First, governments need to strengthen cooperation to meet global challenges, such as turbulence in financial markets, climate change and so on. Second, countries need to strengthen the protection of ordinary people and increase the capabilities of poor people through training and education, targeted innovation, entrepreneurship, job creation, and service and infrastructure provision. Third, a country needs to have the ability to guide and allocate the provision of financial resources and to prevent tax avoidance and speculation. The BRI attaches great importance to the role of government, emphasizing joined-up country policy communication and development strategies, joined-up planning, joined-up projects and an active search for points of agreement and mutual interest. The aim is not just to meet the need to valorize capital and provide for a spatial fix but to do so in ways that meet the needs of less-developed regions and ordinary people, spread the benefits to more regions and more people, and provide for inclusive, win-win adaptation and adjustment.

Inclusive infrastructure development

Inclusive infrastructure development means providing reliable and affordable infrastructure in less-developed areas and countries. Many studies have shown that connectivity is a prerequisite for developing opportunities for a region to benefit from economic globalization (Sheppard, 2016), and that investing in infrastructure bottlenecks can spur economic growth and social and financial returns (Lin Yifu and Wang Yan, 2017). Although modern infrastructure has linked many parts of the globe into a networked small world, with a well-developed market system, there are still however very many regions and billions of people around the world who are not part of this modern system, while in some developed countries such as the United States the infrastructure has become outdated and dilapidated due to a lack of investments.

These problems are closely related to changes in national and global capital markets since the 1980s. Over the past 25 years regional banks and traditional savings organizations have lost out to new financial intermediaries such as pension funds, mutual funds, sovereign wealth funds (SWFs), the funds of private corporations and certain types of insurance companies (Clark, 2017). In many countries of the OECD over the past 50 years, pension funds have been the single most important savings institution. In the 30 years from 1987 to 2016, UK pension fund entitlements rose more than sevenfold from £360 billion to £2.8 trillion. US pension assets are estimated to be worth nearly £20 trillion. According to the Sovereign Wealth Fund Institute, SWFs estimated their assets at more than $7.5 trillion in 2017.

While institutions of the kind considered in the last paragraph do act as intermediaries between savers and lenders, commercial banks do not for the most part act as intermediaries. The importance of commercial banks is that almost all the money in circulation originates as credit or debt that they provide. Rather than acting as intermediaries and lending deposits placed with them, their action of lending money itself creates deposits or bank money. In modern developed economies, savings are not needed to fund investment: a commercial bank can simply create money through its provision of credit. And as Keynes argued, in a well-managed monetary system there need be no limit on the availability of finance or credit for sustainable, income-generating activity.

The fundamental problem is that credit and the funds supplied by financial intermediaries are more likely to be invested in speculative or short-term financial market investments. Hot money that flows from one country to another to earn short-term profits is exemplary, as is the conduct of institutions such as hedge funds. As Stiglitz (2015) noted, "Hedge funds are not noted for their long-term thinking—for them, a quarter [three months] is an eternity".

Infrastructure projects are, however, large scale and capital-intensive, with long turnover times and long payback periods that require patient long-term funding. The gap between these needs and the predominance of short-term finance led Lin Yifu (2017) to emphasize the importance of a serious "maturity mismatch" in the global infrastructure financing market and the need for more "patient capital". One of the priority areas of the Chinese government's BRI is the provision of substantial infrastructure finance for facilities' interconnection, to accelerate access to modern infrastructure networks in less-developed countries and regions and provide opportunities for development. The provision of patient capital is one of the important reasons why the BRI initiative has been welcomed by many developing countries.

Inclusive development paths

Globalization does not require a unified development model. That is, in further promoting globalization best practices, one best way should be abandoned. In the years since the 1980s, the United States, Britain, and other countries have sought to transfer neoliberal ideas and policies often in the shape of conditionality to other countries, especially developing countries. In the 1980s, the Washington Consensus emerged as a set of policy prescriptions adopted by Washington-based institutions such as the International Monetary Fund, the World Bank, and the US Treasury Department. In the 1990s, these and sometimes a wider set of neoliberal measures were imposed on countries in need of financial assistance (Harvey, 2007). At least until the global financial crisis of 2008, the World Bank peddled to developing countries a set of "best practices" whose essence was privatization, marketization, and liberalization.

Nearly two decades of experience have shown that almost all the countries that were forced to adopt Washington Consensus-type measures were subsequently mired for some time in serious economic difficulties and lost their economic independence (which was indeed an objective of the measures). Although they were frequently recommended (but unable to be imposed), China did not adopt these standard prescriptions. Instead, it explored its own development path through "crossing the river while feeling for the stones". As a result of its choices, it achieved high and sustained economic growth. It is precisely for this reason that, unlike the neoliberal globalization model, China's BRI does not involve the identification of one best development path (namely, one centered on contemporary economic, institutional, and political conditions in developed countries). Instead, the BRI stresses that each country should choose a development path that suits its development conditions and its own circumstances. At the Belt and Road International Cooperation Forum, President Xi Jinping said that China will not interfere ideologically in other countries and will not export its own model of development, concentrating instead on mutual benefit, win-win, jointly making the cake bigger and jointly sharing it.

Inclusive participation in globalization

The very concept of globalization embodies the notion that it involves all countries and all of the people in the world. Although global powers are the catalysts of globalization, all countries should have the basic right to equal participation. In historical experiences of global economic expansion, strong countries exercised predominant (hegemonic) influence. The expansion of colonial trade was dominated at various times by the Portuguese, Spanish, Dutch and Great Britain, while the wave of imperial expansion was led by Great Britain and subsequently by the United States. The liberal international order that they, along with subsequently other Western countries, dominated was associated with an extremely unequal system of international trade and investment. In the course of the last phase of economic globalization, multinational corporations and Western-dominated international organizations, along with the United States as the only global superpower, exercised extraordinary power, leaving many countries in a weak position to negotiate with them. Weidong Liu and Peter Dicken (2006) used the theoretical concept of "obligated embeddedness" to show that large countries and a strong state enjoy a natural better position in globalization processes.

In further advancing globalization, a key issue for a path that is inclusive concerns ways of taking care of the weak and limiting the exercise by great powers of predominant influence. The BRI adheres to the principles of "openness, inclusiveness, equality and mutual benefit" and of "joint discussion, joint development, and sharing", placing the largest common development factor in first position and giving predominance to joint development and common prosperity. Moreover, the initiative is not confined to a small group, and is not just for groups with one set of beliefs or civilizational values. The initiative upholds open-mindedness and welcomes all interested countries and regions to participate in appropriate ways on an equal footing. The joint communiqué specifically emphasized the need to pay special attention to the least-developed countries, landlocked developing countries, small island developing states and so on. This is the embodiment of a strong and inclusive BRI.

Cultural inclusiveness

Over the past 300 years, Western European and North American countries took the lead in development, emerging as developed countries and colonial/imperial powers and occupying a leading position in the global economic order. On the one hand, these Western countries have developed a self-centered ideology and an absolute sense of cultural superiority. On the other hand, under severe pressure, many developing countries have developed a sense of cultural inferiority. Especially in recent decades, the increasingly powerful forces of economic globalization and the projection of Western political and ideological power have objectively and subjectively eroded the cultural independence of many countries and non-Western civilizational values. Hollywood movies, McDonald's fast food culture, Western-inspired and supported color revolutions and in some cases wars have swept through many countries and regions, bringing about all kinds of cultural conflicts. The evil consequences of the dominance of Western doctrine and Western cultural superiority are very detrimental to global sustainable development.

The traditional Silk Road principle of mutual respect and mutual learning ("hù xué hù jiàn") is an expression of completely different cultural values. The principle of mutual respect and mutual learning embraces respect for civilizational variety, the drawing of lessons from a variety of development paths and inequalities in levels of development to correct one's own weaknesses and jointly make progress. The BRI also venerates the Silk Road Spirit's respect for the cultural values of harmony and difference ("hé ér bù tóng" – together but different), and it emphasizes principles of common development and common prosperity on the basis of the preservation of cultural pluralism and shared peace. The principle of "harmony and difference" means treating each other equally, learning from each other's experience and supporting the coexistence of diversity and unity. Chinese President Xi Jinping has repeatedly stressed that the BRI does not involve an ideological or political agenda. There is no such thing as civilizational superiority or inferiority. Through equal exchange and mutual learning, civilizations have become more colorful and more innovative.

Summary

At present, economic globalization, as largely shaped by neoliberalism, stands at a crossroad. Antiglobalization voices are heard endlessly, and practical actions are constantly emerging. The question as to how to promote further globalization has become a worldwide challenge. The task of exploring a new type of globalization or an alternative globalization path has been put before political leaders and academic elites in various countries in the world. Against this backdrop, more and more countries have responded positively to the BRI proposed by the Chinese government as a platform for jointly exploring new international economic governance mechanisms. In particular, the Belt and Road International Cooperation Forum attracted more than 130 countries and 70 international organizations. Of these, 74 countries and international organizations have already signed BRI cooperation agreements with China. As an international consensus has emerged around the BRI, the further promotion of this initiative urgently requires underlying discursive concepts and analysis from the perspective of global economic governance.

The idea that the BRI will lead to inclusive globalization has received more and more academic attention and has become a matter of consensus among political leaders at many international summits or forums. In particular, the joint communiqué of the Belt and Road International Cooperation Forum highlights "free and inclusive trade" and globalization that is "open, inclusive, and beneficial to all". Undoubtedly, the idea that economic globalization should benefit all regions and all people is being established as a clear political concept and dream. However, achieving this outcome requires constant practical exploration and discursive construction. Based on a brief analysis of the course and mechanisms of global economic expansion and the limitations of neoliberal globalization, this paper proposes several core dimensions of inclusive globalization in light of the practical development of the BRI: namely, inclusive growth with effective and efficient government regulation; inclusive infrastructure development by resolving the problem of maturity mismatch in capital markets and directing investment resources to productive activities; inclusive development paths that enable countries to choose development paths that suit national conditions; inclusive participation that guarantees the equal participation of all parties in globalization; and cultural inclusiveness that protects cultural diversity in the process of globalization. Although these dimensions are not sufficient fully to characterize inclusive globalization, excluding for the moment the question of environmental sustainability, they do indicate directions for further research and for discursive construction of the BRI.

Notes

1 Originally published in *Progress in Geography* (地理科学进展), 2015: 5.
2 Originally published in *Journal of Chinese Academy of Governance* (国家行政学院学报), 2016: 1.
3 Originally published in *Bulletin of Chinese Academy of Sciences* (中国科学院院刊), 2017: 4.
4 Originally published in *Journal of Geographical Science,* 28, no. 9 (2018): 1–17.

Appendix 2: Relevant interviews

The BRI will create immense economic potential

March 28, 2015, reported by Zhou Rui, ChinaNews.com

On March 28, the Chinese government published the *Vision and Actions* on the promotion of jointly building the BRI. Professor Weidong Liu, assistant director of the Institute of Geographic Sciences and Natural Resources Research, Chinese Academy of Science CAS), in an interview with the China News Service, said that the BRI will create immense economic benefits for countries along the Belt and Road.

Weidong Liu said that strengthening the connection between Western Europe, a developed region, and East Asia, the most dynamic region in the past three or four decades, has immense economic potential. In addition, facility connectivity projects will improve regional transportation and locational conditions, creating a series of new economic growth poles.

This official framework issued by the Chinese government on March 28, 2015, indicates that the Silk Road Economic Belt focuses on bringing together China, Central Asia, Russia and Europe (the Baltic); linking China with the Persian Gulf and the Mediterranean Sea through Central Asia and West Asia; and connecting China with Southeast Asia, South Asia and the Indian Ocean. The 21st-Century Maritime Silk Road is designed to go from China's coastal ports to Europe through the South China Sea and the Indian Ocean on one route, and from China's coastal ports through the South China Sea to the South Pacific on the other.

Weidong Liu said that the BRI is a macro-level strategic concept. The three directions over land and two at sea proposed in the *Vision and Actions* are mainly for transcontinental connectivity and the development of international transport corridors. "Those countries on the international transportation corridors will definitely have more opportunities and better conditions to cooperate with China".

However, Weidong Liu said that the BRI should not be simply be regarded as a concrete linear economy as superficially expressed by the words "Belt and Road". Fundamentally speaking, the Belt and Road, without any specific spatial orientation, is an open and inclusive international cooperation network that welcomes any country to participate. Many fields of cooperation or relevant projects, such as policy design, financing and economic and trade and cultural exchanges, involve cooperation between two or more countries rather than subregional cooperation among neighboring countries.

Furthermore, the improved connectivity facilitated by the BRI will also create new growth poles. He stated that the inland countries of Eurasia are highly dependent on land transport due to their relatively weak infrastructures. The construction of the Silk Road Economic Belt will help these countries significantly improve their transportation and location conditions, thereby creating more economic opportunities and new hot spots for economic growth. The emergence of new economic growth poles, "for example, the Far East region of Russia, the major transportation hubs and resource-abundant regions in Central Asia, the major maritime node cities in Southeast Asia and South Asia, and the node cities in western China, will contribute to the formation of a win-win cooperation landscape for common development and common prosperity, substantially improving the well-being of people along the Belt and Road", said Weidong Liu.

Weidong Liu said that improving facility connectivity among countries is surely not an easy task. Technical standards (such as gauges), financing mechanisms, diplomatic and other issues have hindered highly efficient connectivity among countries in the past. However, it is expected that the aforesaid problems will be resolved in an easier way under the BRI framework.

He also said that it could be expected that under the joint efforts of countries along the Belt and Road, and with the gradual implementation of policy coordination, facilities connectivity, unimpeded trade, financial integration and people-to-people bonds, people in various countries will enjoy more convenience and better efficiency in their exchanges and share the benefits of economic globalization to a greater extent.

The BRI is not just about "going global"

April 23, 2015, reported by Li Boya, *21st Century Business Herald*

On April 22, Chinese president Xi Jinping attended the Asian-African Summit and Activities Commemorating the Sixtieth Anniversary of the Bandung Conference and earlier paid a state visit to Pakistan. The background of this series of diplomatic activities lies in the BRI hereafter that China is promoting.

This initiative is also advancing domestically. With the publication of the *Vision and Actions* and *21st-Century Maritime Silk Road* earlier, provinces, regions and municipalities have been planning their connectivity with the BRI. However, for many regions, some concepts regarding the BRI remain to be further clarified.

Recently, a reporter from *21st Century Business Herald* interviewed Weidong Liu, director and professor of the Center for the Belt and Road Initiative Studies, Institute of Geographic Sciences and Natural Resources Research, Chinese Academy of Science (CAS). It is worth mentioning that he had begun to participate in and lead related studies as early as September 2013.

Weidong Liu believes that the BRI, instead of being a regional development strategy, is a national overall strategy with regional influence, embodying a new concept of governance.

Inform the world of the globalization path China intends to take

REPORTER: The *Vision and Actions* does not look like a plan. What do you think of its interpretation of the BRI?

WEIDONG LIU: The BRI is an initiative proposed by China, but it cannot be accomplished just by China itself. Therefore, President Xi Jinping said at the Boao Forum for Asia that Belt and Road Construction will be a real chorus comprising all countries along the Belt and Road, not a solo performance for China itself. Belt and Road Construction is a historic enterprise that can only be accomplished by all participating countries, rather than planned by a single country.

Therefore, the *Vision and Actions* only proposes what China intends to do in this respect as well as the priorities in its consideration, the implementation of which depends on bilateral or multilateral consultations and connectivity between China and other countries in the future.

Do not simply compare it to most of China's previous plans, which are more about China's internal affairs. The Belt and Road should be jointly built with all participating countries, so we are not willing to use "planning" to describe it.

The Belt and Road conveys a quite important signal that China hopes to follow a path of peace, friendship, cooperation, development and mutual benefit. China, now as the second-largest economy in the world, needs to clearly, explicitly and openly inform the world of what kind of path it will take.

The BRI is not a regional strategy

REPORTER: Ou Xiaoli, a key person in the Belt and Road Initiative office, recently stated that implementation of the BRI will involve the whole country, with provinces left out.

WEIDONG LIU: Since the BRI proposal, there have been misunderstandings. Some cities that used to be on the ancient Silk Road believe that they will play a key role in contemporary Belt and Road Construction, while others in contrast will play a less important role. However, that is not true.

The Third Plenary Session of the Eighteenth Central Committee of the Communist Party of China, when referring to the tasks related to opening up, emphasized promotion of the BRI and building a new pattern for all-around opening up in China.

The BRI is a platform for China's opening up, and should not be regarded as a regional strategy. I do not think those scholars and officials who believe in BRI spatial preferences have correctly understood the connotations of the BRI.

Belt and Road Construction will involve a number of spatial directions in terms of connectivity and the construction of trade routes. Therefore, the *Vision and Actions* has mentioned several different key spatial directions, in which there might be greater investment in infrastructure construction. I do not think it is appropriate for some provinces to have positioned themselves as exclusive areas with a special status on the Belt and Road. The Belt and Road is an open and cooperative network with only nodes but no starting point since it is possible for any node to become a starting point.

REPORTER: What do you think of the relationship between the BRI, the coordinated development of Beijing-Tianjin-Hebei, the construction of the Yangtze River Economic Belt, and the free trade zone?

WEIDONG LIU: The BRI is a top-level and long-term vision that provides a platform for all-around opening up. The coordinated development of Beijing-Tianjin-Hebei and the construction of the Yangtze River Economic Belt, though also national strategies, are about regional development in China.

I do not think that these three strategies can be compared. But they are intertwined in the construction of the opening-up platform, especially free trade zones, which is an important carrier in implementing the BRI from the China side since the facilitation of trade will promote regional development. Moreover, I believe that new free trade zones will emerge in the future at important nodes along the Belt and Road in China.

The BRI is a not one-way path in "going global"

REPORTER: In some important places and nodes, what kind of preferential policies or planned projects will there be?

WEIDONG LIU: I am afraid that there will be no policies specific to certain places like in special economic zones, as that is not in line with the current state governance mode. However, inclusive policies in areas such as financing and enterprises' going global might be designated for Belt and Road Construction. As for some specific areas, certain kinds of policies for the BRI might to be tested first in some places before they are copied and promoted in the entire country.

Chinese capital going global is one of the focuses of Belt and Road Construction, especially for the coastal developed areas. Labor-intensive enterprises that are losing their competitiveness need to shift to other developing countries, while overcapacity of production in a few industries needs a *spatial fix* by investing overseas. Besides, many newly born companies based on new information and communication technologies are eager to expand business globally.

Thus the BRI is by no means a one-way process of Chinese capital going global but a two-way movement of capital. That is, it is a combination of going out and attracting in. China will still make every endeavor to attract FDIs, especially for less-developed regions in the West. Though the *Vision and Actions* has stressed the "going global" side, I think the real situation depends on the conditions in different regions.

It can be expected that Belt and Road Construction, especially the development of major economic corridors and the improvement of infrastructures in these corridors, will have more positive effects on the specific regions along the corridors. However, the transport corridors themselves are just tools for goods transportation, which are not naturally the same as the locations where economic and trade cooperation take place. In fact, economic and trade cooperation may take place in various places all over the country. The construction of these different corridors actually involves opening new paths for China's all-around opening up.

REPORTER: Now China proposes to jointly build the Belt and Road with foreign countries through the model of industrial parks.

WEIDONG LIU: Yes, the development of various industrial parks has been a very successful experience for China in promoting economic growth. However, I suggest that Chinese companies should not build overseas industrial parks on their own but jointly build with partners in cooperative arrangements, promoting the diversity of operations and investments and achieving mutual benefits, which is in line with the principle of the BRI.

The BRI will promote balanced regional development

REPORTER: What impact will the issuance of the *Vision and Actions* have on domestic regional economic development?

WEIDONG LIU: China's regional development is unbalanced, and each national strategy will have an impact on regional development. Therefore, the central government certainly hopes that the BRI will promote the development of lagging regions, thus contributing to overall balanced development in China.

For example, the Northeast China is mentioned relatively often in the *Vision and Actions* because of the emergence of a so-called "new Northeast phenomenon" in the last few years. As scholars, we also hope that the BRI will drive the development of the Northeastern region, and even more, of many places in the Western region.

Other cities and areas that are not directly mentioned in the *Vision and Actions* should not feel neglected. In fact, every area will have opportunities to participate in the BRI. The BRI is about international cooperation. How can cooperation in trade, investment and culture be limited to a few special areas? However, I do believe that the central government is concerned about whether the BRI can play an effective role in promoting China's relatively balanced development.

REPORTER: So you think that it is not a regional strategy, but that its implementation in China requires the support of relevant regional policies?

WEIDONG LIU: An initiative needs uniformity. If the BRI is publicized as a regional strategy at home, it will bring confusion to countries along the Belt and Road that are interested in participating. So I have always opposed calling it a regional strategy, or interpreting it as a regional strategy. This is contrary to the purpose of the initiative. It is a platform for international cooperation. The development of the BRI does have an impact on China's regional development, but I have to emphasize that it is definitely not a regional development strategy of China.

REPORTER: In the *Vision and Actions*, some nodal cities or city clusters in China have been mentioned in developing the BRI. What kind of role will these play in the Belt and Road?

WEIDONG LIU: I think it reflects a hope of promoting balanced regional development inside China through the BRI, while cities with better foundations for openness act as nodes. However, I do not think the BRI just has a special and significant impact on certain cities or regions. It offers an opportunity shared by all. How much is gained will depend on the capacity of each area or city, such as the surplus of capital or the level of technological development.

However, connectivity improvement will surely have some impact on certain regions. For example, the development of transportation corridors may attract some companies to certain areas. For instance, although the current transportation volume on the Chongqing-Xinjiang-Europe line is not large, it is a signal that goods can be transported by railway to Europe. Such notable improvement of location conditions will naturally attract capital inflow.

For example, border cities such as Suifenhe, Heihe, Manzhouli, and Erenhot have become the frontier of opening up due to their increasingly better locations brought about by the opening of trade passageways or the improvement of facilities connectivity.

Local governments and enterprises should not rush forward

REPORTER: Now we have clearly explained what the Belt and Road is at home and abroad. How can we proceed in the next step?

WEIDONG LIU: This question should be addressed from two parts – the domestic part and the foreign part. For the domestic part, we have to do our own work, and we have already begun to do what we currently can. The Chinese parts of many cross-border projects that have been negotiated bilaterally should be promoted.

The next important task is to connect some specific projects in a bilateral or multilateral manner with relevant countries. The implementation of such a project can start once a common interest is found.

Finding common interests is a process of adjustment. China's confidence should not be substantially affected if it encounters a few twists and turns in a particular project. Such volatility is inevitable since it naturally exists in international projects and China is inexperienced at working with other countries on international projects and confronts much interference. However, I do believe that there is a large need for mutual cooperation, a big wish for win-win outcomes and a great possibility of finding common interests.

REPORTER: What is your biggest concern about the promotion of the BRI?

WEIDONG LIU: I am much concerned about local governments' or enterprises' rushed actions, since they tend to respond with great enthusiasm once the central government has called for going global. Without patience and a clear and in-depth understanding of the other party, the common interests we find might be not appropriate, and it might even lead to some mistakes.

Therefore, I suggest that every party concerned should respond positively, but there is no need to rush forward. The first thing is to deeply understand and thoroughly communicate with the other party. The "going global" strategy is not simply about the action of going out but also about intensive homework.

The BRI involves many countries and requires mutual consultation between or among different parties. Therefore, China should not be too impatient. It is a long-term process that will last at least 20 or 30 years. The last three decades have witnessed a rapid development of China, which has caused the country to pursue everything with speed. However, the BRI after all is a joint project with other countries that requires mutual consultations. China should take its time to prepare thoroughly at the initial stage, working on policy communication, planning and consultation, and finding common interests.

"Open development"

A series of interviews about the five development concepts

December 16, 2015, reported by Liao Wengen, *People's Daily*
(Selected part of the interview on "Building the Chinese Dream and Achieving the World Dream")

I. Since the Third Plenary Session of the Eleventh CPC Central Committee, "opening up" has become a theme. The Fifth Plenary Session of the Eighteenth CPC Central Committee highlighted the need to adhere to the "opening-up" strategy in China's development. What is the deep meaning of this theme?

Reform and *opening up* have been the two magic tools leading to China's remarkable achievements in economic development since the Third Plenary Session of the Eleventh Central Committee. Since the 1980s, China has continuously and deeply participated in the process of economic globalization through gradual reform and opening up, which has driven economic growth through the introduction of capital, technology, management experience and so forth into the country. Arguably, China, whose rapid economic development has benefited from economic globalization, has also made tremendous contributions to world economic growth. Today, China's economy is so closely connected with the world that neither could develop without the other's involvement. Therefore, only by adhering to a concept of development with opening up can China correctly plan its future development path.

On the other hand, *opening up* in the past three decades has been mainly a one-way street. That is, China actively adapted to the trend of global industrial shift and attracted foreign investment to participate in our economic development. In the past ten years, especially since the global financial crisis in 2008, with the rapidly increasing scale of its outflow of direct investments, China has gradually entered the stage of capital and industry "going global", which is driving the formation of the second round of global industrial shift. This means that China has entered a stage emphasizing both "going global" and "attracting in", that is, a new era of two-way opening up. In this context, only with a deeper implementation of the opening-up strategy and an organic combination of "going global" and "attracting in", can the transformation and upgrading of Chinese industries and sustainable and sound economic development be facilitated through international economic and trade cooperation.

In addition, China, as the world's second-largest economy and the world's largest current importer and exporter of goods has to assume greater and more international responsibilities, playing a role as an engine driving world economic growth. This also requires China to think about problems and plan its future path from the perspective of open development, cooperative development and win-win development.

II. What is the biggest change brought to China by "opening up"? What is the essence of "open development"?

Opening up has brought enormous and remarkable changes to China. The first has to do with the change in ideas. We have changed from having little understanding of the operation of the market to using the market as the main force of resource allocation, and from only following established plans to familiarizing ourselves with the rules of the international market, which are all inseparable from opening up. Furthermore, a set of governance mechanisms compatible with economic globalization has been established. Through protracted and unremitting effort made in more than 30 years of opening up, China has established a relatively complete socialist market economy system that not only meets the needs of domestic and foreign investors but also basically adapts to global economic competition. The third is the rapid growth of economic strength. Undoubtedly, foreign capital and foreign trade have made great contributions to China's economic growth over the past three decades. China's share of the world economy, which was only about 5 percent at the beginning of reform and opening up, reached 13 percent in 2014.

Open development, highlighted in the "Fifth Plenary Session", embodies not only the continuation of opening up as in the past but also adds some brand-new connotations, the essence of which is fourfold. The first is two-way opening up, which promotes an orderly flow of domestic and international factors. That is to say, under the new development situation and development stage, resource allocation should be considered from a global perspective to ensure China's deeper integration into the global economic system. The second is win-win cooperation, that is, establishing a broad community of shared interests and destiny, so as to achieve inclusive development on a larger scale and to drive the world economic growth. The third is opening up. It is necessary, on the one hand, to improve the domestic business environment and develop institutional mechanisms that are compatible with international trade and investment rules, and on the other hand, it is necessary to promote overseas investment service systems and protection mechanisms. The fourth is international responsibility, that is, assuming more responsibility as the world's second-largest economy, including promoting the establishment of a more equitable global economic governance system, maintaining international peace, assisting poor countries and so on.

III. Since the "Twelfth Five-Year Plan" period, especially since the Eighteenth National Congress of CPC, with the further deepening and broadening of China's opening up, a higher-level opening structure has been in the process of formation. In respect of "open development", what other problems do we need to solve and what potential remains to be explored?

Since the "Twelfth Five-Year Plan", China's opening up has displayed a new trend, that is, two-way opening up. After more than 30 years of open development characterized by "attracting in", we have accumulated a lot of governance experience in adapting to the need to "attract investment" from foreign investors. However, in so doing, it is hard to satisfy the need for Chinese capital to "go global". Therefore, in the new round of open development, the first problem that needs to be solved is our insufficient experience in "going global". The developed countries have accumulated experience in this regard for decades or even hundreds of years, while China's experience of "going global" on a large scale amounts to less than one decade. Both the government and enterprises need to learn the rules of international maneuvering by employing great concentration and an open mind, so as to accumulate more and better experience in promoting overseas investments. The academic community should change their concepts regarding values and support mechanisms as soon as possible, in order to establish an academic atmosphere proud of serving Chinese capital going global, and strengthen research into the relevant national governance structures, investment environments, market demand and so on.

The second problem to be solved concerns coordination. Under our current governance structure, the central government has such a strong convening and mobilizing power that all departments, regions and sectors of society will positively respond to a strategy as soon as the government releases it. However, a key issue is how to coordinate actions when all these forces are mobilized. Many cases of malignant competition among enterprises have been witnessed in the process of Chinese capital going global. At present, there have been emerging signs of inconsistency among sectors and regions in relation to overseas investment, cooperation and assistance. Some cases that reflect bad practice will have extremely bad demonstration effects that negatively affect subsequent cooperation. Therefore, a new round of open development urgently requires an integrated coordinating body.

The third problem that needs to be solved has to do with balance. On the one hand, China should balance the implementation of "going global" and "attracting in" as open development aims for complementary advantages in the international arena. With a large technology gap between China and developed countries, attracting more foreign investment still warrants China's intense attention. On the other hand, there is a need to balance the large-scale "going global" of enterprises and the creation of domestic manufacturing jobs, so as to prevent China's manufacturing industry from "hollowing out" due to the implementation of the "going global" strategy.

IV. An active participation in global economic governance would be an important sign that China has become an influential power in the world. What should we do in this regard?

With the improvement of economic strength and status, our ability to participate in global economic governance is gradually improving. For example, China initiated the establishment of the Asian Infrastructure Investment Bank and the BRICS New Development Bank, and Chinese voices in the World Bank and the International Monetary Fund are to some extent more influential. In this regard, however, it should be clearly recognized that a greater voice in global economic governance does not necessarily mean reinventing the wheel. On the one hand, we need to maintain the mechanism of economic globalization; on the other hand, we should promote the reform of the globalization mechanism to allow globalization to benefit more countries and regions. The active promotion of inclusive globalization and of win-win cooperation tis one of the important contributions that China can make to the development of the global economic governance system. As for whether China will have a greater voice in global economic governance, that crucially depends on whether our global development philosophy and its practice are recognized by more countries.

5. The Belt and Road now is becoming a worldwide topic. What will the Belt and Road bring to China and the world?

Fundamentally, the BRI is an initiative for win-win cooperation and inclusive globalization. The "Silk Road" is a historical and cultural heritage shared by all countries along the Belt and Road. And China, drawing on the historical and cultural connotations of the Silk Road, has presented to the world a path of development that it will take in the future, namely, "peace, development, cooperation and mutual benefit". For China itself, the BRI is a leading strategy for coordinating its all-around opening up and the major flag and carrier for achieving open development, which will bring two-way investments, convenience in trade and shape the development path and model of China in the coming decades. As for the world, the BRI represents an attempt to reform the existing global economic governance, achieve inclusive development and transform the world development model from a binary structure of "core-periphery" to a ternary integration (that is, to closely connect developed and developing countries with emerging countries acting as the link), which may change the global economic landscape in the next few decades. Therefore, the BRI is not just about the construction of a few roads and several corridors. It is a platform for our country to deepen its integration into the global economic system and play a greater leading role therein. The Belt and Road construction will bring peace, prosperity and inclusive development to the world, benefiting all countries involved.

Interview on the BRI and multiscale spatial planning

Lv Bin, author of the interview, Human Settlements Forum in West China, 2016, 1.

I. How to correctly understand the BRI?

The BRI is a major national vision of China to coordinate its all-a round opening up to the world and the major flag and carrier for achieving "open development" in the new era. The *Vision and Actions*, jointly issued by the National Development and Reform Commission, the Ministry of Foreign

Affairs, and the Ministry of Commerce of the People's Republic of China, states that "the initiative to jointly build the Belt and Road is aimed at promoting the orderly and free flow of economic factors, highly efficient allocation of resources and deep integration of markets, encouraging the countries along the Belt and Road to achieve economic policy coordination and carry out broader and deeper regional cooperation, and jointly creating an open, inclusive and balanced regional economic cooperation architecture that benefits all". Therefore, the BRI is an international cooperation platform to promote regional development that benefits all regions and countries under the economic globalization mechanism, which can be seen as a proposal for inclusive globalization.

Over the past 30–40 years, economic globalization has profoundly changed the world economic landscape. However, the inherent contradictions of the economic globalization mechanism have also led to a dramatically widening gap between the rich and the poor in the world. Therefore, how to avoid the deepening of the gap between the rich and the poor while promoting the development of economic globalization is an important question that needs to be answered to achieve sustainable world development. Since the 1980s, China has continuously and deeply participated in the process of economic globalization through gradual reform and opening up. The rise of the national economy and the lifting of 700 million people out of poverty have made China a bright star in the process of global development. China should thus make greater contributions to the development of the global economic governance mechanism and play a more active role in leading the development of the world economy. This is the context for the emergence of the BRI. It is designed to uphold the global free trade regime and the open world economy. It is not a simple continuation of the economic globalization of the past, but a new type of globalization notably characterized by the inclusion of the cultural connotations of the "Silk Road", that is, by the advocacy of inclusive globalization.

II. Several misunderstandings about the Belt and Road

There have been various misunderstandings about the BRI. First, the BRI, though stressing the historical and cultural connotations of the "Silk Road", is not aimed at rebuilding former international trade routes. Second, the BRI is not a regional strategy of China but a long-term national strategy for coordinating an all-around opening up. The former is about domestic affairs, while the latter focuses on international cooperation. Third, the BRI is not a one-way "going global" strategy, but a closely interwoven approach of "going global" and the "attracting in". Fourth, the BRI is not a traditional geopolitical strategy but an attempt to explore new methods of international cooperation such as connected development and win-win cooperation. Fifth, the BRI is not a simple linear economy but a platform for international economic cooperation based on the cultural connotations of the "Silk Road".

III. What is the relationship between the BRI and the Coordinated Development of Beijing-Tianjin-Hebei and the Construction of the Yangtze River Economic Belt?

It is very common to compare the BRI with the coordinated development of Beijing-Tianjin-Hebei and the construction of the Yangtze River Economic Belt. Although these are all important national-level strategies of China in the new era, these three should not be equated.

The BRI is a long-term national strategy for coordinating an all-around opening up in the new era that will determine the development path and model of China in the coming decades, and an attempt to reform the existing mode of international economic governance in order to achieve inclusive development, which may change the global economic landscape in the next few decades. By contrast, the coordinated development of Beijing-Tianjin-Hebei and the construction of the Yangtze River Economic Belt are largely about domestic regional development. Although they involve open development, they are not long-term strategies in the same sense as the BRI. In a word, the BRI is a leading and long-term globalization process of China, while the other two are regional and relatively short-term strategies.

IV. What impact will the BRI have on regional economic development domestically?

The BRI does have significant regional impacts. For example, the building of the six major economic corridors and the construction of leading areas of opening up in inland regions (see *Vision and Actions*) will drive the development of certain areas in the central and western regions, forming new growth poles. In particular, the connectivity and trade facilitation of Eurasia will play an important role in promoting the development of the western border areas, providing significant opportunities and a starting point for the Western Development Strategy to enter a new stage. In addition, the deepening and expansion of economic and trade exchanges with countries along the Belt and Road will promote the sustainable development of coastal economic centers, improving their international competitiveness. This is why the *Suggestions of the CPC Central Committee on the Thirteenth Five-Year Plan for National Economic and Social Development* stated in its suggestions on expanding and developing a new spatial structure that China will form vertical and horizontal economic axial lines mainly comprised of economic belts along its coastline and major rivers, based on its overall regional development strategy and guided by the BRI; the integrated development of Beijing, Tianjin and Hebei; and the Yangtze River Industrial Belt. Generally speaking, the BRI will help China achieve a more balanced land development pattern.

It should be noted that "Belt and Road" construction is an open development platform in which all regions in the country can participate, rather than a strategy that yields "dividends" particularly for a few areas along the ancient Silk Road. Connectivity and improved trade facilitation will bring new opportunities to the development of various regions in China and major port cities along the border. These areas will surely have more opportunities to become new growth poles.

V. It has been mentioned that the BRI will build some nodal cities or strategic propellers as well as city clusters. What kind of role will these play in implementing the BRI?

The BRI is a platform for international economic cooperation fundamentally based on the connectivity of infrastructure and economic, trade and cultural cooperation projects. From the spatial structure perspective, the BRI is associated with a network structure consisting of economic corridors and nodes in which the corridors mainly undertake the function of circulation, that is, they are channels for exchanges of personnel, goods, information, technology, culture and so on, while the nodes are the intersections of various flows, and especially places where various economic and trade cooperation and cultural exchanges take place. Therefore, the nodal cities or city clusters, as the place where specific cooperation projects occur, are the footholds and support points for the BRI

VI. What is your main concern about advancing the BRI?

My first concern relates to China's insufficient experience of "going global". Developed countries have accumulated experience in this regard for many decades or even hundreds of years, while China's experience of "going global" consists by and large of less than one decade. Both the government and enterprises need to learn the rules of the international game with great concentration and an open mind, so as to accumulate more experience related to overseas investment. The academic community should strengthen their studies of the relevant national governance structures, investment environments, market demand and so forth.

The second concerns coordination. Under our current governance structure, the central government has strong convening and mobilizing power so that all departments, regions and sectors of society will positively respond to a strategy once the government releases it. However, the subsequent coordination of these forces requires attention. Many cases of malignant competition among enterprises have been witnessed in the process of China's "going global". As a result, the BRI has been in urgent need of a powerful integrated coordinating body.

The BRI is a chorus of countries along the route

September 12, 2016, reported by Wen Yuan, Guangming Daily

After attending the symposium on promoting the BRI and delivering a speech as the sole expert representative, Weidong Liu, director of the Center for the

Belt and Road Studies, IGSNRR-CAS (Chinese Academy of Sciences), has been quite busy every day. However, this conference on August 17 remains fresh in his memory. He said, "I was most impressed by the confidence and determination to promote the BRI expressed in the speech delivered by President Xi Jinping".

The BRI: Opening a new era of inclusive globalization

REPORTER: You once said that the BRI presents a new path of globalization that China expects to take. How do you understand this path?

WEIDONG LIU: Over the past 30–40 years, economic globalization has profoundly changed the world economic landscape. On the one hand, the economies of developed countries have been financialized and shifted to high-tech industries, while their low-end manufacturing industries have been hollowed out; on the other hand, some developing countries, represented by China, have risen to become major manufacturing powers. This has changed the traditional binary structure of core-periphery to a ternary structure of "developed countries-emerging countries-less-developed countries". In the meantime, with continuously declining trade, sluggish economic growth and the rising tide of trade protectionism and populism, the world economy has not yet emerged from the shadow of the 2008 international financial crisis. Therefore, how to promote the recovery of the world economy in this new situation is the "maximum common denominator" of all countries' concerns.

Since reform and opening up, China has deeply participated in the process of economic globalization, making remarkable development achievements. China has already become the world's second-largest economy, the largest manufacturing country, the largest commodity exporter, and the third-largest foreign investor. A second global industrial shift characterized by Chinese capital "going global" has started, in which context China needs to make greater contributions to safeguarding the achievements and developing the mechanisms of economic globalization, assuming greater responsibility in promoting the economic growth of the world.

The BRI, which emerged in the context of major changes in the world economic landscape, is an effort to promote inclusive development of economic globalization that will open a new era of inclusive globalization, where inclusiveness largely refers to the principles of "openness and inclusiveness", "equality and mutual benefit", "achieving shared growth through discussion and collaboration", and "harmony in diversity". The BRI stresses the quest for common development, prosperity, and peace on the basis of maintaining cultural diversity, rather than building a small circle with only one voice. It is not a solo performance for China itself, but a real chorus comprising all countries along the routes, which not only meets China's needs of "going global" but also will allow people in more countries and regions to benefit from globalization.

To avoid misunderstandings of the BRI

REPORTER: The BRI is a leading vision involving all aspects of work. With various understandings among different communities of our society, is there any misunderstanding?

WEIDONG LIU: Some misunderstandings about the BRI do exist today. First, the BRI is not aimed at rebuilding former international trade routes. It is notable that the usage of the Silk Road concept in the BRI has caused some regions to become keen to explore their own role in the ancient Silk Road, as starting points, passages, and links. However, in fact, the Silk Road, from perspective of history, is actually a quite dense trade network rather than a set of fixed routes. The so-called Silk Road today is a historical and cultural heritage shared by all countries along the Belt and Road that is associated with the development concepts of "peace, development, cooperation, and mutual benefit". The BRI is not aimed at rebuilding the ancient trade routes, but at building an international cooperation platform for China and the countries along the Road to achieve common development and shared prosperity.

Second, the BRI is interpreted by many as a regional development strategy of China. Some provinces believe they enjoy a special and exclusive status in relation to the Belt and Road, while others consider themselves irrelevant to it. However, the BRI is indeed a long-term, top-level strategy of China to coordinate its all-around opening up, and a national strategic vision that involves international cooperation. Instead of being a regional development strategy, it is a project in which all regions in the country can and should participate.

Third, the BRI is not a matter of "going global" in one direction. "Going global" is a key part of the BRI, and also its strategic foundation. However, due to the large technology gap between China and developed countries, "attracting in" will remain deserving of China's great attention for a long time to come. Economic globalization indeed is a deepening process of mutual investments between countries. Over the past three decades, European and American developed countries have been both major investors in foreign countries and major recipients of foreign capital. Therefore, to advance the BRI, China should not only encourage domestic capital to "go global" but also attach great importance to attracting capital.

REPORTER: As the only participating expert, what opinions did you express at the meeting?

WEIDONG LIU: I mainly talked about my experiences in studying the BRI. First, the BRI is a brand-new national vision. In the last three decades,

China's opening up and opening-up mechanisms have largely focused on attracting foreign direct investment. Now it is more a matter of "going global", that is, of "being a guest" in other people's homes. Only by deepening the reform of institutional mechanisms can the BRI be better advanced.

Second, it is necessary to balance the role of the state and market in advancing the BRI, while the latter should be better used. The BRI has been considered by many outsiders as a project of the Chinese government, which it is actually not. The BRI is a global public service platform initiated by the Chinese government for world capital flows, in which enterprises from all over the world can participate.

Third, there is an urgent need for more theoretical and academic discourses on the BRI, so as to have a better understanding of it.

Strengthening studies on the BRI

REPORTER: President Xi Jinping said that the BRI should be advanced step-by-step in "nailing" spirit and with the purpose of benefiting the people of all countries along the Belt and Road. How do you understand this spirit?

WEIDONG LIU: My understanding of the "nailing" spirit is that it refers to perseverance and the solid implementation of relevant measures step-by-step so that people along the Belt and Road will truly appreciate the benefits and well-being brought by the BRI.

REPORTER: President Xi Jinping proposed "strengthening academic studies, theoretical support, and discourses about the Belt and Road Initiative". What are your current studies focused on?

WEIDONG LIU: Generally speaking, theoretical study on the BRI in China has fallen behind practice, and there is also a lack of understanding and study of neighboring countries along the Belt and Road and relevant talent reserves. As researchers, we need to promote the establishment of corresponding academic discourses in the world through active academic study, and to build an academic discourse concerning "inclusive globalization".

The BRI: Leading a new era of inclusive globalization[1]

Weidong Liu

In 2016, with the deeply changing international landscape, it has been increasingly recognized that the BRI is becoming a new platform for countries to promote the deepening of economic globalization and the reform of corresponding mechanisms, which will lead a new era of inclusive globalization.

This might be a turning point in history. Brexit, the presidential election in the United States, and other events reflecting the rise of populism and protectionism all indicate that neoliberal economic globalization, which has caused severe social conflict over the past three decades, is coming to an end. Bittersweet results seem inevitable because of the internal contradiction between the fact that capital can flow freely, while labor cannot easily move. According to studies by Oxfam (a charity institution), in 2016 the richest 1 percent of the global population were wealthier than the remaining 99% percent. Therefore, in the process of neoliberal economic globalization, capital was the winner, while large sections of the population bore the costs. This is the reason why economic globalization is increasingly questioned in the world today, and also the key to understanding a series of "black swan" events in 2016.

Against this background, addressing equity and justice issues in the process of promoting economic globalization is a major concern and the source of difficulties confronting sustainable global development. The BRI has thus attracted more attention. Though China was only trying to make a few contributions to the global economic governance when it first put forward the BRI, the current international situation has raised the significance of this new initiative.

At a time when driving economic globalization in a more inclusive direction is increasingly urgent, the fact that the BRI is aimed at building an open, inclusive, and balanced regional economic cooperation framework that benefits all will surely open the way to new philosophical thinking about the development of economic globalization, promoting a new era of inclusive economic globalization.

The inclusive connotation of the BRI is reflected in several aspects of the proposal. First, the BRI emphasizes the quest for common interests in the development strategies of countries along the Belt and Road, meeting not only capital's needs for a spatial fix but also benefiting more regions. Second, the connections between national development strategies will enable countries along the Belt and Road to learn from China's experience in promoting economic development and poverty alleviation, and enable them to find more effective ways to facilitate their own poverty alleviation and modernization. Third, the BRI, adhering to the concepts of "openness and inclusiveness" and "equality and mutual benefit", welcomes the equal participation of different countries and regions. Fourth, the BRI takes the pursuit of the "biggest developmental common denominator" as the top priority of common development and prosperity with the principle of "achieving shared growth through discussion and collaboration". Fifth, the BRI, deeply influenced by the cultural values of "harmony in diversity", advocates inclusiveness, peaceful coexistence, and common prosperity on the basis of maintaining the diversity in civilizations. Last but not least, the BRI will include more underdeveloped regions within the modern infrastructure networks, bringing them more economic development opportunities.

As mentioned above, the practice of jointly building the Belt and Road is one of inclusive globalization and an essential exploration in promoting the healthy development of globalization. The last three years have proved that this is not a "maverick" move of China but an international cooperation platform to promote shared regional development that benefits all countries under economic globalization conditions. From a long-term perspective, improving economic globalization through jointly building the Belt and Road will not only meet China's own development needs but also will allow economic globalization to benefit more countries and regions.

The BRI, driving the development of a more balanced and inclusive world economic structure

January 18, 2017, reported by Wang Moying, Fu Yuwei, and Zhang Xiao, Xinhua News Agency

With the frequent occurrence of "black swan events" on the world political and economic stage and certain setbacks today to globalization, there is an urgent need to introduce new thinking and innovative cooperation models into international cooperation, so as to stimulate the growth of the world economy. At the 2017 annual meeting of the World Economic Forum, there were heated discussions by participants about China's BRI, which has been stimulating regional economic cooperation and enhancing the prospects for the recovery of the world economy.

With respect to related topics, Weidong Liu, director with the Center for the Belt and Road Initiative Studies, IGSNRR-CAS (Chinese Academy of Sciences), said in an exclusive interview with the Xinhua News Agency that, in the new circumstances, countries urgently need to break through stereotypes and abandon old models. The BRI, as a good example of innovative international cooperation, is conductive to bringing the world economy into a new realm of balance, inclusiveness, and mutual benefit.

Weidong Liu stated that the BRI, with its core concept of "inclusive globalization", has achieved greater than expected results since it was proposed three years ago. It now has been written into United Nations (UN) resolutions and gained the support of more than 100 countries and international organizations. By 2016, China had signed cooperation agreements with more than 40 countries along the Belt and Road and with international organizations. Designed to jointly build the Belt and Road, these agreements indicate that the cooperation concepts and models advocated by the BRI have gradually attracted the attention, recognition, and support of the international community.

Weidong Liu pointed out that the frequent occurrence of "black swan events" all over the world in 2016 is likely to lead to the stagnation, even retrogression, of economic globalization. In the meantime, after more than 30 years of development, China has become the world's second-largest economy, the largest commodity-trading nation, and the second-largest foreign investor.

Weidong Liu said that in the above-mentioned new situation, China should lead globalization toward more inclusiveness by advancing the BRI and stimulate new growth of the world economy by promoting cooperation among countries along the Belt and Road.

He suggested that, first, China should deepen the connections between its development strategy and countries along the Belt and Road under the BRI framework. In addition, it needs to start building those economic corridors that have comparatively matured, such as the China-Pakistan Economic Corridor and the China-Indochina Peninsula Economic Corridor. Meanwhile, it is advisable to improve the infrastructure conditions and investment and trade facilitation in neighboring countries, both bilateral and multilateral, by deepening infrastructure connectivity.

Weidong Liu noted that the BRI should follow market principles with a focus on the actions of enterprises, so as to effectively mitigate risks. He suggested that a third-party cooperation platform to jointly promote the BRI should be introduced to strengthen the cooperation with European and American enterprises.

As for the Sino-foreign manufacturing capacity cooperation under the BRI framework, Weidong Liu emphasized that the spatial shift of manufacturing is a type of market behavior. China's manufacturing capacity cooperation with other countries has effectively stimulated the shift of manufacturing activities to them, tremendously powering the economic and social development of these countries.

The five connectivity priorities are the key to advancing the BRI. Weidong Liu pointed out in this regard that the five priorities, though equally important in respect of their status, will play subtly different roles in advancing the BRI, which should be deliberately handled by all parties involved.

He said that, since there are huge differences between China and other countries along the Belt and Road in terms of development level and model, political and economic regime, and religious culture, in order to achieve effective cooperation, policy coordination is the precondition, unimpeded trade is the goal, facilities connectivity is the foundation, financial integration is the guarantee, and people-to-people bonds are the essence.

The BRI will be a strong driving force for the further development of economic globalization

May 8, 2017, reported by Fan Sili, China Economic Times

"The BRI is a *dao* (a sort of philosophy), that is, a new concept of and way of thinking about cooperation, whose key word is inclusive globalization". Weidong Liu has been talking about inclusive globalization for the past two years. And he believes that the biggest change since the BRI was proposed more than three years ago is its transformation from a Chinese initiative to an international consensus.

Weidong Liu, the director with the Center for the Belt and Road Initiative Studies, IGSNRR-CAS (Chinese Academy of Sciences), said in an interview with the *China Economic Times* on the eve of the Belt and Road Forum for International Cooperation that, regarding the world, Belt and Road construction is an attempt to reform the existing mode of international economic governance to achieve inclusive development, an effort to drive the world development model from a binary (core-peripheral) division to a ternary integration model, which may change the global economic landscape in the next few decades

The limitations of economic globalization give birth to the proposal of the BRI.

REPORTER: The BRI has entered a stage of comprehensive implementation and has made a lot of important progress. You have repeatedly said that the BRI was proposed in the macro context when the limitations of economic globalization and antiglobalization movements have notably hindered the sustainable development of the world economy. How should one understand the significance of this initiative and its role?

WEIDONG LIU: The BRI was proposed in the macro context of economic globalization. To correctly understand the significance and role of this initiative requires a deep understanding of the mechanisms of economic globalization and their limitations.

Economic globalization is a historical phenomenon that emerged from the combined effects of institutional, economic, and technological forces, involving both objective forces and institutional factors. In terms of objective forces, on the one hand, endless spatial expansion and spatial restructuring are inherent needs of capital accumulation, and, on the other hand, the shift of production organization from Fordism to post-Fordism has increased the prevalence of parts and components outsourcing, which has made many regions in the world closely connected by supply chain relationships, forming various production networks. In addition, advances in transportation and communication technologies over the past half-century have led to a significant drop in the cost of organizing economic activities across space, resulting in so-called time-space compression. However, all of these developments only create possibilities. The decisive factor lies in the investment and trade liberalization policies embraced by many countries in the world, including developed and developing countries, which were convinced of the benefits of free trade.

Economic globalization over the past three decades has actually been a set of international economic governance mechanisms developed on the basis of neoliberalism by developed countries in Europe and America to address the economic crisis they had encountered in 1970s. In the process of promoting economic globalization, these developed countries, convinced that the market afforded a one-size-fits-all solution to all problems and that the development path they had taken was the best in the world, have continuously exported these ideas to developing countries. It was the "Washington Consensus" policies of the 1990s (a product of neoliberal policy) that caused the Soviet Union and Eastern European countries to experience economic recessions. Moreover, proponents of Western mainstream economics and development economics argue based on their mathematical models that free trade will enable countries to achieve balanced development. The reality, however, has been quite the opposite at many spatial scales. The reason is that free trade theory is based on epistemological individualism, and all people in a country are averaged. The absence of attention to social and regional differentiation that is associated with significant variations around average outcomes is an important reason why developed countries have gained huge benefits from globalization while their ordinary citizens have lost out.

Therefore, neoliberal globalization is a set of mechanisms that mainly meets the needs of capital's spatial fix, and from which capital and large companies have gained enormously, while society, especially average people, has paid huge costs, causing serious social problems. Moreover, neoliberal globalization has resulted in the coexistence of prosperity and precarity because capital can flow freely cross countries while labor cannot, which is the internal contradiction of neoliberal globalization. If the same mechanisms continue to dominate world economic governance, social conflicts around the world will by no means be solved, and global sustainable development goals will hardly be achievable. In fact, a series of "black swan events", including Brexit, have manifested the great need of the world to reform the economic governance mechanism. In such a sense, inclusive globalization is the essence of the BRI.

REPORTER: How should one carry out an effective reform of the economic globalization when an antiglobalization trend has emerged?

WEIDONG LIU: Economic globalization is a "double-edged sword", which has not only has promoted world economic growth but also brought serious social problems. However, most countries in the world have been so closely interconnected by modern production organization, global production networks, and modern communications technologies that each has a stake in the others. It is impossible for the world to return to complete isolationism and closed borders. Therefore, at this historical point in time, what the world needs is to reform the mechanisms of economic globalization rather than to reject it and restart it again.

It is notable that in the world today many voices are seeking reform. Reform requires new thinking and new models. As the world's second-largest economy and as a big country with successful development experience, China should provide a possible scheme for the reform and development of economic globalization. From the perspective of addressing the negative effects of globalization, the interests of ordinary grassroots people should be taken into account in the new international economic governance model. It is also necessary to extend modern infrastructures to lagging regions, allowing economic growth to benefit more people.

The practice of the past three decades has proved that it is difficult to achieve such a goal by relying entirely on market mechanisms. It is thus necessary to carry out reforms while retaining the beneficial side of economic globalization.

Fundamentally speaking, neoliberal thinking should be abandoned, while the banner of inclusive globalization should be established. This is exactly the core connotation and essence of the BRI proposed by President Xi Jinping. The BRI will be a banner leading to inclusive globalization.

REPORTER: You believe that the BRI will become a stabilizer and engine driving world economic growth, as well as a banner promoting the reform and development of globalization. How will the BRI lead to inclusive globalization?

WEIDONG LIU: The BRI advocates inclusive globalization. Inclusive globalization can be understood in the light of at least the following points.

First, the state should play an important role, especially in maintaining social equity and reducing poverty, as it is impossible to just rely on the market to solve all of these problems. Second, the diversity of development paths chosen by different countries should be respected, with each country exploring suitable development paths based on their own characteristics and conditions. In the past, neoliberal globalization only advocated the path that developed countries had already adopted. Third, the BRI emphasizes the connections between the development strategies of countries involved in seeking common interests, which not only meet capital's needs for a spatial fix but also benefit more regions and people. Fourth, the BRI has made its top priority pursuit of the biggest common denominator for development and promoting common development and prosperity while adhering to the principles of "openness and inclusiveness", "equality and mutual benefit", and "achieving shared growth through discussion and collaboration". Fifth, the BRI stresses the search for common development, prosperity, and peace on the basis of maintaining cultural diversity following the cultural value of "harmony in diversity".

Therefore, the BRI has provided new thinking for promoting the deep development of economic globalization, that is, inclusive globalization. From the perspective of historical trends, inclusive globalization might be regarded as the economic globalization 2.0 that will incorporate Chinese wisdom and China's plan for world peace and development. Perhaps it will be a new governance model after Keynesianism and neoliberalism.

To clear up misunderstandings of the BRI

REPORTER: The BRI has achieved remarkable results since its proposal more than three years ago. However, there are still various understandings of the initiative, some of which are even misunderstandings. You have earlier pointed out that avoiding such misunderstandings of the BRI is still of significance for promoting the initiative.

WEIDONG LIU: Some misunderstandings in society in respect of the BRI that I noted at the beginning of last year now still exist. These misunderstandings are mainly as follows.

The BRI is not simply about international trade routes. Some scholars and local officials have misunderstood the BRI in that they think that the aim is to rebuild former international trade routes, because the concept of the Silk Road is used. It is notable that some regions have been keen to explore their own roles in the ancient Silk Roads as starting points, passages, and links, so as to establish a special position in current Belt and Road development. Although it is hard to completely deny the practical meaning of these perspectives, especially the significance of such an approach to learning from the past to deal with current issues, it is clearly a misunderstanding of the underlying meaning of the reference to the Silk Road in the BRI.

The BRI is not about one way of going global, although going global is an inherent part of the BRI and its strategic foundation. At present, there has been a misunderstanding in society that the BRI is just about going global. Correspondingly, the expectation that they should accelerate steps in going global has been rising in some local governments, while some enterprises are eager to "go global" as soon as possible. Indeed, a few local governments even consider that the results of "going global" should be a criterion of administrative performance. This is a quite risky misunderstanding.

The BRI is not a geopolitical strategy. The emergence of the BRI can be attributed to internal reasons relating to changes in China's development stage and seen as the inevitable result of the changes in the international economic structure in the past three decades. Among others, China has become the second-largest economy in the world, the largest manufacturing country, and a significant capital exporting country. These changes are important foundations for the BRI. In this context, some scholars tend to interpret the BRI as China's geopolitical strategy, which is what it fundamentally entails.

The BRI is not a simple linear economy. Almost everyone who reads the term "Belt and Road" will unconsciously ask, "Where are the belt and the road?" This is actually another misunderstanding. The term "Belt and Road", though including the direct meaning of linear economies, is an abstract and metaphorical concept, whose core connotation is, rather than just building a few roads, creating a platform for international economic cooperation by using the cultural connotations of the "Silk Road". Linear economies are just important parts and representations of this platform.

In brief, advancing the BRI to improve the mechanisms of economic globalization meets not only China's need to "go global" but also the need for inclusive globalization so as to benefit more countries and regions. Thus, the BRI will open a door to inclusive economic globalization.

The Belt and Road: Leading to inclusive globalization

May 11, 2017, reported by Wang Xiaoying, www.cctv.com

For more than three years, China has proved to the world through practical actions that the BRI is helpful in promoting the reform of the international economic governance and deepening development of economic globalization.

Weidong Liu, assistant director of the Institute of Geographic Sciences and Natural Resources Research, Chinese Academy of Sciences (CAS), and the director of the Center for the Belt and Road Initiative Studies, said in an interview with CCTV.com that the Belt and Road Forum for International Cooperation held in this context is of great significance, not only in advancing the BRI but also for countries in the world seeking solutions to address the results of the global financial crisis and promote the reform of global economic governance.

Finding a "new prescription" for the economic downturn of the world

Over the past three years, the BRI has entered a stage of full implementation, having had an extensive impact on the international arena and made significant progress.

Weidong Liu noted that the BRI has been recognized by more and more countries and international organizations, developing from an initiative by China to an international consensus as it has not only gained wide support from the countries along the Belt and Road but also begun to be reexamined by some developed countries that used to display a wait-and-see attitude.

The BRI is an open and inclusive initiative that welcomes all interested countries to participate in an appropriate way. With the increase in the number of participating countries, an issue that must be addressed is finding an appropriate construction mechanism to accommodate various forms of participation and development.

Weidong Liu argued that, in this context, it is expected that in the upcoming Forum the participating countries will reach a stronger consensus, through the new cooperation concept and cooperation model proposed by the BRI, regarding deepening international economic cooperation and finding new paths and "new prescriptions" for getting the world economy out of its downturn.

Another expected result is the establishment of an institutionalized dialogue mechanism by relevant countries under the framework of the BRI, providing a new platform for global economic governance. "For example, such a Forum could be held regularly. And if an international organization like the Belt and Road Council could be established in the future, it would be much better".

In a briefing held on April 18, 2017, by the Ministry of Foreign Affairs for Chinese and foreign media on activities related to the Belt and Road

Forum for International Cooperation that President Xi Jinping will attend and preside over, the foreign minister of China, Wang Yi, said that the Forum will focus four issues, including improving the support system and clarifying the cooperation direction; determining key cooperation fields in the next phase, both bilateral and multilateral; formulating cooperation plans for the next five years or for even longer time periods; and refining specific implementation plans.

The BRI: Leading to inclusive globalization

It is notable that in the world today many voices are seeking reform, and reforms in particular require new thinking and new models. As the world's second-largest economy and a big country with a successful development experience, China should provide possible schemes for the reform and development of economic globalization. Therefore, as Weidong Liu pointed out, China proposed to jointly build the Belt and Road, promoting cooperation among countries along the Belt and Road in the Spirit of the Silk Road, to achieve mutual benefit.

He also stated that the core connotation and essence of the BRI is inclusive globalization and that the BRI will be a banner leading to inclusive globalization.

Weidong Liu explained that the BRI respects the diversity of development paths chosen by each country and should explore suitable development paths based on their own characteristics and conditions. Moreover, the BRI emphasizes the connecting up of the development strategies of the countries with the aim of identifying common interests.

The BRI makes the pursuit of the biggest common denominator for development and the promotion of common development and prosperity its top priority, while adhering to the principles of "openness and inclusiveness", "equality and mutual benefit", and "achieving shared growth through discussion and collaboration". Moreover, under the influence of the cultural values of "harmony in diversity", it emphasizes common development, prosperity, and peace on the basis of maintaining cultural diversity.

"Therefore, the BRI has provided new thinking for deepening the development of economic globalization toward more inclusiveness. The BRI will lead to inclusive globalization, which will bring Chinese wisdom and a scheme for world peace and development", Weidong Liu said.

[195]

Pursuing the *Dao* of the BRI

Exclusive interview with Weidong Liu, professor at the Institute of Geographic Sciences and Natural Resources Research, CAS

Reported by Zhang Xingfei, *China United Front*, 2017, 6.

REPORTER: At the conference for promoting the Belt and Road Initiative held by the Party's Central Committee on August 17 last year, you, as the only representative of the academic community, gave a talk together with the director of the National Development and Reform Commission, the foreign minister, and secretaries of several provincial Party committees. It seems that you have attracted a lot of attention in major media reports.

WEIDONG LIU: Actually, it is not me, but the BRI that has attracted a lot of attention. As a scholar, I am honored to participate in and make contributions to the BRI. At that meeting, I was sitting in an important place diagonally opposite President Xi Jinping, which I had not expected. And after the meeting, President Xi held my hand and urged me to strengthen BRI studies. I deeply felt the central government has attached great importance to intellectuals and realized the great responsibility that I should assume.

REPORTER: Did you attend the Belt and Road Forum for International Cooperation just held in Beijing? If yes, could you please share something about your perceptions?

WEIDONG LIU: I participated in the opening ceremony, a high-level plenary meeting, the policy communication parallel session, the welcome dinner, and watched the performance that formed a part of it. I think this Forum is a milestone in the development of the BRI over the past four years. The BRI has been widely recognized around the world, and seen the emergence of an international consensus. Many heads of state pointed out in their speeches in the Forum that the BRI, with its strong emphasis on inclusiveness, will allow more regions to share the benefits of globalization. For example, Pakistani prime minister Sharif noted that the BRI has demonstrated rich cultural diversity and great inclusiveness, providing development opportunities for people on the margins of globalization. Former French prime minister de Villepin stated that the BRI is a bridge that connects the past, the present, and the future, aiming to leave no one behind on the path of development. The presidents of Chile, Turkey, the Czech Republic, and Ethiopia also expressed the same expectations. Secretary General António Guterres of the United Nations pointed out that the BRI is significant and will unite the world in driving globalization in a more equitable direction. It might be said that promoting inclusive globalization is one of the consensuses reached by political elites at this Forum. By the end of the Forum, China had signed cooperation MOUs for jointly building the Belt and Road with some 60 countries and international organizations. The success of this Forum has demonstrated that the BRI fits with the expectations of many countries and people in the world, and is also a great contribution that China has made to global economic governance as well as peace and development in the world in the twenty-first century.

REPORTER: I have seen "inclusive globalization" many times in your articles and interviews. The book entitled *A Study of the Belt and Road*

Initiative, led by you, was published at the beginning of this year. It received great coverage in newspapers and journals such as *People's Daily*, *China Youth Daily*, and *Chinese Social Science Today*. You also mentioned in multiple interviews that the core point of this study is "inclusive globalization".

WEIDONG LIU: Yes, just as President Xi Jinping proposed, the BRI is designed to promote cooperation among countries along the Belt and Road in the Spirit of the Silk Road. I would like to argue that BRI is a result of the "Silk Road Spirit plus Globalization", and it involves new thinking about development that will allow more regions and people to benefit from globalization, that is, inclusive globalization. Since China proposed the BRI, many foreign scholars have been trying to figure out where the belt and road are. However, to do so is to misunderstand the BRI. In fact, the "Silk Road" concept we use today largely refers to its cultural symbols rather than a spatial phenomenon of fixed lines. It is both a historical phenomenon and a cultural metaphor. This metaphor is what we call the "spirit of the Silk Road". It is a cultural heritage shared by countries along the Belt and Road and a common story shared by many countries in Eurasia. Therefore, the BRI is first and foremost an open and inclusive international cooperation platform, followed by such keys as economic corridors and cooperative parks.

REPORTER: Was the "Spirit of the Silk Road" first proposed at this Forum?

WEIDONG LIU: President Xi Jinping had elaborated on the Spirit of the Silk Road in important speeches during his earlier foreign visits. In the opening speech of this Forum, President Xi put forward a comprehensive and profound interpretation of the Spirit of the Silk Road. He pointed out in his speech that "history is our best teacher. The glory of the ancient silk routes shows that geographical distance is not insurmountable. If we take the first courageous step toward each other, we can embark on a path leading to friendship, shared development, peace, harmony, and a better future". In the opening speech for the Roundtable Summit, he stressed that "we can fully draw wisdom and strength from the ancient Silk Road to promote cooperation and common development in the Silk Spirit of peace and cooperation, openness and inclusiveness, mutual learning, and mutual benefit for a brighter future". I think more foreign leaders have clearly understood the fundamental meaning of the BRI and recognized the role and significance of this initiative in addressing global challenges.

REPORTER: Some concepts associated with the BRI, such as inclusiveness, mutual understanding, and ideas such as that the BRI is a real chorus comprising all countries along the routes, not a solo performance for China itself, are not unfamiliar to the readers of our journals.

WEIDONG LIU: There are indeed many similar concepts. At the Forum, President Xi Jinping stressed that the BRI is not designed to engage in group politics and make confrontational alliances but to create a community of shared interests and destiny to achieve common development and prosperity that benefits all. On the eve of the Forum, Foreign Minister Wang Yi pointed out that the BRI is a "friendship circle" in which every participant who recognizes the spirit of Silk Road can participate in jointly building the Belt and Road in a way that s/he thinks appropriate. In my personal opinion, the BRI is the path for pursuing common development, prosperity, and peace.

REPORTER: You have participated in the twentieth training class for nonparty personages, and many activities of nonparty study and service groups. In addition, you are a member of the economic group of nonparty intellectuals offering advice and suggestions.

WEIDONG LIU: Yes, in 2012, I participated in the nonparty field trip to Yunnan for the first time. I then went to Guizhou, Fujian, Jilin, Heilongjiang, Guangxi, and Hebei. I just took part in a Guangdong field trip. We also went to Mianyang and Hangzhou for a field investigation with the economic group of nonparty personages offering advice and suggestions.

REPORTER: I have talked with you about several activities, and also communicated with other accompanying reporters. I have built a "profile" for you. You always straightforwardly express your sharp insights on problems with a serious poker face, and never say anything superficial . . . Well, our nonparty friend is such a "cold face king".

WEIDONG LIU: Ha, am I that cold? When providing service to local people, I feel obligated to offer real advice from their side with a genuine and sincere desire to help solve some problems for them. To point out the problem without evading it is a contribution to finding together a better solution. It is a matter of maintaining independent thinking rather than echoing groundless hearsay, which is the real contribution a scholar should make to the country. I have gained a lot from frequent participation in the collective activities of nonparty experts and have learned a great deal from field studies and investigations, while enjoying a sense of self-worth and pride from being consulted. With the continuous improvement in political consultation, communication methods will surely become more mature and acceptable. I do like the nonparty group because everyone expresses their ideas frankly. In particular, Professor Justin Yifu Lin has always been an example for me. I was so touched when I recently read his article reminiscing about his 30 years of teaching experience after he returned to China . . . It is only with a group of intellectuals of this kind, who have learned and who understand rather than copying the Western theories, that one can explore a "Chinese path" of our own.

REPORTER: Many of our grass-roots groups and industrial and commercial associations have been actively participating in and organizing a series of activities around the BRI. Can you give them some work guidance and advice?

WEIDONG LIU: To participate in the BRI, one must first correctly understand it, avoiding misunderstandings and the dissemination of wrong ideas. Attention and participation are favorable for creating a good "ecological circle" for the BRI. However, some problems should not be overlooked. We should not consider the BRI a basket into which one can put everything. In addition, it is also necessary to pay more attention to the consistency of expression used in publicity with the central spirit. On the one hand, the advantages of China's fast-growing economy will be more widely understood through actively disseminating the benefits that the BRI have brought to people in China and the countries along the Belt and Road. On the other hand, it will be recognized that the BRI is not a project of the Chinese government but a global platform that China provides to the world, which can only be taken advantage of through the joint efforts of all countries involved. Second, enterprises participating in the BRI should understand, under proper guidance, that it is not just about going global but rather a close combination of the "going global" and "attracting in". The key issue lies in determining which kind of enterprises are suitable for "going global" and how to "go global". I believe that haste makes waste, and that enterprises, instead of simply pursuing the honor of "going global", should take pride in domestic upgrading and job creation. As for those enterprises with the need and capacity to "go global", I suggest they organize some study visits to countries along the Belt and Road, and that more valuable information services be provided for them.

Note

1 Originally published in *People's Daily*, December 27, 2016, pp. 14–15.

References

Agnew J. "The Territorial Trap: The Geographical Assumptions of International Relations Theory". *Review of International Political Economy* 1, no. 1 (1994): 53–80.

Baoquan, H. "Chang'an in the Han and Tang Dynasties and the Silk Road" (in Chinese text), *Wenbo*, no. 6 (2006): 52–55.

Chetty, R., Grusky D., Hell M., Hendren N., Manduca R., Narang J. "The Fading American Dream: Trends in Absolute Income Mobility Since 1940". *Science* 356, no. 6336 (2017): 398–406.

Clark, G. L. "Financial Intermediation, Infrastructure Investment and Regional Growth". *Area Development and Policy* 2, no. 3 (2017): 217–236.

Coe, N. M. and Yeung, W. C. H. *Global Production Network*. Oxford: Oxford University Press, 2015.

Daniel, W. "Richthofen's 'Silk Roads': Toward the Archaeology of a Concept". *The Silk Road* 5, no. 1 (2007): 4.

Debu, G. and Jue, W. *An Economic History of the World* (in Chinese text), Beijing: China Renmin University Press, 2001.

Dicken, P. *Global Shift* (6th ed.). London: SAGE, 2010.

Guogang, Z. "The Silk Road and Cultural Exchanges between the East and the West" (in Chinese text). *The Western Regions Studies*, no. 1 (2010): 1–3.

Harvey, D. "The Geography of Capitalist Accumulation: A Reconstruction of the Marxian Theory". *Antipode* 2, S (1975): 9–12.

Harvey, D. "The Spatial Fix: Hegel, Von Thunen and Marx". *Antipode* 13 (1981): 1–12.

Harvey, D. *The Limits to Capital*. Chicago: University of Chicago Press, 1982.

Harvey, D. *A Brief History of Neoliberalism*. New York: Oxford University Press, 2007.

Henderson, J. and Jepson, N. "Critical Transformations and Global Development: Materials for a New Analytical Framework". *Area Development and Policy* 3, no. 1 (2018): 1–23.

Issawi, C. *An Economic History of the Middle East and North Africa*. New York: Columbia University Press, 1982.

Jiadong, T. and Cheng, L. "The Origin and Trend of Anti-globalization: Based on the Perspective of Historical Comparison" (in Chinese text). *China Industrial Economics*, no. 6 (2017): 6: 5–59.

Jing, Z. "The Muslim Culture along the Silk Road" (in Chinese text). *Journal of Ethnic Art*, no. 1 (2016): 27–32.

Maddison, A. "Statistics on World Population, GDP and Per Capita GDP, 1-2008 AD". "Maddison Project", 2009. www.ggdc.net/maddison/ortndex.htm

Mingde, C. "Peace-Making Marriage in Ancient China and the Expansion of the Silk Road". *China's Borderland History and Geography Studies* 2 (2005):

Morse, H. B. *The International Relations of the Chinese Empire*. London, New York [etc.]: Longmans, Green, and Co., 1910.

National Development and Reform Commission, Ministry of Foreign Affairs, and Ministry of Commerce of the People's Republic of China. *Vision and Actions on Jointly Building Silk Road Economic Belt and 21st-Century Maritime Silk Road*. Beijing: Foreign Language Press, 2015.

Ping, Z. "The Concept of the Construction of Historical and Geographic Information System for the Silk Road and Its Value and Significance" (in Chinese Text). *Journal of Shaanxi Normal University* (Philosophy and Social Sciences Edition), no. 1 (2016): 5–11.

Qinsheng, L. "Historical Review on the Formation of the Silk Road" (in Chinese text). *Silk Monthly*, no. 3 (1999): 43–45.

Richthofen, F. V. *China, Ergebnisseeigner Reisen und daraufgegrundeter Studien* [China: The results of my travels and the studies based thereon], 1877–1912. 5 vols.

Shaohua, Z. "On the Cultural Significance of the Silk Road" (in Chinese text). *Theoretic Observation*, no. 6 (2005): 74–75.

Sheppard, E. *Limits to Globalization: Disruptive Geographies of Capitalist Development*. Oxford: Oxford University Press, 2016.

Stein, M. A. *Ancient Khotan: Detailed Report of Archaeological Explorations in Chinese Turkestan*. New York: Hacker Art Books, 1975.

Stiglitz, J. E. "A Nobel Laureate Explains How Trump Could Nuke the Economy", *Vanity Fair*, December 27, 2016 (quoted from Lin Yifu and Wang Yan, 2017).

Taylor, J. G. *Williamson, Globalization in Historical Perspective*. Chicago: University of Chicago Press, 2005.

Wakeman, F. "The Canton Trade and the Opium War". In *The Cambridge History of China,* edited by Denis Twitchett and John K. Fairbank, 163–212. Cambridge: Cambridge University Press, 1978.

Weidong, L. "Scientific Connotations and Scientific Issues of the Belt and Road Initiative" (in Chinese text). *Progress in Geography* 34, no. 5 (2015): 538–544.

Weidong, L. "Misunderstanding on the Belt and Road Initiative" (in Chinese text). *Journal of Chinese Academy of Governance*, no. 1 (2016): 30–34.

Weidong, L. and Dicken, P. "Transnational Corporations and 'Obligated Embeddedness': Foreign Direct Investment in China's Automobile Industry". *Environment and Planning A* 38, no. 7 (2006): 1229–1247.

Weiqiang, W. "Who Won the Battle between Hayek and Keynes? Comments on the Rise and Fall of Neo-Liberalism and Keynesianism and Its Enlightenment to China's Economy" (in Chinese text). *Theoretic Observation*, no. 6 (2006): 20–22.

Wenli, L. "Richthofen named the 'Silk Road'", www.globalpeople.com.cn/.

Wuyi, Z. "The New Trends of Studies in the Silk Road" (in Chinese Text). *China Numismatics* no. 1 (2005): 77–77.

Xiaoying, M. "Some Thoughts on Cultural Identity in the Tourism Cooperation in the Hexi Corridor" (in Chinese text). *The Silk Road*, no. 2 (2016): 37–39.

Xinhua, W. "The Silk Road in the Western Regions: The Ancient Route Nurturing Civilizations" (in Chinese text), *China Cultural Heritage*, no. 1 (2007): 22–31.

Yan, Z. and Youwen, W. "The General of Ili in the Qing Dynasty and Political Considerations on the Development of the Silk Road in the Kazakh Steppe" (in Chinese Text). *Social Sciences in Guangxi*, no. 10 (2015): 118–123.

Yaopeng, Q. “Analysis on Eastern Factors in the Formation of the Silk Road – Cultural Diversity and Common Progress of Human Society” (in Chinese text). *Journal of Northwest University* (Philosophy and Social Sciences Edition), no. 4 (2007): 37–42.

Yifu, L. and Yan, W. “New Structural Economics: Making Patient Capital as a Comparative Advantage” (in Chinese text). *Development Finance Research*, no. 1 (2017): 3–15.

Yule, H. *The Book of Ser Marco Polo the Vinetian, Concerning the Kingdoms and the Marveis of the East*. London: J. Murray, 1871.

Zhi, J. “The Silk Road, the Channel for Exchanges of the Eastern and Western Civilizations” (in Chinese text). *New Silk Road Horizon*, no. 10 (2006): 12–14.

Zhijiang, W. and Ce, L. “On the Construction of China’s Disciplinary Theoretical System in Respect of the Silk Road” (in Chinese text). *Journal of Xinjiang Normal University* (Edition of Philosophy and Social Sciences), no. 2 (2016).

Index

For Product Safety Concerns and Information please contact our
EU representative GPSR@taylorandfrancis.com Taylor & Francis
Verlag GmbH, Kaufingerstraße 24, 80331 München, Germany